ADDRESSES ON WAR

BY

CHARLES SUMNER

WITH AN INTRODUCTION BY

EDWIN D. MEAD

PUBLISHED FOR THE INTERNATIONAL UNION

GINN & COMPANY, BOSTON

1904

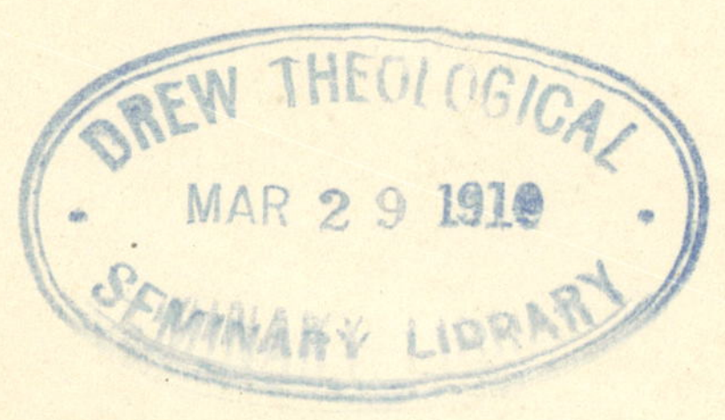
DREW THEOLOGICAL
MAR 29 1910
SEMINARY LIBRARY

CONTENTS.

INTRODUCTION.

Charles Sumner began his public life by what he himself called a *declaration of war against war.* His great oration in Tremont Temple on "The True Grandeur of Nations" marked, his biographer rightly observes, the most important epoch in Sumner's life. "Had he died before this event, his memory would have been only a tradition with the few early friends who survive him. The 4th of July, 1845, gave him a national, and more than a national, fame." Epoch-making in Sumner's own life, we think it may be safely said that no oration which he ever gave has greater intrinsic importance, and perhaps no other will be read so long. Of all pleas made by American men for the rule of peace on earth, it is the noblest and the most comprehensive, save Sumner's own later address on "The War System of Nations." There is almost no argument against war which these orations and their successor do not somehow make use of; and the advocate of peace in all the years returns to them, and returns again, for support and inspiration. The bringing together in a single volume, as is now done for the first time, of all of Sumner's three great addresses on war and peace is a distinct public service; and every philanthropist and every true philo-American will wish the volume the widest currency and influence.

There was nothing upon which Sumner dwelt with greater emphasis in his first famous oration than upon the cost and waste of war and the incalculable advantage that would result from the diversion of these misapplied resources to purposes of education and the real development and progress of society. Passing from the fearful cost of war itself, he discussed the regular, permanent expense of the war footing, — the preparations for war in time of peace. His survey of the armies and navies and fortifications of Europe is interesting to-day chiefly as revealing how startlingly the burden has increased in the fifty years between then and now. In the United States he found that the average annual appropriation for military and naval purposes was eighty per cent of the total annual expenses of the government. "Yes, eighty cents in every dollar were applied in this unproductive manner. The remaining twenty cents sufficed to maintain the government in all its branches, executive, legislative, and judicial, the administration of justice, our relations with foreign nations, the post-office, and all the light-houses, which, in happy, useful contrast with the forts, shed their cheerful signals over the rough waves beating upon our long coast." In the years from the formation of our government, in 1789, down to the time when Sumner spoke, almost twelve times as much was sunk under the sanction of the national government in mere peaceful preparations for war as was dedicated by the government during the same period to all other purposes whatever. Of the military expenses of the United States from that time to this all of us know something.

But "the passage which was most striking at the time," says Sumner's biographer, "according to the testimony of hearers still living, was the one where, treating of the immense waste of war defences, he compared the cost of the *Ohio*, a ship-of-the-line lying in the harbor, and, on account of its decorations, a marked spectacle of the day, with that of Harvard College." He spoke of Harvard's library, the oldest and most valuable in the country, its museums, its schools of law, divinity, and medicine, its body of professors and teachers, many of them known in every part of the globe, and its distinguished president, Josiah Quincy, who had rendered such high public service in so many fields. "Such," he said, "is Harvard University; and it appears," he added, "from the last report of the treasurer, that the whole available property of the University, the various accumulations of more than two centuries of generosity, amounts" — 1845 was still the day of small things at Harvard — "to $703,175."

"Change the scene," said Sumner, "and cast your eyes upon another object. There now swings idly at her moorings in this harbor a ship-of-the-line, the *Ohio*, carrying ninety guns, finished as late as 1836 at an expense of $547,888, repaired only two years afterwards for $233,012, with an armament which has cost $53,945, making an aggregate of $834,845" — 1845 was still the day of small things in battle-ships — "as the actual outlay at this moment for that single ship, more than $100,000 beyond all the available wealth of the richest and most ancient seat of learning in the land."

He continued in that masterly array of comparative statistics which is well known and which the reader will study in the following pages. He did not fail to urge the great moral arguments against war; no one has ever presented them, not only in this early address, but in later ones, more strongly. But the argument that stays with us most influentially is that for the generous constructive use of national resources as the means of making destructiveness and war unnecessary and impossible. In the powerful use of this argument Sumner was the great forerunner of Jean de Bloch. In the line of Sumner's thought lies the hope of the world; and those who think as Sumner thought should, without recourse to generalities, to anything remote in time or place, apply that principle to the situation through which our Anglo-Saxon world has been passing.

We have spent $300,000,000 in the war with Spain about Cuba. We have spent more than that in the conquest of the Philippines. We are in the outer circles of the maelstrom of a policy which means larger armies, larger navies, costlier forts, and more of them, and all the paraphernalia of the Old World militarism which we have prided ourselves on being free from,—with the corresponding burdens of taxation, the devotion to waste and destruction of the immense resources which might otherwise go to development and progress. The man who, seeing this, has no forebodings, is not a student of history. Is this way of spending money a wise way? Is it protective, is it constructive, is it good business, is it common sense, does it pave a good road into the future, is it the economical and promising way to secure the results we claim to aim at, will it make us a truer and safer democracy, and will it help the world? Was Sumner right, was Longfellow right, or were they not, in claiming that, if half the wealth bestowed on camps, given to maintain armies and navies, were given to redeem the human mind, to educate the human race, there would soon be no need of armies and navies?

We have spent $300,000,000 in a war with Spain. Have we spent it well? Have we done the most that could be done with $300,000,000 to accomplish what we claimed to want to accomplish? Our object in going to war with Spain was to make Cuba free, to make it a better place to live in, to insure it better government, and make its people comfortable and happy. Have we got our money's worth? Has our way of spending our $300,000,000 been best, or would Sumner's way have been best? If in the midst of our perplexities half a dozen years ago, the senator who sits in Sumner's seat had addressed words like the following to the Senate and the nation, would they have been foolish or fallacious words?

We are clearly drifting towards a war with Spain in behalf of Cuba. Unless we show wisdom greater than the past has shown, we shall soon be in the midst of war. That war will cost us $300,000,000. Is there not a better way of spending $300,000,000? Is there not a better way of achieving what we aim at, — the freedom, good government, and development of Cuba? I propose that we submit to Cuba and to Spain this offer and request: Let us establish at Havana a university as well equipped as Harvard University, with an endowment of $10,000,000, free to every young man and woman of Cuba, with the best professors who can be secured from America and Spain and England and France and Germany. Let us establish at Santiago and Matanzas and Puerto Principe colleges like Amherst and Williams, with a total endowment of $10,000,000; and in each of the twenty largest towns a high school or academy, at a cost of $10,000,000. Let us devote $20,000,000 —$1,000,000 a year for twenty years—to the thorough planting in Cuba of our American common-school system; $10,000,000 to the promotion of a system of free public libraries, making books as accessible and common in each Cuban town and village as in Barnstable or Berkshire; and $6,000,000 for the maintenance in each of the six provinces of a newspaper conducted by the best men who can be enlisted in the service, bringing all Cuban men and women into touch with all the world, giving them those things which will feed them, and not giving them those things which would poison them. Let us build a Cuban Central Railroad through the whole length of the island, from Mantua to Maysi; and let us devote the balance of $100,000,000 to the scientific organization, by proper bureaus, of Cuban agriculture, industry, and commerce. Let there be a truce for ten years, till these things are done and begin to show their fruits; and then let the representatives of the United States and Spain meet at Havana to settle the "Cuban question" as it then exists. This seems to me worth trying. If it succeeds, we should at least have saved $200,000,000; and it would be, I think, a kind of success more pregnant with good for Cuba and Spain and America and humanity than the success which we may be celebrating next year or the year after. There are those who will laugh and scoff, and say this thought is all chimerical and fallacious; but I say that with those who do not think so lies the hope of the world. I say that the kingdom of God can come in this world, that peace and justice and fraternity can come among men, that democracy itself has a safe future, only as some elect people, with sublime abandon, in a great opportunity, does this thing, — taking, in this world of undeniable and conflicting risks, the heroic risk, the risk which alone has in it hope for the world and relish of salvation.

But, it will be urged, this is to make the nation a missionary; and that is not to be expected. Unhappily it is not to be expected; but the time will come when nothing else is to be expected. The constructive way instead of the wasteful way will obtain alike in national and international policies, — and in the latter for the sake of the nation's own welfare. The constructive way is in every aspect and in every field the profitable way.

With vastly greater force than to our war with Spain does this argument apply to our war in the Philippines; and I do not here discuss the aims of our government or the politics of the situation, but merely the question of method. What would the hundreds of millions which we have spent there not have accomplished if it had been applied, lovingly and sympathetically, in simple coöperation with the leaders of the Filipino people, to purposes of construction instead of destruction? Compare the results of the few millions lately spent in education with all that war has done. Yet — how horrible the satire — all the money spent for schools and roads and all constructive purposes is money which we have forced themselves to pay out of their own scant revenues; we have been generous and lavish only for slaughter and destruction.

I shall not push this consideration into the recent war in South Africa and ask how the billion dollars wasted there could have been well spent, spent so as to have advanced the true interests of England and of humanity. The American instances suffice. The consideration should sink deeply into the hearts of all the educated youth of America and all the people of America. If our republic is to be true to itself, if we are to help civilization forward and not backward, then the young men of our universities and all those who look at war and national defence and national grandeur in the old way have got to be born again, — nothing less than that, — baptized with the spirit wherewith Charles Sumner was baptized, and have our eyes opened to see that his way is the only right or sensible or efficient way, and that now we are wasting our substance and defeating ourselves. The revolution in the point of view is as radical as the difference between Ptolemy and Copernicus; but, when we go through it, things fall at once into order, we find ourselves in a rational world with right means for right ends, and our old notions of what is wise and prudent and necessary for the defence and upbuilding and influence of the nation instantly dissolve, stamped all as vicious and fallacious. Our thoughts on what it is that makes a nation strong need almost all of them to be turned inside out. Our economics and generosities are all Ptolemaic. We boast of public and private munificences in education and philanthropy. We need to understand that we are yet in the kindergarten of munificence as concerns all positive, constructive, and real things. It would sometimes seem as if, were the devil privileged to organize the world so as to thwart struggling men most effectually, wasting their accumulations and cutting forever the margin of civilization, he would choose precisely what he now sees, — the dominance of false political ideals and of gross unintelligence as to how men and nations should spend their money. If an eleventh commandment were to be added to the decalogue, it should be one addressed to nations, and should be: Thou shalt not waste thy substance.

Every war gives new life to that old notion which

died so hard, but which is responsible for so much mischief in the world, that patriotism is somehow bound up with war, — the patriotic man, the man who fights or wants to fight for his country. Congress, "in a great wave of patriotism," we read, appropriates fifty million dollars for gun-boats and torpedoes. No "wave of patriotism" is reported when Massachusetts appropriates a million dollars for good roads, when New York appropriates five millions for new school-houses, or Chicago ten millions for an exposition, when Boston builds a library, when the Adirondack forests are secured, when the college is endowed, and when good wages are paid in the factory. There may be exigencies when the appropriation of fifty million dollars or five hundred millions for national defence or for national offence is the duty imposed upon the patriot; but the man who votes for guns and gun-boats with a glow and an excitement which he does not feel when he has opportunity to help on the great interests of education, science, art, and industry, may be very sure that his glow is not the honest glow of patriotism, but is very likely the excitement of the tiger and the savage, which still lives on in good society and dies so hard in half-civilized and even civilized men. It happens every day that a council, a legislature, or a congress will buoyantly, without computation, without protest, and without debate, vote the people's thousands or millions of money for some great waste, some great destruction — new cruisers and new forts — when some poor pittance is grudgingly doled out or grudgingly denied, each dollar pinched and challenged, for the measure of philanthropy, of conservation, of construction, of education, of relief, of encouragement or high emprise, whose generous and bold advancement would do so much to hasten the day when forts and cruisers shall be unnecessary and obsolete. Society is zealous and lavish on its displays and its defences, its dams and sewers and police and armament, and blind and niggardly a thousand times as to the things which affect its fountains and its real vitality, the interests of the discipline and the construction which make protection needless.

The lifelong position of Charles Sumner upon the subject of armies and navies and forts and wars is to be commended to the educated youth of America at this time as a position peculiarly worthy of their adoption, imperatively worthy of their earnest thought. Sumner was not a non-resistant, not a man of "peace at any price." We know how warmly and efficiently, in his place in the Senate, he supported the government in the Civil War; and we know how otherwise he appealed to force when that appeal was necessary and just. We know how he believed in strong government and hated imbecile police, how he spoke of "the sword of the magistrate" in the very record of his services for peace. But the great principles of his "True Grandeur of Nations" were the principles of his whole life, from a time long before that oration to the last hour, when he bequeathed a thousand dollars to Harvard University for an annual prize for the best essay on Universal Peace. I do not remember any autobiographical passage in his writings so impressive as that in which, replying to unfriendly criticism, he gives an account of his devotion to the peace movement.

"My name," he wrote, "is connected somewhat with two questions, which may be described succinctly as those of peace and slavery. That which earliest enlisted me, and which has always occupied much of my thoughts, is the peace question. When scarcely nine years old, it was my fortune to listen to President Quincy's address before the Peace Society, delivered in the Old South Church. It made a deep and lasting impression on my mind; and though, as a boy and youth, I surrendered myself to the illusions of battles and wars, still, as I came to maturity, I felt too keenly their wickedness and woe. A lecture which I heard from William Ladd, in the old courthouse at Cambridge, shortly after I left college, confirmed these impressions." He tells how he expressed his ripened convictions to his friends, and how, going to Europe, he often dwelt upon them there. In Paris, when M. Victor Foucher submitted for his criticism the manuscript of his treatise upon the law of nations, Sumner, observing that he had adopted, among his fundamental principles, that war was recognized as the necessary arbitrament between nations, ventured to discuss this dogma, and, while admitting that it was accepted by every publicist up to that time, suggested to him to be the first to brand it as unchristian and barbarous and to declare that the institution of war, defined and sanctioned by the law of nations as a mode of determining justice between them, was but another form of the ordeal by battle, which was once regarded as a proper mode of determining justice between individuals. Returning to Boston after his two years and a half in Europe, he tells of the little meeting of the American Peace Society to which he found his way in the very month of his arrival. "The Rev. Henry Ware was in the chair. I think there were not more than twelve persons present. We met in a small room under the Marlboro Chapel. On motion of Dr. Gannett, I was placed on the executive committee." He tells of his humble efforts for the cause in the next few years; and then he comes to the oration on the 4th of July, 1845. "The position taken by me on this occasion has drawn upon me not a little criticism,

—perhaps I might use a stronger expression. Convinced of its intrinsic propriety and importance, I have been drawn, on subsequent occasions, by an inevitable necessity, to sustain and fortify it. I hope that I shall always be willing to maintain it."

Universal peace, the methods by which war may be permanently superseded,—these were ever the burden of his thought and study, of addresses to the public and letters to friends; and ever the economic argument is at the front. "I wish our country would cease to whet its tusks," he writes to Doctor Howe in 1843. "The appropriations of the navy last year were nine million dollars. Imagine half—nay, a tithe—of this sum given annually to objects of humanity, education, and literature! I know of nothing in our government that troubles me more than this thought." To his brother George in 1844: "I would not vote a dollar for any engine of war. One war-steamer costs more than all the endowments of Harvard College. Nations keep standing armies and Paixhan guns—sharpen their tusks—that they may be prepared for war. Far better to be always prepared for peace." Again: "What a boon to France, if her half million of soldiery were devoted to the building of railways and other internal improvements, instead of passing the day in carrying superfluous muskets! What a boon to Paris, if the immense sums absorbed in her fortifications were devoted to institutions of benevolence! She has more to fear from the poverty and wretchedness of her people than from any foreign foe." No crime was to him so great as that of the country which "entered into war for the sordid purpose of securing a few more acres of land." No letter that came to him among the many drawn out by "The True Grandeur of Nations" was more welcome than that from Theodore Parker, — his first letter to Sumner, the beginning of their friendship, — defending him from the attacks of "men of low morals, who can only swear by their party and live only in public opinion," and exclaiming: "The Church and State are both ready to engage in war, however unjust, if a little territory can be added to the national domain thereby. The great maxims of Christianity — the very words of Christ — are almost wholly forgotten." Full of faith in the republic, confident in the influence its institutions were destined to exert over the ancient establishments of Europe, he prayed "that a race of men may be reared among us competent to understand the destinies of the country, to abjure war, and to give extension and influence to our institutions by cultivating the arts of peace, by honesty, and by dignity of life and character." In the cause of peace lay to him the hope of the world. "It is destined," he said, "to a triumph much earlier than many imagine. It is so necessary to meet the financial embarrassments of Europe and the humane aspirations of the age, that it must succeed. Let it be presented carefully and clearly, let the incalculable good it has in store be unfolded, and people must feel its practicability. . . . I have full faith in a coming era of humanity; but I believe it is to be brought about by removing existing evils, by education, and especially by removing the great evil and expense of war preparations or the war system. If the friends of progress in Europe would aim at the armies and navies, direct all their energies at these monster evils, all else that can reasonably be desired will soon follow. Why not sound the idea in the ears of Europe?" It was to his brother, then in Europe, that he wrote, in 1849. His call was heard, fifty years afterward, by Jean de Bloch and the Czar of Russia.

In 1849, four years after the oration on "The True Grandeur of Nations," he delivered an address on "The Abolition of the War System in the Commonwealth of Nations," advocating instead of the arbitrament of arms a Congress of Nations with a high court of judicature or arbitration. In many respects this address is stronger than the earlier one. No more powerful arraignment of the war system exists in brief compass. Its survey of the history of the peace movement shows the breadth of Sumner's knowledge; and its use of statistics in the economic argument is masterly and most impressive.

The next year, 1850, as Chairman of the United States Committee of the International Peace Congress, which had held its sessions in Paris in 1849 under the presidency of Victor Hugo, Sumner issued an address to the people of the United States, with a view to securing a proper representation at the next Congress, at Frankfort. This address was so important an expression of Sumner's views that it is here given entire.

"The month of August last witnessed at Paris a Congress or Convention of persons from various countries, to consider what could be done to promote the sacred cause of Universal Peace. France, Germany, Belgium, England, and the United States were represented by large numbers of men eminent in business, politics, literature, religion, and philanthropy. The

Catholic Archbishop of Paris and the eloquent Protestant preacher, M. Athanase Coquerel; Michel Chevalier, Horace Say, and Frédéric Bastiat, distinguished political economists; Émile de Girardin, the most important political editor of France; Victor Hugo, illustrious in literature; Lamartine, whose glory it is to have turned the recent French Revolution, at its beginning, into the path of peace; and Richard Cobden, the world-renowned British statesman, the unapproached model of an earnest, humane, and practical reformer, — all these gave to this august assembly the sanction of their presence or approbation. Victor Hugo, on taking the chair as President, in an address of persuasive eloquence, shed upon the occasion the illumination of his genius; while Mr. Cobden, participating in all the proceedings, impressed upon them his characteristic common sense.

"The Congress adopted, with entire unanimity, a series of resolutions, asserting the duty of governments to submit all differences between them to Arbitration, and to respect the decisions of the Arbitrators; also asserting the necessity of a general and simultaneous disarming, not only as a means of reducing the expenditure absorbed by armies and navies, but also of removing a permanent cause of disquietude and irritation. The Congress condemned all loans and taxes for wars of ambition or conquest. It earnestly recommended the friends of Peace to prepare public opinion, in their respective countries, for the formation of a Congress of Nations, to revise the existing International Law and to constitute a High Tribunal for the decision of controversies among nations. In support of these objects, the Congress solemnly invoked the representatives of the press, so potent to diffuse truth, and also all ministers of religion, whose holy office it is to encourage good-will among men.

"The work thus begun has been continued since. In England and the United States large public meetings have welcomed the returning delegates. Men have been touched by the grandeur of the cause. Not in the aspirations of religion and benevolence only, but in the general heart and mind, has it found reception, filling all who embrace it with new confidence in the triumph of Christian truth.

"Another Congress or Convention has been called to meet at Frankfort-on-the-Main, in the month of August next, to do what is possible, by mutual counsels and encouragement, to influence public opinion, and to advance still further the cause which has been so well commended by the Congress at Paris. To promote the objects of this Congress generally, and particularly to secure the attendance of a delegation from the United States, in number and character not unworthy of the occasion, a Committee, representing friends of Peace throughout the country, various in opinion, has been appointed, under the name of "Peace Congress Committee for the United States." This Committee now appeal to their fellow-citizens for coöperation in this work. The Committee hope, in the first place, to interest our Government at Washington in the objects contemplated by the proposed Congress. As this can be done only through the prompting of the people, they recommend petitions like the following:—

"Petition for Peace

"To the Honorable Senate (or H. of R.) of the United States.

"The undersigned, inhabitants (or citizens, or legal voters) of ——, in the State of ——, deploring the manifold evils of War, and believing it possible to supersede its alleged necessity, as an Arbiter of Justice among Nations, by the timely adoption of wise and feasible substitutes, respectfully request your honorable body to take such action as you may deem best in favor of Stipulated Arbitration, or a Congress of Nations, for the accomplishment of this most desirable end.

"As the number of delegates to the proposed Congress is not limited, the Committee hope to see States, Congressional Districts, Towns, and other bodies represented. Every delegate will be a link between the community, large or small, from which he comes and the cause of Universal Peace. The Committee recommend a State Convention in each State to choose a State Committee, and also two delegates at large from the State; also a Convention in each Congressional District to choose a delegate; also public meetings in towns and other smaller localities to explain the objects of the Congress and to choose local delegates. The Committee also recommend to the religious and literary bodies of the country, as churches and colleges, to send delegates to the Congress.

"In making this appeal, the Committee desire to impress upon their fellow-citizens the practical character of the present movement. Instead of the *custom* or *institution* of War, now recognized by International Law, as the Arbiter of Justice between Nations, they propose, by the consent of nations, to substitute a System of Arbitration, or a permanent Congress of Nations. With this change will necessarily follow a general disarming down to that degree of force required for internal police. The barbarous and incongruous War System, which now encases our Christian civilization as with a cumbrous coat of mail, will be destroyed. The enormous means thus released from destructive industry and purposes of hate will be appropriated to productive industry and purposes of beneficence. To help this consummation who will not labor? The people in every part of the country, East and West, North and South, of all political parties and all religious sects, are now invited to join in this endeavor. So doing, while confident of the blessing of God, they will become fellow-laborers of wise and good men in other lands, and will secure to themselves the inexpressible satisfaction of aiding the advent of that happy day when Peace shall be *organized* among nations."

This appeal, in its general features, our people should regard as addressed to them to-day. There has been a distinct falling-off in American attention to the International Peace Congresses. At the Paris Congress of 1849, of which Sumner speaks, a score of American delegates were in attendance. At recent Congresses there have not been half so many. Our churches, universities, and scientific and political societies should take this matter up with energy and see to it that our representation and influence in the coming Congresses be strong and worthy. There is much talk nowadays about America as a "world power." There is no place where she can make herself a greater power for the real welfare of the world than in these International Peace Congresses.

In 1870 Sumner was still enforcing the truths which he enforced in 1845. He gave in many places, in the autumn of that year, a lecture on the war between France and Prussia, the third address printed in the present volume, pointing as its moral that the war system should be discarded and the nations should disarm themselves. In 1872 he introduced in the Senate the following resolutions concerning International Arbitration; and he presented them once more a few days before his death:

"Whereas by International Law and existing custom War is recognized as a form of Trial for the determination of differences between nations; and

"Whereas for generations good men have protested against the irrational character of this arbitrament, where force instead of justice prevails, and have anxiously sought for a substitute in the nature of a judicial tribunal, all of which was expressed by Franklin in his exclamation, 'When will mankind be convinced that all wars are follies, very expensive and very mischievous, and agree to settle their differences by Arbitration?' and

"Whereas war once prevailed in the determination of differences between individuals, between cities, between counties, and between provinces, being recognized in all these cases as the arbiter of justice, but at last yielded to a judicial tribunal, and now, in the progress of civilization, the time has come for the extension of this humane principle to nations, so that their differences may be taken from the arbitrament of war, and, in conformity with these examples, submitted to a judicial tribunal; and

"Whereas Arbitration has been formally recognized as a substitute for war in the determination of differences between nations, being especially recommended by the Congress of

Paris, where were assembled the representatives of England, France, Russia, Prussia, Austria, Sardinia, and Turkey, and afterward adopted by the United States in formal treaty with Great Britain for the determination of differences arising from depredations of British cruisers, and also from opposing claims with regard to the San Juan boundary; and

"Whereas it becomes important to consider and settle the true character of this beneficent tribunal, thus commended and adopted, so that its authority and completeness as a substitute for war may not be impaired, but strengthened and upheld, to the end that civilization may be advanced and war be limited in its sphere: Therefore,

"1. *Resolved*, That in the determination of international differences Arbitration should become a substitute for war in reality as in name, and therefore coëxtensive with war in jurisdiction, so that any question or grievance which might be the occasion of war or of misunderstanding between nations should be considered by this tribunal.

"2. *Resolved*, That any withdrawal from a treaty recognizing Arbitration, or any refusal to abide the judgment of the accepted tribunal, or any interposition of technicalities to limit the proceedings, is to this extent a disparagement of the tribunal as a substitute for war, and therefore hostile to civilization.

"3. *Resolved*, That the United States, having at heart the cause of peace everywhere, and hoping to help its permanent establishment between nations, hereby recommend the adoption of Arbitration as a just and practical method for the determination of international differences, to be maintained sincerely and in good faith, so that war may cease to be regarded as a proper form of trial between nations."

In 1873 Sumner was invited to be one of the speakers at the public meeting held at Steinway Hall, New York, to stimulate a war spirit against Spain at the time of the seizure of the *Virginius*,—a meeting at which Mr. Evarts presided, and made an inflammatory speech; but he declined, and instead sent a letter of a spirit directly opposite to that of the meeting, in which he insisted on waiting for evidence and on considerate treatment of the Spanish republic, and discountenanced the belligerent preparations then under way in our navy yards, which involved burdensome expenditure and encouraged an unhealthy war fever. In 1873, also, in the last summer of his life, he sent a letter of congratulation to Henry Richard, who had succeeded in carrying through the House of Commons a motion in favor of international arbitration. "It marks an epoch in a great cause. There is no question so supremely practical; for it concerns not merely one nation, but every nation, and even its discussion promises to diminish the terrible chances of war. Its triumph would be the greatest reform of history." At the same time he wrote to his English friend, Robert Ingham: —

I have been cheered by the vote of the House of Commons on Mr. Richard's motion. . . . It cannot fail to exert a prodigious influence. I know no reform which promises such universal good as the release of any considerable portion of present war expenditures or expenditure on armaments, so that they can be applied to purposes of civilization. It is absurd to call this Utopian. . . . Here is an open and incessant waste. Why not stop it? Here is something which keeps human thoughts on bloodshed, and rears men to slay each other. Why not turn their thoughts to things which contribute to human happiness? Mr. Richard has done a great work, and so has the House of Commons. . . . Such a presentation of the case must have an effect on the continent as well as in England, teaching reason. I shall not live to see the great cause triumph. I often wish I had been born a few years later, and one reason is because I long to witness the harmony of nations, which I am sure is near. When an evil so great is recognized and discussed, the remedy must be at hand.

But it was to Harvard University that Charles Sumner addressed his first striking message and his last, in behalf of the rule of peace. The first message was through Henry Ware. Mr. Ware, a graduate of Harvard of the Class of 1843, writes: —

I went with Professor Felton one day, just after our Commencement parts had been assigned, into Sumner's office; and he, kindly asking what I had got, and being told that I had to *do* a Latin oration, asked me what subject I had chosen. I replied that I had not yet found a text to my mind. "Then," said he, "I will give you one, — *De imperio pacis:* talk about *that.*" And, says Mr. Ware, I did.

His last message was through his will, the most memorable provision of which was as follows: —

I bequeath to the President and Fellows of Harvard College one thousand dollars in trust, for an annual prize for the best dissertation by any student of the College, or any of its schools, undergraduate or graduate, on Universal Peace and the methods by which war may be permanently superseded. I do this in the hope of drawing the attention of students to the practicability of organizing peace among nations, which I sincerely believe may be done. I cannot doubt that the same modes of decision which now prevail between individuals, between towns, and between smaller communities, may be extended to nations.

Who can doubt that more and more, as days go on, the attention of the students of Harvard University will be drawn to Sumner's last solemn call and charge, — that this "most ancient, most interesting, and most important seat of learning in the land," to which in the sweep of his great oration he could not allude without pausing to pay his tribute of filial affection, will more and more become a centre where educated and aspiring youth, with their hearts kindled by Sumner's gospel and with great visions of a better future, will provoke each other to high argument, and in times of war prepare for peace? Upon each student's desk shall lie, as a book of each student's Bible, the great orations of the greatest son of Harvard who in the memory of men now living has gone forth from Harvard's halls into the councils of the nation. And no page will be pondered more than that which sets forth how, if we would transfer to the offices of education and development the millions now appropriated so lavishly for destruction and defence, the need of destruction and defence would quickly cease.

With two causes the name of the great Harvard senator is identified, — the cause of freedom and the cause of peace. From the wall of the memorial hall which Harvard built to commemorate the services of her sons in the cause of freedom, Sumner's face looks down upon the hundreds of students gathering daily in that most holy place, and upon the hundreds of alumni who, "in the memories of a youth nurtured in her classic retreats," come up to the ancient University as each Commencement week comes round. As that face looks down on them in the years to come, may it not speak chiefly to them of the past, of the victory of the cause of freedom, whose fruits we enjoy to-day, but of the future, the triumph, which he so longed to live to see and which the educated youth of America can do so much to hasten, of the cause of universal peace! Ever and ever may Harvard consider wherein the true grandeur of nations lies, and ever and ever hear the first and last message of her great statesman, giving a new burden and new power to her great singer's gospel: —

"Were half the power that fills the world with terror,
Were half the wealth bestowed on camps and courts,
Given to redeem the human mind from error,
There were no need of arsenals or forts."

May the message of Sumner to Harvard be heard equally by every university and every school in the broad land! for it is in the educated youth of the country that the hope of the republic lies. In this day of generous benefactions, it would be well if some rich man who loves his country and mankind would endow every college in America as Sumner endowed Harvard, and decree that the annual prizes thus provided everywhere should be called the Sumner prizes. But the thing of importance is that all our people, young and old, should ponder ever and ever the great prophet's words, and consecrate themselves ever anew to the high duty of making the republic the greatest of world powers in the work of their fulfilment.

EDWIN D. MEAD.

Boston, 1902.

THE TRUE GRANDEUR OF NATIONS.

An Oration before the Authorities of the City of Boston, July 4, 1845.

O, yet a nobler task awaits thy hand,
(For what can war but endless war still breed?)
Till truth and right from violence be freed.

Milton, *Sonnet to Fairfax.*

Pax optima rerum
Quas homini novisse datum est; pax una triumphis
Innumeris potior; pax custodire salutem
Et cives æquare potens.

SILIUS ITALICUS, *Punica*, Lib. XI. vv. 592 - 595.

Sed majoris est gloriæ *ipsa bella verbo occidere* quam homines ferro, et acquirere vel obtinere pacem pace, non bello. — AUGUSTINI *Epistola* CCLXII., *ad Darium Comitem.*

Certainly, if all who look upon themselves as men, not so much from the shape of their bodies as because they are endowed with reason, would listen awhile unto Christ's wholesome and peaceable decrees, and not, puffed up with arrogance and conceit, rather believe their own opinions than his admonitions, the whole world long ago (turning the use of iron into milder works) should have lived in most quiet tranquillity, and have met together in a firm and indissoluble league of most safe concord. — ARNOBIUS AFER, *Adversus Gentes*, Lib. I. c. 6.

And so for the first time [three hundred years after the Christian era] the meek and peaceful Jesus became a God of Battle, and the cross, the holy sign of Christian redemption, a banner of bloody strife. This irreconcilable incongruity between the symbol of universal peace and the horrors of war, in my judgment, is conclusive against the miraculous or supernatural character of the transaction [the vision of Constantine]. — I was agreeably surprised to find that Mosheim concurred in these sentiments, for which I will readily encounter the charge of Quakerism. — MILMAN, *History of Christianity*, Book III. chap. 1.

When you see fighting, be peaceable; for a peaceable disposition shuts the door of contention. Oppose kindness to perverseness; the sharp sword will not cut soft silk. By using sweet words and gentleness you may lead an elephant with a hair. — SAADI, *The Gulistan*, translated by Francis Gladwin, Chap. III. Tale 28.

Si l'on vous disait que tous les chats d'un grand pays se sont assemblés par milliers dans une plaine, et qu'après avoir miaulé tout leur saoul, ils se sont jetés avec fureur les uns sur les autres, et ont joué ensemble de la dent et de la griffe, que de cette mêlée il est demeuré de part et d'autre neuf à dix mille chats sur la place, qui ont infecté l'air à dix lieues de là par leur puanteur, ne diriez-vous pas, "Voilà le plus abominable sabbat dont on ait jamais ouï parler"? Et si les loups en faisaient de même, quels hurlements! quelle boucherie! Et si les uns ou les autres vous disaient *qu'ils aiment la gloire*, ... ne ririez-vous pas de tout votre cœur de l'ingénuité de ces pauvres bêtes? — LA BRUYÈRE, *Les Caractères: Des Jugements.*

He was disposed to dissent from the maxim, which had of late years received very general assent, that the best security for the continuance of peace was to be prepared for war. That was a maxim which might have been applied to the nations of antiquity, and to society in a comparatively barbarous and uncivilized state. . . . . Men, when they adopted such a maxim, and made large preparations in time of peace that would be sufficient in time of war, were apt to be influenced by the desire to put their efficiency to the test, that all their great preparations and the result of their toil and expense might not be thrown away. — EARL OF ABERDEEN, *Hansard's Parliamentary Debates*, July 20, 1849.

Bellum para, si pacem velis, was a maxim regarded by many as containing an incontestable truth. It was one, in his opinion, to be received with great caution, and admitting of much qualification. . . . . We should best consult the true interests of the country by husbanding our resources in a time of peace, and, instead of a lavish expenditure on all the means of defence, by placing some trust in the latent and dormant energies of the nation. — SIR ROBERT PEEL, *Hansard's Parliamentary Debates*, March 12, 1850.

Let us terminate this disastrous system of rival expenditure, and mutually agree, with no hypocrisy, but in a manner and under circumstances which can admit of no doubt, — by a reduction of armaments, — that peace is really our policy. — MR. D'ISRAELI, *Hansard's Parliamentary Debates*, July 21, 1859.

All high titles of honor come hitherto from fighting. Your *Herzog* (Duke, *Dux*) is Leader of Armies; your Earl (*Jarl*) is Strong Man; your Marshal, Cavalry Horseshoer. A Millennium, or Reign of Peace and Wisdom, having from of old been prophesied, and becoming now daily more and more indubitable, may it not be apprehended that such fighting titles will cease to be palatable, and new and higher need to be devised? — CARLYLE, *Sartor Resartus*, Book III. chap. 7.

After the memorable conflict of June, 1848, in which, as *Chef de Bataillon*, he [Ary Scheffer] had shown a capacity for military conduct not less remarked than his cool courage, General Changarnier, then commanding the National Guard of Paris, tendered to Scheffer's acceptance the cross of *Commandeur*. He replied, "Had this honorable distinction been offered to me in my quality of Artist, and as a recognition of the merit of my works, I should receive it with deference and satisfaction. But to carry about me a decoration reminding me only of the horrors of civil war is what I cannot consent to do." — ARY SCHEFFER, *Life by Mrs. Grote*, Appendix.

ORATION.

IN accordance with uninterrupted usage, on this Sabbath of the Nation, we have put aside our daily cares, and seized a respite from the never-ending toils of life, to meet in gladness and congratulation, mindful of the blessings transmitted from the Past, mindful also, I trust, of our duties to the Present and the Future.

All hearts turn first to the Fathers of the Republic. Their venerable forms rise before us, in the procession of successive generations. They come from the frozen rock of Plymouth, from the wasted bands of Raleigh, from the heavenly companionship of Penn, from the anxious councils of the Revolution, — from all those fields of sacrifice, where, in obedience to the spirit of their age, they sealed their devotion to duty with their blood. They say to us, their children, "Cease to vaunt what you do, and what has been done for you. Learn to walk meekly and to think humbly. Cultivate habits of self-sacrifice. Never aim at what is not RIGHT, persuaded that without this every possession and all knowledge will become an evil and a shame. And may these words of ours be ever in your minds! Strive to increase the inheritance we have bequeathed to you, — bearing in mind always, that, if we excel you in virtue, such a victory will be to us a mortification, while defeat will bring happiness. In this way you may conquer us. Nothing is more shameful for a man than a claim to esteem, not on his own merits, but on the fame of his ancestors. The glory of the fathers is doubtless to their children a most precious treasure; but to enjoy it without transmission to the next generation, and without addition, is the extreme of ignominy. Following these counsels, when your days on earth are finished, you will come to join us, and we shall receive you as friend receives friend; but if you neglect our words, expect no happy greeting from us."[1]

Honor to the memory of our fathers! May the turf lie lightly on their sacred graves! Not in words only, but in deeds also, let us testify our reverence for their name, imitating what in them was lofty, pure, and good, learning from them to bear hardship and privation. May we, who now reap in strength what they sowed in weakness, augment the inheritance we have received! To this end, we must not fold our hands in slumber, nor abide content with the past. To each generation is appointed its peculiar task; nor does the heart which responds to the call of duty find rest except in the grave.

Be ours the task now in the order of Providence cast upon us. And what is this duty? What can we do to make our coming welcome to our fathers in the skies, and draw to our memory hereafter the homage of a grateful posterity? How add to the inheritance received? The answer must interest all, particularly on

[1] This is borrowed almost literally from the words attributed by Plato to the Fathers of Athens, in the beautiful funeral discourse of the Menexenus.

this festival, when we celebrate the Nativity of the Republic. It well becomes the patriot citizen, on this anniversary, to consider the national character, and how it may be advanced, — as the good man dedicates his birthday to meditation on his life, and to resolutions of improvement. Avoiding, then, all exultation in the abounding prosperity of the land, and in that freedom whose influence is widening to the uttermost circles of the earth, I would turn attention to the character of our country, and humbly endeavor to learn what must be done that the Republic may best secure the welfare of the people committed to its care, — that it may perform its part in the world's history, — that it may fulfil the aspirations of generous hearts, — and, practising that righteousness which exalteth a nation, attain to the elevation of True Grandeur.

With this aim, and believing that I can in no other way so fitly fulfil the trust reposed in me to-day, I purpose to consider *what, in our age, are the true objects of national ambition, — what is truly National Honor, National Glory,* — WHAT IS THE TRUE GRANDEUR OF NATIONS. I would not depart from the modesty that becomes me, yet I am not without hope that I may do something to rescue these terms, now so powerful over the minds of men, from mistaken objects, especially from deeds of war, and the extension of empire, that they may be applied to works of justice and beneficence, which are better than war or empire.

The subject may be novel, on an occasion like the present; but it is comprehensive, and of transcendent importance. It raises us to the contemplation of things not temporary or local, but belonging to all ages and countries, — things lofty as Truth, universal as Humanity. Nay, more; it practically concerns the general welfare, not only of our own cherished Republic, but of the whole Federation of Nations. It has an urgent interest from transactions in which we are now unhappily involved. By an act of unjust legislation, extending our power over Texas, peace with Mexico is endangered, — while, by petulant assertion of a disputed claim to a remote territory beyond the Rocky Mountains, ancient fires of hostile strife are kindled anew on the hearth of our mother country. Mexico and England both avow the determination to vindicate what is called the *National Honor;* and our Government calmly contemplates the dread Arbitrament of War, provided it cannot obtain what is called an honorable peace.

Far from our nation and our age be the sin and shame of contests hateful in the sight of God and all good men, having their origin in no righteous sentiment, no true love of country, no generous thirst for fame, "that last infirmity of noble mind," but springing manifestly from an ignorant and ignoble passion for new territory, strengthened, in our case, in a republic whose star is Liberty, by unnatural desire to add new links in chains destined yet to fall from the limbs of the unhappy slave! In such contests God has no attribute which can join with us. Who believes that the national honor would be promoted by a war with Mexico or a war with England? What just man would sacrifice a single human life to bring under our rule both Texas and Oregon? An ancient Roman, ignorant of Christian truth, touched only by the relation of fellow-countryman, and not of fellow-man, said, as he turned aside from a career of Asiatic conquest, that he would rather save the life of a single citizen than win to his power all the dominions of Mithridates.[1]

A war with Mexico would be mean and cowardly; with England it would be bold at least, though parricidal. The heart sickens at the murderous attack upon an enemy distracted by civil feud, weak at home, impotent abroad; but it recoils in horror from the deadly shock between children of a common ancestry, speaking the same language, soothed in infancy by the same words of love and tenderness, and hardened into vigorous manhood under the bracing influence of institutions instinct with the same vital breath of freedom. The Roman historian has aptly pictured this unnatural combat. Rarely do words of the past so justly describe the present. *Curam acuebat, quod adversus Latinos bellandum erat, lingua, moribus, armorum genere, institutis ante omnia militaribus congruentes: milites militibus, centurionibus centuriones, tribuni tribunis compares collegæque, iisdem præsidiis, sæpe iisdem manipulis permixti fuerant.*[2]

Can there be in our age any peace that is not honorable, any war that is not dishonorable? The true honor of a nation is conspicuous only in deeds of justice and beneficence, securing and advancing human happiness. In the clear eye of that Christian judgment which must yet prevail, vain are the victories of War, infamous its spoils. He is the benefactor, and worthy of honor, who carries comfort to wretchedness, dries the tear of sorrow, relieves the unfortunate, feeds the hungry, clothes the naked, does justice, enlightens the ignorant, unfastens the fetters of

[1] Plutarch, *Lucullus*, Cap. VIII.

[2] Livy, Hist., Lib. VIII. c. 6.

the slave, and finally, by virtuous genius, in art, literature, science, enlivens and exalts the hours of life, or, by generous example, inspires a love for God and man. This is the Christian hero; this is the man of honor in a Christian land. He is no benefactor, nor worthy of honor, whatever his worldly renown, whose life is absorbed in feats of brute force, who renounces the great law of Christian brotherhood, whose vocation is blood. Well may the modern poet exclaim, "The world knows nothing of its greatest men!" — for thus far it has chiefly honored the violent brood of Battle, armed men springing up from the dragon's teeth sown by Hate, and cared little for the truly good men, children of Love, guiltless of their country's blood, whose steps on earth are noiseless as an angel's wing.

It will not be disguised that this standard differs from that of the world even in our day. The voice of man is yet given to martial praise, and the honors of victory are chanted even by the lips of woman. The mother, rocking the infant on her knee, stamps the images of War upon his tender mind, at that age more impressible than wax; she nurses his slumber with its music, pleases his waking hours with its stories, and selects for his playthings the plume and the sword. From the child is formed the man; and who can weigh the influence of a mother's spirit on the opinions of his life? The mind which trains the child is like a hand at the end of a long lever; a gentle effort suffices to heave the enormous weight of succeeding years. As the boy advances to youth, he is fed like Achilles, not on honey and milk only, but on bears' marrow and lions' hearts. He draws the nutriment of his soul from a literature whose beautiful fields are moistened by human blood. Fain would I offer my tribute to the Father of Poetry, standing with harp of immortal melody on the misty mountain-top of distant Antiquity, — to those stories of courage and sacrifice which emblazon the annals of Greece and Rome, — to the fulminations of Demosthenes and the splendors of Tully, — to the sweet verse of Virgil and the poetic prose of Livy; fain would I offer my tribute to the new literature, which shot up in modern times as a vigorous forest from the burnt site of ancient woods, — to the passionate song of the Troubadour in France and the Minnesinger in Germany, — to the thrilling ballad of Spain and the delicate music of the Italian lyre: but from all these has breathed the breath of War, that has swept the heart-strings of men in all the thronging generations.

And when the youth becomes a man, his country invites his service in war, and holds before his bewildered imagination the prizes of worldly honor. For him the pen of the historian and the verse of the poet. His soul is taught to swell at the thought that he, too, is a soldier, — that his name shall be entered on the list of those who have borne arms for their country; and perhaps he dreams that he, too, may sleep, like the Great Captain of Spain, with a hundred trophies over his grave. The law of the land throws its sanction over this frenzy. The contagion spreads beyond those subject to positive obligation. Peaceful citizens volunteer to appear as soldiers, and affect, in dress, arms, and deportment, what is called the "pride, pomp, and circumstance of glorious war." The ear-piercing fife has to-day filled our streets, and we have come to this church, on this National Sabbath, by the thump of drum and with the parade of bristling bayonets.

It is not strange, then, that the Spirit of War still finds a home among us, nor that its honors continue to be regarded. All this may seem to illustrate the bitter philosophy of Hobbes, declaring that the natural state of mankind is War, and to sustain the exulting language of the soldier in our own day, when he wrote, "War is the condition of this world. From man to the smallest insect, all are at strife; and the glory of arms, which cannot be obtained without the exercise of honor, fortitude, courage, obedience, modesty, and temperance, excites the brave man's patriotism, and is a chastening corrective for the rich man's pride."[1] This is broad and bold. In madder mood, another British general is reported as saying, "Why, man, do you know that a grenadier is the *greatest character* in this world," — and after a moment's pause, with the added emphasis of an oath, "and, I believe, in the next, too."[2] All these spoke in harmony. If one is true, all are true. A French voice has struck another note, chanting nothing less than the divinity of war, hailing it as "divine" in itself, — "divine" in its consequences, — "divine" in mysterious glory and seductive attraction, — "divine" in the manner of its declaration, — "divine" in the results obtained, — "divine" in the undefinable force by which its triumph is determined;[3] and the whole earth, continually imbibing blood, is nothing but an immense altar, where life is immolated without end, without measure, without respite. But this oracle is not saved from rejection even by the magistral style in which it is delivered.

[1] Napier, Peninsular War, Book XXIV. ch. 6, Vol. VI. p. 688.

[2] Southey, Colloquies on the Progress and Prospects of Society, Coll. VIII., Vol. I. p. 211.

[3] Joseph de Maistre, Soirées de Saint-Pétersbourg, Tom. II. pp. 27, 32 – 35.

Alas! in the existing attitude of nations, the infidel philosopher and the rhetorical soldier, to say nothing of the giddy general and the French priest of Mars, find too much support for a theory which degrades human nature and insults the goodness of God. It is true that in us are impulses unhappily tending to strife. Propensities possessed in common with the beast, if not subordinated to what in man is human, almost divine, will break forth in outrage. This is the predominance of the animal. Hence wars and fightings, with the false glory which crowns such barbarism. But the true civilization of nations, as of individuals, is determined by the extent to which these evil dispositions are restrained. Nor does the teacher ever more truly perform his high office than when, recognizing the supremacy of the moral and intellectual, he calls upon nations, as upon individuals, to declare independence of the bestial, to abandon practices founded on this part of our nature, and in every way to beat down that brutal spirit which is the Genius of War. In making this appeal, he will be startled as he learns, that, while the municipal law of each Christian nation, discarding the Arbitrament of Force, provides a judicial tribunal for the determination of controversies between individuals, International Law expressly *establishes* the Arbitrament of War for the determination of controversies between nations.

Here, then, in unfolding the True Grandeur of Nations, we encounter a practice, or *custom,* sanctioned by the Law of Nations, and constituting a part of that law, which exists in defiance of principles such as no individuals can disown. If it is wrong and inglorious when individuals *consent and agree* to determine their petty controversies by combat, it must be equally wrong and inglorious when nations *consent and agree* to determine their vaster controversies by combat. Here is a positive, precise, and specific evil, of gigantic proportions, inconsistent with what is truly honorable, making within the sphere of its influence all true grandeur impossible, which, instead of proceeding from some uncontrollable impulse of our nature, is *expressly established and organized by law.*

As all citizens are parties to Municipal Law, and responsible for its institutions, so are all the Christian nations parties to International Law, and responsible for its provisions. By recognizing these provisions, nations *consent and agree* beforehand to the Arbitrament of War, precisely as citizens, by recognizing Trial by Jury, *consent and agree* beforehand to the latter tribunal. As, to comprehend the true nature of Trial by Jury, we first repair to the Municipal Law by which it is established, so, to comprehend the true nature of the Arbitrament of War, we must first repair to the Law of Nations.

Writers of genius and learning have defined this arbitrament, and laid down the rules by which it is governed, constituting a complex code, with innumerable subtile provisions regulating the resort to it and the manner in which it must be conducted, called the *Laws of War.* In these quarters we catch our first authentic glimpses of its folly and wickedness. According to Lord Bacon, whose authority is always great, "Wars are no massacres and confusions, but they are the highest *Trials of Right,* when princes and states, that acknowledge no superior upon earth, shall put themselves upon the justice of God *for the deciding of their controversies* by such success as it shall please him to give on either side."[1] This definition of the English philosopher is adopted by the American jurist, Chancellor Kent, in his Commentaries on American Law.[2] The Swiss publicist, Vattel, whose work is accepted as an important repository of the Law of Nations, defines War as "that state in which a nation *prosecutes its right by force.*"[3] In this he very nearly follows the eminent Dutch authority, Bynkershoek, who says, "Bellum est eorum, qui suæ potestatis sunt, *juris sui persequendi ergo,* concertatio per vim vel dolum."[4] Mr. Whewell, who has done so much to illustrate philosophy in all its departments, says, in his recent work on the Elements of Morality and Polity, "Though war is appealed to, because there is no other ULTIMATE TRIBUNAL to which states can have recourse, *it is appealed to for justice.*"[5] And in our country, Dr. Lieber says, in a work of learning and sagacious thought, that war is undertaken "in order to obtain right,"[6] — a definition which hardly differs in form from those of Vattel and Bynkershoek.

In accordance with these texts, I would now define the evil which I arraign. *War is a public armed contest between nations, under the sanction of International Law, to establish* JUSTICE *between them:* as, for instance, to determine a disputed boundary, the title to territory, or a claim for damages.

This definition is confined to contests between nations.

1 Observations upon a Libel, etc., Works, Vol. III. p. 40.
2 Lecture III., Vol. I. p. 45.
3 Book III. ch. 1, sec. 1.
4 Quæst. Jur. Pub., Lib. I. cap. 1.
5 Book VI. ch. 2. art. 1146.
6 Political Ethics, Book VII. sec. 19, Vol. II. p. 643.

It is restricted to International War, carefully excluding the question, often agitated, concerning the right of revolution, and that other question, on which friends of peace sometimes differ, the right of personal self-defence. It does not in any way throw doubt on the employment of force in the administration of justice or the conservation of domestic quiet.

It is true that the term *defensive* is always applied to wars in our day. And it is creditable to the moral sense that nations are constrained to allege this seeming excuse, although its absurdity is apparent in the equal pretensions of the two belligerents, each claiming to act on the defensive. It is unreasonable to suppose that war can arise in the present age, under the sanctions of International Law, except to determine an *asserted right.* Whatever its character in periods of barbarism, or when invoked to repel an incursion of robbers or pirates, "enemies of the human race," war becomes in our day, *among all the nations parties to existing International Law,* simply a mode of litigation, or of deciding a *lis pendens.* It is a mere TRIAL OF RIGHT, an appeal for justice to force. The wars now lowering from Mexico and England are of this character. On the one side, we assert a *title* to Texas, *which is disputed;* on the other, we assert a *title* to Oregon, *which is disputed.* Only according to "martial logic," or the "flash language" of a dishonest patriotism, can the Ordeal by Battle be regarded in these causes, on either side, as *Defensive War.* Nor did the threatened war with France in 1834 promise to assume any different character. Its professed object was to obtain the payment of five million dollars, — in other words, to determine by this *Ultimate*

Tribunal a simple question of justice. And going back still farther in our history, the avowed purpose of the war against Great Britain in 1812 was to obtain from the latter power an abandonment of the claim to search American vessels. Unrighteous as was this claim, it is plain that war here was invoked only as a *Trial of Right.*

It forms no part of my purpose to consider individual wars in the past, except so far as necessary by way of example. My aim is higher. I wish to expose an irrational, cruel, and impious *custom,* sanctioned by the Law of Nations. On this account I resort to that supreme law for the definition on which I plant myself in the effort I now make.

After considering, in succession, *first,* the character of war, *secondly,* the miseries it produces, and, *thirdly,* its utter and pitiful insufficiency, as a mode of determining justice, we shall be able to decide, strictly and logically, whether it must not be ranked as crime, from which no true honor can spring to individuals or nations. To appreciate this evil, and the necessity for its overthrow, it will be our duty, *fourthly,* to consider in succession the various prejudices by which it is sustained, ending with that prejudice, so gigantic and all-embracing, at whose command uncounted sums are madly diverted from purposes of peace to preparations for war. The whole subject is infinitely practical, while the concluding division shows how the public treasury may be relieved, and new means secured for human advancement.

I.

First, as to the essential character and root of war, or that part of our nature whence it proceeds. Listen to the voice from the ancient poet of Bœotian Ascra: —

> "This is the law for mortals, ordained by the Ruler of Heaven:
> Fishes and beasts and birds of the air devour each other;
> JUSTICE *dwells not among them: only to* MAN *has he given*
> JUSTICE *the Highest and Best*."[1]

These words of old Hesiod exhibit the distinction between man and beast; but this very distinction belongs to the present discussion. The idea rises to the mind at once, that war is a resort to brute force, where nations strive to overpower each other. Reason, and the divine part of our nature, where alone we differ from the beast, where alone we approach the Divinity, where alone are the elements of that *justice* which is the professed object of war, are rudely dethroned. For the time men adopt the nature of beasts, emulating their ferocity, like them rejoicing in blood, and with lion's paw clutching an asserted right. Though in more recent days this character is somewhat disguised by the skill and knowledge employed, war is still the same, only more destructive from the genius and intellect which have become its servants. The primitive poets, in the unconscious simplicity of the world's childhood, make this boldly apparent. The heroes of Homer are likened to animals in ungovernable fury, or to things devoid of reason or affection. Menelaus presses his

[1] Hesiod, Works and Days, vv. 276-279. Cicero also says, "Neque ulla re longius absumus a natura ferarum, in quibus inesse fortitudinem sæpe dicimus, ut in equis, in leonibus; justitiam, æquitatem, bonitatem non dicimus." — De Offic., Lib. I. cap. 16.

way through the crowd "like a wild beast." Sarpedon is aroused against the Argives, "as a lion against the crooked-horned oxen," and afterwards rushes forward "like a lion nurtured on the mountains, for a long time famished for want of flesh, but whose courage impels him to attack even the well-guarded sheep-fold." In one and the same passage, the great Telamonian Ajax is "wild beast," "tawny lion," and "dull ass"; and all the Greek chiefs, the flower of the camp, are ranged about Diomed, "like raw-eating lions, or wild-boars, whose strength is irresistible." Even Hector, the model hero, with all the virtues of war, is praised as "tamer of horses"; and one of his renowned feats in battle, indicating brute strength only, is where he takes up and hurls a stone which two of our strongest men could not easily lift into a wagon; and he drives over dead bodies and shields, while the axle is defiled by gore, and the guard about the seat is sprinkled from the horses' hoofs and the tires of the wheels;[1] and in that most admired passage of ancient literature, before returning his child, the young Astyanax, to the arms of the wife he is about to leave, this hero of war invokes the gods for a single blessing on the boy's head, — "that he may excel his father, and bring home *bloody spoils*, his enemy being slain, and *so make glad the heart of his mother!*"

From early fields of modern literature, as from those of antiquity, might be gathered similar illustrations, showing the unconscious degradation of the soldier, in vain pursuit of *justice*, renouncing the human character,

[1] Little better than Trojan Hector was the "great" Condé ranging over the field and exulting in the blood of the enemy, which defiled his sword-arm to the elbow. — Mahon, Essai sur la Vie du Grand Condé, p. 60.

to assume that of brute. Bayard, the exemplar of chivalry, with a name always on the lips of its votaries, was described by the qualities of beasts, being, according to his admirers, *ram in attack, wild-boar in defence, and wolf in flight.* Henry the Fifth, as represented by our own Shakespeare, in the spirit-stirring appeal to his troops exclaims, —

> " When the blast of war blows in our ears,
> *Then imitate the action of the tiger.*"

This is plain and frank, revealing the true character of war.

I need not dwell on the moral debasement that must ensue. Passions, like so many bloodhounds, are unleashed and suffered to rage. Crimes filling our prisons stalk abroad in the soldier's garb, unwhipped of justice. Murder, robbery, rape, arson, are the sports of this fiendish Saturnalia, when

> " The gates of mercy shall be all shut up,
> And the fleshed soldier, rough and hard of heart,
> In liberty of bloody hand shall range
> *With conscience wide as hell.*"

By a bold, but truthful touch, Shakespeare thus pictures the foul disfigurement which war produces in man, whose native capacities he describes in those beautiful words: " How noble in reason! how infinite in faculties! in form and moving how express and admirable! in action how like an angel! in apprehension how like a god!" And yet this nobility of reason, this infinitude of faculties, this marvel of form and motion, this nature so angelic, so godlike, are all, under the transforming power of War, lost in the action of the beast, or the license of the fleshed soldier with bloody hand and conscience wide as hell.

II.

The immediate effect of war is to sever all relations of friendship and commerce between the belligerent nations, and every individual thereof, impressing upon each citizen or subject the character of enemy. Imagine this instant change between England and the United States. The innumerable ships of the two countries, the white doves of commerce, bearing the olive of peace, are driven from the sea, or turned from peaceful purposes to be ministers of destruction; the threads of social and business intercourse, so carefully woven into a thick web, are suddenly snapped asunder; friend can no longer communicate with friend; the twenty thousand letters speeded each fortnight from this port alone are arrested, and the human affections, of which they are the precious expression, seek in vain for utterance. Tell me, you with friends and kindred abroad, or you bound to other lands only by relations of commerce, are you ready for this rude separation?

This is little compared with what must follow. It is but the first portentous shadow of disastrous eclipse, twilight usher of thick darkness, covering the whole heavens with a pall, broken only by the lightnings of battle and siege.

Such horrors redden the historic page, while, to the scandal of humanity, they never want historians with feelings kindred to those by which they are inspired. The demon that draws the sword also guides the pen. The favorite chronicler of modern Europe, Froissart, discovers his sympathies in his Prologue, where, with something of apostleship, he announces his purpose, "that the honorable enterprises and noble adventures and feats of arms which happened in the wars of France and England be notably registered and put in perpetual memory," and then proceeds to bestow his equal admiration upon bravery and cunning, upon the courtesy which pardoned as upon the rage which caused the flow of blood in torrents, dwelling with especial delight on "beautiful incursions, beautiful rescues, beautiful feats of arms, and beautiful prowesses"; and wantoning in pictures of cities assaulted, "which, being soon gained by force, were robbed, and men and women and children put to the sword without mercy, while the churches were burnt and violated."[1] This was in a barbarous age. But popular writers in our own day, dazzled by false ideas of greatness, at which reason and humanity blush, do not hesitate to dwell on similar scenes even with rapture and eulogy. The humane soul of Wilberforce, which sighed that England's "bloody laws sent many unprepared into another world," could hail the slaughter of Waterloo, by which thousands were hurried into eternity on the Sabbath he held so holy, as a "splendid victory."[2]

My present purpose is less to judge the historian than to expose the horrors on horrors which he applauds. At Tarragona, above six thousand human beings, almost all defenceless, men and women, gray hairs and infant innocence, attractive youth and wrinkled age, were butchered by the infuriate troops in one night, and the morning sun rose upon a city whose streets and houses

[1] Froissart, Les Chroniques, Ch. 177, 179, Collection de Buchon, Tom. II. pp. 87, 92.

[2] Life of William Wilberforce, by his Sons, Ch. 30, Vol. IV. pp 256, 261.

were inundated with blood: and yet this is called a "glorious exploit."[1] Here was a conquest by the French. At a later day, Ciudad Rodrigo was stormed by the British, when, in the license of victory, there ensued a savage scene of plunder and violence, while shouts and screams on all sides mingled fearfully with the groans of the wounded. Churches were desecrated, cellars of wine and spirits were pillaged, fire was wantonly applied to the city, and brutal intoxication spread in every direction. Only when the drunken dropped from excess, or fell asleep, was any degree of order restored: and yet the storming of Ciudad Rodrigo is pronounced "one of the most brilliant exploits of the British army."[2] This "beautiful feat of arms" was followed by the storming of Badajoz, where the same scenes were enacted again, with accumulated atrocities. The story shall be told in the words of a partial historian, who himself saw what he eloquently describes. "Shameless rapacity, brutal intemperance, savage lust, cruelty, and murder, shrieks and piteous lamentations, groans, shouts, imprecations, the hissing of fires bursting from the houses, the crashing of doors and windows, and the reports of muskets used in violence, resounded for two days and nights in the streets of Badajoz. On the third, when the city was sacked, when the soldiers were exhausted by their own excesses, the tumult rather subsided than was quelled. The wounded men were then looked to, the dead disposed of."[3] All this is in the nature of confession, for the historian is a partisan of battle.

The same terrible war affords another instance of atrocities at a siege crying to Heaven. For weeks be-

[1] Alison, Hist. of Europe, Ch. 61, Vol. VIII. p. 237.
[2] Ibid., Ch. 64, Vol. VIII. p. 482.
[3] Napier, Hist. Peninsular War, Book XVI. ch. 5, Vol. IV. p. 431.

fore the surrender of Saragossa, the deaths daily were from four to five hundred; and as the living could not bury the increasing mass, thousands of carcasses, scattered in streets and court-yards, or piled in heaps at the doors of churches, were left to dissolve in their own corruption, or be licked up by the flames of burning houses. The city was shaken to its foundations by sixteen thousand shells, and the explosion of forty-five thousand pounds of powder in the mines, — while the bones of forty thousand victims, of every age and both sexes, bore dreadful testimony to the unutterable cruelty of War.[1]

These might seem pictures from the life of Alaric, who led the Goths to Rome, or of Attila, general of the Huns, called the Scourge of God, and who boasted that the grass did not grow where his horse had set his foot; but no! they belong to our own times. They are portions of the wonderful, but wicked, career of him who stands forth the foremost representative of worldly grandeur. The heart aches, as we follow him and his marshals from field to field of Satanic glory,[2] finding everywhere, from Spain to Russia, the same carnival of woe. The picture is various, yet the same. Suffering, wounds, and death, in every form, fill the terrible canvas. What scene more dismal than that of Albuera, with its horrid piles of corpses, while all night the rain pours down, and river, hill, and forest,

[1] Napier, Book V. ch. 3, Vol. II. p. 46.

[2] A living poet of Italy, who will be placed by his prose among the great names of his country's literature, in a remarkable ode which he has thrown on the urn of Napoleon invites posterity to judge whether his career of battle was True Glory.

"Fu vera gloria? Ai posteri
L' ardua sentenza." — **Manzoni**, *Il Cinque Maggio.*

When men learn to appreciate moral grandeur, the easy sentence will be rendered.

on each side, resound with the cries and groans of the dying?[1] What scene more awfully monumental than Salamanca, where, long after the great battle, the ground, strewn with fragments of casques and cuirasses, was still white with the skeletons of those who fell?[2] What catalogue of horrors more complete than the Russian campaign? At every step is war, and this is enough: soldiers black with powder; bayonets bent with the violence of the encounter; the earth ploughed with cannon-shot; trees torn and mutilated; the dead and dying; wounds and agony; fields covered with broken carriages, outstretched horses, and mangled bodies; while disease, sad attendant on military suffering, sweeps thousands from the great hospitals, and the multitude of amputated limbs, which there is no time to destroy, accumulate in bloody heaps, filling the air with corruption. What tongue, what pen, can describe the bloody havoc at Borodino, where, between rise and set of a single sun, one hundred thousand of our fellow-men, equalling in number the whole population of this city, sank to earth, dead or wounded?[3] Fifty days after the battle, no less than thirty thousand are found stretched where their last convulsions ended, and the whole plain is strewn with half-buried carcasses of men and horses, intermingled with garments dyed in blood, and bones gnawed by dogs and vultures.[4] Who can follow the French army in dismal retreat, avoiding the spear of the pursuing Cossack only to sink beneath the sharper frost and ice,

1 Napier, Book XII. ch. 7, Vol. III. p. 543.

2 Alison, Ch. 64, Vol. VIII. p. 589.

3 Ibid., Ch. 67, Vol. VIII. p. 871.

4 Ibid., Ch. 68, Vol. VIII. p. 930. Ségur, Hist. de Napoléon, Liv. IX. ch. 7, Tom. II. p. 153. Labaume, Rel. de la Campagne de Russie, Liv. VII.

in a temperature below zero, on foot, without shelter for the body, famishing on horse-flesh and a miserable compound of rye and snow-water? With a fresh array, the war is upheld against new forces under the walls of Dresden; and as the Emperor rides over the field of battle — after indulging the night before in royal supper with the Saxon king — he sees ghastly new-made graves, with hands and arms projecting, stark and stiff, above the ground; and shortly afterwards, when shelter is needed for the troops, the order to occupy the Hospitals for the Insane is given, with the words, "Turn out the mad." [1]

Here I might close this scene of blood. But there is one other picture of the atrocious, though natural, consequences of war, occurring almost within our own day, that I would not omit. Let me bring to your mind Genoa, called the Superb, City of Palaces, dear to the memory of American childhood as the birth-place of Christopher Columbus, and one of the spots first enlightened by the morning beams of civilization, whose merchants were princes, and whose rich argosies, in those early days, introduced to Europe the choicest products of the East, the linen of Egypt, the spices of Arabia, and the silks of Samarcand. She still sits in queenly pride, as she sat then, — her mural crown studded with towers, — her churches rich with marble floors and rarest pictures, — her palaces of ancient doges and admirals yet spared by the hand of Time, — her close streets thronged by a hundred thousand inhabitants, — at the foot of the Apennines, as they approach the blue and tideless waters of the Mediterranean Sea,

[1] Alison, Ch. 72, Vol. IX. pp. 469, 553.

— leaning her back against their strong mountain-sides, overshadowed by the foliage of the fig-tree and the olive, while the orange and the lemon with pleasant perfume scent the air where reigns perpetual spring. Who can contemplate such a city without delight? Who can listen to the story of her sorrows without a pang?

At the opening of the present century, the armies of the French Republic, after dominating over Italy, were driven from their conquests, and compelled, with shrunken forces, to find shelter under Massena, within the walls of Genoa. Various efforts were made by the Austrian general, aided by bombardment from the British fleet, to force the strong defences by assault. At length the city was invested by a strict blockade. All communication with the country was cut off, while the harbor was closed by the ever-wakeful British watch-dogs of war. Besides the French troops, within the beleaguered and unfortunate city are the peaceful, unoffending inhabitants. Provisions soon become scarce; scarcity sharpens into want, till fell Famine, bringing blindness and madness in her train, rages like an Erinnys. Picture to yourselves this large population, not pouring out their lives in the exulting rush of battle, but wasting at noonday, daughter by the side of mother, husband by the side of wife. When grain and rice fail, flaxseed, millet, cocoa, and almonds are ground by hand-mills into flour, and even bran, baked with honey, is eaten, less to satisfy than to deaden hunger. Before the last extremities, a pound of horse-flesh is sold for thirty-two cents, a pound of bran for thirty cents, a pound of flour for one dollar and seventy-five cents. A single bean is soon sold for two cents, and a biscuit of three ounces for two dollars and a quarter, till finally none can be had at any price. The wretched soldiers, after devouring the horses, are reduced to the degradation of feeding on dogs, cats, rats, and worms, which are eagerly hunted in cellars and sewers. "Happy were now," exclaims an Italian historian, "not those who lived, but those who died!" The day is dreary from hunger, — the night more dreary still, from hunger with delirious fancies. They now turn to herbs, — dock, sorrel, mallows, wild succory. People of every condition, with women of noble birth and beauty, seek upon the slope of the mountain within the defences those aliments which Nature designed solely for beasts. Scanty vegetables, with a scrap of cheese, are all that can be afforded to the sick and wounded, those sacred stipendiaries of human charity. In the last anguish of despair, men and women fill the air with groans and shrieks, some in spasms, convulsions, and contortions, yielding their expiring breath on the unpitying stones of the street, — alas! not more unpitying than man. Children, whom a dead mother's arms had ceased to protect, orphans of an hour, with piercing cries, supplicate in vain the compassion of the passing stranger: none pity or aid. The sweet fountains of sympathy are all closed by the selfishness of individual distress. In the general agony, some precipitate themselves into the sea, while the more impetuous rush from the gates, and impale their bodies on the Austrian bayonets. Others still are driven to devour their shoes and the leather of their pouches; and the horror of human flesh so far abates, that numbers feed like cannibals on the corpses about them.[1]

[1] This account is drawn from the animated sketches of Botta (Storia

At this stage the French general capitulated, claiming and receiving what are called "the honors of war," — but not before twenty thousand innocent persons, old and young, women and children, having no part or interest in the contest, had died the most horrible of deaths. The Austrian flag floated over captured Genoa but a brief span of time; for Bonaparte had already descended like an eagle from the Alps, and in nine days afterwards, on the plains of Marengo, shattered the Austrian empire in Italy.

But wasted lands, famished cities, and slaughtered armies are not all that is contained in "the purple testament of bleeding war." Every soldier is connected with others, as all of you, by dear ties of kindred, love, and friendship. He has been sternly summoned from the embrace of family. To him there is perhaps an aged mother, who fondly hoped to lean her bending years on his more youthful form; perhaps a wife, whose life is just entwined inseparably with his, now condemned to wasting despair; perhaps sisters, brothers. As he falls on the field of war, must not all these rush with his blood? But who can measure the distress that

d' Italia dal 1789 al 1814, Tom. III. Lib. 19), Alison (History of Europe, Vol. IV. ch. 30), and Arnold (Modern History, Lect. IV.). The humanity of the last is particularly aroused to condemn this most atrocious murder of innocent people, and, as a sufficient remedy, he suggests a modification of the Laws of War, permitting non-combatants to withdraw from a blockaded town! In this way, indeed, they may be spared a languishing death by starvation; but they must desert firesides, pursuits, all that makes life dear, and become homeless exiles, — a fate little better than the former. It is strange that Arnold's pure soul and clear judgment did not recognize the truth, that the whole custom of war is unrighteous and unlawful, and that the horrors of this siege are its natural consequence. Laws of War! Laws in what is lawless! rules of wrong! There can be only *one Law of War*,— that is, the great law which pronounces it unwise, unjust, and unchristian.

radiates as from a bloody sun, penetrating innumerable homes? Who can give the gauge and dimensions of this infinite sorrow? Tell me, ye who feel the bitterness of parting with dear friends and kindred, whom you watch tenderly till the last golden sands are run out and the great hour-glass is turned, what is the measure of your anguish? Your friend departs, soothed by kindness and in the arms of Love: the soldier gasps out his life with no friend near, while the scowl of Hate darkens all that he beholds, darkens his own departing soul. Who can forget the anguish that fills the bosom and crazes the brain of Lenore, in the matchless ballad of Bürger, when seeking in vain among returning squadrons for her lover left dead on Prague's ensanguined plain? But every field of blood has many Lenores. All war is full of desolate homes, as is vividly pictured by a master poet of antiquity, whose verse is an argument.

"But through the bounds of Grecia's land,
Who sent her sons for Troy to part,
See mourning, with much suffering heart,
On each man's threshold stand,
On each sad hearth in Grecia's land.
Well may her soul with grief be rent;
She well remembers whom she sent,
She sees them not return:
Instead of men, to each man's home
Urns and ashes only come,
And the armor which they wore, —
Sad relics to their native shore.
For Mars, the barterer of the lifeless clay,
Who sells for gold the slain,
And holds the scale, in battle's doubtful day,
High balanced o'er the plain,
From Ilium's walls for men returns
Ashes and sepulchral urns, —
Ashes wet with many a tear,
Sad relics of the fiery bier.
Round the full urns the general groan
Goes, as each their kindred own:

One they mourn in battle strong,
And one that 'mid the armed throng
He sunk in glory's slaughtering tide,
And for another's consort died.

. . . . .

Others they mourn whose monuments stand
By Ilium's walls on foreign strand;
Where they fell in beauty's bloom,
There they lie in hated tomb,
Sunk beneath the massy mound,
In eternal chambers bound." [1]

III.

But all these miseries are to no purpose. War is utterly ineffectual to secure or advance its professed object. The wretchedness it entails contributes to no end, helps to establish no right, and therefore in no respect determines *justice* between the contending nations.

The fruitlessness and vanity of war appear in the great conflicts by which the world has been lacerated. After long struggle, where each nation inflicts and receives incalculable injury, peace is gladly obtained on the basis of the condition before the war, known as the *status ante bellum.* I cannot illustrate this futility better than by the familiar example — humiliating to both countries — of our last war with Great Britain, where the professed object was to obtain a renunciation of the British claim, so defiantly asserted, to impress our seamen. To overturn this injustice the Arbitrament of War was invoked, and for nearly three years the whole country was under its terrible ban. American commerce was driven from the seas; the re-

[1] Agamemnon of Æschylus: *Chorus.* This is from the beautiful translation by John Symmons.

sources of the land were drained by taxation; villages on the Canadian frontier were laid in ashes; the metropolis of the Republic was captured; while distress was everywhere within our borders. Weary at last with this rude trial, the National Government appointed commissioners to treat for peace, with these specific instructions: "Your first duty will be to conclude a peace with Great Britain; and you are authorized to do it, *in case* you obtain a satisfactory stipulation against impressment, one which shall secure under our flag protection to the crew. . . . . If this encroachment of Great Britain is not provided against, *the United States have appealed to arms in vain.*"[1] Afterwards, finding small chance of extorting from Great Britain a relinquishment of the unrighteous claim, and foreseeing from the inveterate prosecution of the war only an accumulation of calamities, the National Government directed the negotiators, in concluding a treaty, to "*omit any stipulation on the subject of impressment.*"[2] These instructions were obeyed, and the treaty that restored to us once more the blessings of peace, so rashly cast away, but now hailed with intoxication of joy, contained no allusion to impressment, nor did it provide for the surrender of a single American sailor detained in the British navy. Thus, by the confession of our own Government, "the United States *had appealed to arms* IN VAIN."[3] These important words are not mine; they are words of the country.

[1] Mr. Monroe to Commissioners, April 15, 1813: American State Papers, Vol. VIII. pp. 577, 578.

[2] Mr. Monroe to Commissioners, June 27, 1814: Ibid., Vol. VIII. p. 593.

[3] Mr. Jefferson, in more than one letter, declares the peace *an armistice only*, "because no security is provided against the impressment of our seamen." — Letter to Crawford, Feb. 11, 1815; to Lafayette, Feb. 14, 1815: Works, Vol. VI. pp. 420, 427.

All this is the natural result of an appeal to war for the determination of *justice.* Justice implies the exercise of the judgment. Now war not only supersedes the judgment, but delivers over the pending question to superiority of *force,* or to *chance.*

Superior force may end in conquest; this is the natural consequence; but it cannot adjudicate any right. We expose the absurdity of its arbitrament, when, by a familiar phrase of sarcasm, we deride *the right of the strongest,* — excluding, of course, all idea of right, except that of the lion as he springs upon a weaker beast, of the wolf as he tears in pieces the lamb, of the vulture as he devours the dove. The grossest spirits must admit that this is not justice.

But the battle is not always to the strong. Superiority of force is often checked by the proverbial contingencies of war. Especially are such contingencies revealed in rankest absurdity, where nations, as is the acknowledged *custom,* without regard to their respective forces, whether weaker or stronger, voluntarily appeal to this mad umpirage. Who beforehand can measure the currents of the heady fight? In common language, we confess the "chances" of battle; and soldiers devoted to this harsh vocation yet call it a "game." The Great Captain of our age, who seemed to drag victory at his chariot-wheels, in a formal address to his officers, on entering Russia, says, "In war, *fortune* has an equal share with ability in success."[1] The famous victory of Marengo, accident of an accident, wrested unexpectedly at close of day from a foe at an earlier hour successful, taught him the uncertainty of war. Afterwards, in bitterness of spirit, when his immense forces were

[1] Alison, Ch. 67, Vol. VIII. p. 815.

shivered, and his triumphant eagles driven back with broken wing, he exclaimed, in that remarkable conversation recorded by his secretary, Fain, — "Well, this is War! High in the morning, — low enough at night! From a triumph to a fall is often but a step."[1] The same sentiment is repeated by the military historian of the Peninsular campaigns, when he says, "*Fortune* always asserts her supremacy in war; and often from a slight mistake such disastrous consequences flow, that, in every age and every nation, the *uncertainty* of arms has been proverbial."[2] And again, in another place, considering the conduct of Wellington, the same military historian, who is an unquestionable authority, confesses, "A few hours' delay, an accident, a turn of fortune, and he would have been foiled. Ay! but this is War, *always dangerous and uncertain*, an ever-rolling wheel, and armed with scythes."[3] And will intelligent man look for justice to an ever-rolling wheel armed with scythes?

Chance is written on every battle-field. Discerned less in the conflict of large masses than in that of individuals, it is equally present in both. How capriciously the wheel turned when the fortunes of Rome were staked on the combat between the Horatii and Curiatii! — and who, at one time, augured that the single Horatius, with two slain brothers on the field, would overpower the three living enemies? But this is not alone. In all the combats of history, involving the fate of individuals or nations, we learn to revolt at the frenzy which carries questions of property, freedom, or life to a judgment so uncertain and senseless. The humorous poet fitly exposes its hazards, when he says, —

1 Alison, Ch. 72, Vol. IX. p. 497.

2 Napier, Book XXIV. ch. 6, Vol. VI. p. 687.

3 Ibid., Book XVI. ch. 7, Vol. IV. p. 476.

"that a turnstile is more certain
Than, in events of war, Dame Fortune."[1]

During the early modern centuries, and especially in the moral night of the Dark Ages, the practice prevailed extensively throughout Europe of invoking this adjudication for controversies, whether of individuals or communities. I do not dwell on the custom of Private War, though it aptly illustrates the subject, stopping merely to echo that joy which, in a time of ignorance, before this arbitrament yielded gradually to the ordinances of monarchs and an advancing civilization, hailed its temporary suspension as *The Truce of God.* But this beautiful term, most suggestive, and historically important, cannot pass without the attention which belongs to it. Such a truce is still an example, and also an argument; but it is for nations. Here is something to be imitated; and here also is an appeal to the reason. If individuals or communities once recognized the Truce of God, why not again? And why may not its benediction descend upon nations also? Its origin goes back to the darkest night. It was in 1032 that the Bishop of Aquitaine announced the appearance of an angel with a message from Heaven, engaging men to cease from war and be reconciled. The people, already softened by calamity and disposed to supernatural impressions, hearkened to the sublime message, and consented. From sunset Thursday to sunrise Monday each week, also during Advent and Lent, and at the great festivals, all effusion of blood was interdicted, and no man could molest his adversary. Women, children, travellers, merchants, laborers, were assured perpetual peace. Every church was made an asylum,

[1] Hudibras, Part I. Canto 3, vv. 23, 24.

and, by happy association, the plough also sheltered from peril all who came to it. This respite, justly regarded as marvellous, was hailed as the Truce of God. Beginning in one neighborhood, it was piously extended until it embraced the whole kingdom, and then, by the authority of the Pope, became coextensive with Christendom, while those who violated it were put under solemn ban. As these things passed, bishops lifted their crosses, and the people in their gladness cried, *Peace! Peace.!*[1] Originally too limited in operation and too short in duration, the Truce of God must again be proclaimed for all places and all times, — proclaimed to all mankind and all nations, without distinction of person or calling, on all days of the week, without distinction of sacred days or festivals, and with one universal asylum, not merely the church and the plough, but every place and thing.

From Private Wars, whose best lesson is the Truce of God, by which for a time they were hushed, I come to the *Judicial Combat,* or Trial by Battle, where, as in a mirror, we behold the barbarism of War, without truce of any kind. Trial by Battle was a formal and legitimate mode of deciding controversies, principally between individuals. Like other ordeals, by walking barefoot and blindfold among burning ploughshares, by holding hot iron, by dipping the hand in hot water or hot oil, and like the great Ordeal of War, it was a presumptuous appeal to Providence, under the apprehension and hope that Heaven would give the victory to him who had the right. Its object was the

1 Robertson, Hist. of Charles V., Vol. I. note 21. Semichon, La Paix et la Trève de Dieu, Tom. II. pp. 35, 53.

very object of War, — *the determination of Justice.* It was sanctioned by Municipal Law as an arbitrament for individuals, as War, to the scandal of civilization is still sanctioned by International Law as an arbitrament for nations. "Men," says the brilliant Frenchman, Montesquieu, "subject even their prejudices to rules"; and Trial by Battle, which he does not hesitate to denounce as a "monstrous usage," was surrounded by artificial regulations of multifarious detail, constituting an extensive system, determining how and when it should be waged, as War is surrounded by a complex code, known as the Laws of War. "Nothing," says Montesquieu again, "could be more contrary to good sense, but, once established, it was executed with a certain prudence," — which is equally true of War. No battle-field for an army is selected with more care than was the field for Trial by Battle. An open space in the neighborhood of a church was often reserved for this purpose. At the famous Abbey of Saint-Germain-des-Prés, in Paris, there was a tribune for the judges, overlooking the adjoining meadow, which served for the field.[1] The combat was inaugurated by a solemn mass, according to a form still preserved, *Missa pro Duello,* so that, in ceremonial and sanction, as in the field, the Church was constantly present. Champions were hired, as soldiers now.[2]

No question was too sacred, grave, or recondite for this

[1] Sismondi, Hist. des Français, Part. V. ch. 9, Tom. X. p. 514.

[2] The pivotal character of Trial by Battle, as an illustration of War, will justify a reference to the modern authorities, among which are Robertson, who treats it with perspicuity and fulness (History of Charles V., Vol. I. note 22), — Hallam, always instructive (Middle Ages, Vol. I. Chap. II. pt. 2), — Blackstone, always clear (Commentaries, Book III. ch. 22, sec. 5, and Book IV. ch. 27, sec. 3), — Montesquieu, who casts upon it a flood of

tribunal. In France, the title of an Abbey to a neighboring church was decided by it; and an Emperor of Germany, according to a faithful ecclesiastic, "desirous of dealing *honorably* with his people and nobles" (mark here the standard of honor!), waived the judgment of the court on a grave question of law concerning the descent of property, and referred it to champions. Human folly did not stop here. In Spain, a subtile point of theology was submitted to the same determination.[1] But Trial by Battle was not confined to particular countries or to rare occasions. It prevailed everywhere in Europe, superseding in many places all other ordeals, and even *Trials by Proofs*, while it extended not only to criminal matters, but to questions of property. In Orléans it had an exceptional limitation, being denied in civil matters where the amount did not exceed five sous.[2]

Like War in our day, its justice and fitness as an arbitrament were early doubted or condemned. Liutprand, a king of the Lombards, during that middle period neither ancient nor modern, in a law bearing date A. D.

light (Esprit des Lois, Liv. XXVIII. ch. 18-33), — Sismondi, humane and interesting (Histoire des Français, Part. IV. ch. 11, Tom. VIII. pp. 72-78), — Guizot, in a work of remarkable historic beauty, more grave than Montesquieu, and enlightened by a better philosophy (Histoire de la Civilisation en France depuis la Chute de l'Empire Romain, Tom. IV. pp. 89, 149-166), — Wheaton, our learned countryman (History of the Northmen, Chap. III. and XII.), — also the two volumes of Millingen's History of Duelling, if so loose a compend deserves a place in this list. All these, describing Trial by Battle, testify against War. I cannot conceal that so great an authority as Selden, a most enlightened jurist of the Long Parliament, argues the lawfulness of the Duel from the lawfulness of War. After setting forth that "a duel may be granted in some cases by the law of England," he asks, "But whether is this lawful?" and then answers, "*If you grant any war lawful*, I make no doubt but to convince it." (Table-Talk: *Duel.*) But if the Duel be unlawful, how then with War?

1 Robertson, Hist. Charles V., Vol. I. note 22.

2 Montesquieu, Esprit des Lois, Liv. XXVIII. ch. 19.

724, declares his distrust of it as a mode of determining justice; but the monarch is compelled to add, that, considering the *custom* of his Lombard people, he cannot forbid the *impious law.* His words deserve emphatic mention: "*Propter consuetudinem gentis nostræ Langobardorum* LEGEM IMPIAM *vetare non possumus.*"[1] The appropriate epithet by which he branded Trial by Battle is the important bequest of the royal Lombard to a distant posterity. For this the lawgiver will be cherished with grateful regard in the annals of civilization.

This custom received another blow from Rome. In the latter part of the thirteenth century, Don Pedro of Aragon, after exchanging letters of defiance with Charles of Anjou, proposed a personal combat, which was accepted, on condition that Sicily should be the prize of success. Each called down upon himself all the vengeance of Heaven, and the last dishonor, if, at the appointed time, he failed to appear before the Seneschal of Aquitaine, or, in case of defeat, refused to consign Sicily undisturbed to the victor. While they were preparing for the lists, the Pope, Martin the Fourth, protested with all his might against this new Trial by Battle, which staked the sovereignty of a kingdom, a feudatory of the Holy See, on a wild stroke of chance. By a papal bull, dated at Civita Vecchia, April 5th, 1283, he threatened excommunication to either of the princes who should proceed to a combat which he pronounced *criminal* and *abominable.* By a letter of the same date, the Pope announced to Edward the First of England, Duke of Aquitaine, the agreement of the two princes, which he most earnestly declared to

[1] Liutprandi Leges, Lib. VI. cap. 65: Muratori, Rerum Italic. Script., Tom. I. pars 2, p. 74.

be full of indecency and rashness, hostile to the concord of Christendom, and reckless of Christian blood; and he urged upon the English monarch all possible effort to prevent the combat, — menacing him with excommunication, and his territories with interdict, if it should take place. Edward refusing to guaranty the safety of the combatants in Aquitaine, the parties retired without consummating their duel.[1] The judgment of the Holy See, which thus accomplished its immediate object, though not in terms directed to the suppression of the *custom*, remains, nevertheless, from its peculiar energy, a perpetual testimony against Trial by Battle.

To a monarch of France belongs the honor of first interposing the royal authority for the entire suppression within his jurisdiction of this *impious custom*, so universally adopted, so dear to the nobility, and so profoundly rooted in the institutions of the Feudal Age. And here let me pause with reverence as I pronounce the name of St. Louis, a prince whose unenlightened errors may find easy condemnation in an age of larger toleration and wider knowledge, but whose firm and upright soul, exalted sense of justice, fatherly regard for the happiness of his people, respect for the rights of others, conscience void of offence toward God or man, make him foremost among Christian rulers, and the highest example for Christian prince or Christian people, — in one word, a model of True Greatness. He was of angelic conscience, subjecting whatever he did to the single and exclusive test of moral rectitude, disregarding every consideration of worldly advantage, all fear of worldly consequences.

[1] Sismondi, Hist. des Français, Part. IV. ch. 15, Tom. VIII. pp. 338 - 347.

His soul, thus tremblingly sensitive to right, was shocked at the judicial combat. It was a sin, in his sight, thus to *tempt God,* by demanding of him a miracle, whenever judgment was pronounced. From these intimate convictions sprang a royal ordinance, promulgated first at a Parliament assembled in 1260: "*We forbid to all persons throughout our dominions the* TRIAL BY BATTLE; . . . . *and instead of battles, we establish proofs by witnesses.* . . . . AND THESE BATTLES WE ABOLISH IN OUR DOMINIONS FOREVER."[1]

Such were the restraints on the royal authority, that this beneficent ordinance was confined in operation to the demesnes of the king, not embracing those of the barons and feudatories. But where the power of the sovereign did not reach, there he labored by example, influence, and express intercession, — treating with the great vassals, and inducing many to renounce this unnatural usage. Though for years later it continued to vex parts of France, its overthrow commenced with the Ordinance of St. Louis.

Honor and blessings attend this truly Christian king, who submitted all his actions to the Heaven-descended sentiment of Duty, — who began a long and illustrious reign by renouncing and restoring conquests of his predecessor, saying to those about him, whose souls did not ascend to his heights, "I know that the predecessors of the King of England lost altogether by right the conquest which I hold; and the land which I give him I do not give because I am bound to him or his heirs, *but to put love between my children and his children, who are cousins-german;* and it seems to me that what I

[1] Guizot, Hist. de la Civilisation en France, Leçon 14, Vol. IV. pp. 162 - 164.

thus give I employ to good purpose."[1] Honor to him who never by force or cunning grasped what was not his own, — who sought no advantage from the turmoil and dissension of his neighbors, — who, first of Christian princes, rebuked the Spirit of War, saying to those who would have him profit by the strifes of others, "Blessed are the peacemakers,"[2] — who, by an immortal ordinance, abolished Trial by Battle throughout his dominions, — who extended equal justice to all, whether his own people or his neighbors, and in the extremity of his last illness, before the walls of Tunis, under a burning African sun, among the bequests of his spirit, enjoined on his son and successor, "in maintaining justice, to be inflexible and loyal, turning neither to the right hand nor to the left."[3]

To condemn Trial by Battle no longer requires the sagacity above his age of the Lombard monarch, or the intrepid judgment of the Sovereign Pontiff, or the ecstatic soul of St. Louis. An incident of history, as curious as it is authentic, illustrates this point, and shows the certain progress of opinion; and this brings me to England, where this trial was an undoubted part of the early Common Law, with peculiar ceremonies sanctioned by the judges robed in scarlet. The learned Selden, not content with tracing its origin, and exhibiting its forms, with the oath of the duellist, "As God me help, and his saints of Paradise," shows also the copartnership of the Church through its liturgy appointing prayers for the occasion.[4] For some time it was the

1 Guizot, Hist. de la Civilisation en France, Leçon 14, Vol. IV. p. 151.

2 "*Benoist soient tuit li apaiseur.*" — Joinville, p. 143.

3 Sismondi, Hist. des Français, Part. IV. ch. 12, Tom. VIII. p. 196.

4 Selden, The Duello, or Single Combat, from Antiquity derived into this

only mode of trying a writ of right, by which the title to real property was determined, and the fines from the numerous cases formed no inconsiderable portion of the King's revenue.[1] It was partially restrained by Henry the Second, under the advice of his chief justiciary, the ancient law-writer, Glanville, substituting the Grand Assize as an alternative, on the trial of a writ of right; and the reason assigned for this substitution was the uncertainty of the Duel, so that after many and long delays justice was scarcely obtained, in contrast with the other trial, which was more convenient and swift.[2] At a later day, Trial by Battle was rebuked by Elizabeth, who interposed to compel the parties to a composition, — although, for the sake of their *honor*, as it was called, the lists were marked out and all the preliminary forms observed with much ceremony.[3] It was awarded under Charles the First, and the proceeding went so far that a day was proclaimed for the combatants to appear with spear, long sword, short sword, and dagger, when the duel was adjourned from time to time, and at last the king compelled an accommodation without bloodshed.[4] Though fallen

Kingdom of England; also, Table Talk, *Duel:* Works, Vol. III. col. 49 – 84, 2027.

1 Madox, Hist. of Exchequer, Vol. I. p. 349.

2 "Est autem magna Assisa regale quoddam beneficium, ... quo vitæ hominum et status integritati tam salubriter consulitur, ut in jure quod quis in libero soli tenemento possidet retinendo, duelli casum declinare possunt homines ambiguum. . . . . Jus enim, *quod post multas et longas dilationes vix evincitur per duellum*, per beneficium istius constitutionis commodius et acceleratius expeditur." (Glanville, Tractatus de Legibus et Consuetudinibus Regni Angliæ, Lib. II. cap. 7.) These pointed words are precisely applicable to our Arbitrament of War, with its many and long delays, so little productive of justice.

3 Robertson, Hist. Charles V., Vol. I. note 22.

4 Proceedings in the Court of Chivalry, on an Appeal of High Treason by

into desuetude, quietly overruled by the enlightened sense of successive generations, yet, to the disgrace of English jurisprudence, it was not legislatively abolished till near our own day, — as late as 1819, — the right to it having been openly claimed in Westminster Hall only two years previous. An ignorant man, charged with murder, — whose name, Abraham Thornton, is necessarily connected with the history of this monstrous usage, — being proceeded against by the ancient process of appeal, pleaded, when brought into court, as follows: "Not guilty; and I am ready to defend the same by my body": and thereupon taking off his glove, he threw it upon the floor. The appellant, not choosing to accept this challenge, abandoned his proceedings. The bench, the bar, and the whole kingdom were startled by the infamy; and at the next session of Parliament Trial by Battle was abolished in England. In the debate on this subject, the Attorney-General remarked, in appropriate terms, that, "if the appellant had persevered in the Trial by Battle, he had no doubt the legislature would have felt it their imperious duty at once to interfere, and pass *an ex post facto law to prevent so degrading a spectacle from taking place.*" [1]

These words evince the disgust which Trial by Battle excites in our day. Its folly and wickedness are conspicuous to all. Reverting to that early period in which it prevailed, our minds are impressed by the general barbarism; we recoil with horror from the awful subjection of justice to brute force, — from the impious profanation

Donald Lord Rea against Mr. David Ramsay, 7 Cha. I., 1631: Hargrave's State Trials, Vol. XI. pp. 124–131.

[1] Hansard, Parl. Debates, XXXIX. 1104. Blackstone, Com., III. 337, Chitty's note.

of God in deeming him present at these outrages, — from the moral degradation out of which they sprang, and which they perpetuated; we enrobe ourselves in self-complacent virtue, and thank God that we are not as these men, — that ours is an age of light, while theirs was an age of darkness!

But remember, fellow-citizens, that this criminal and impious custom, which all condemn in the case of individuals, is openly avowed by our own country, and by other countries of the great Christian Federation, nay, that it is expressly *established* by International Law, as the proper mode of determining *justice* between nations, — while the feats of hardihood by which it is waged, and the triumphs of its fields, are exalted beyond all other labors, whether of learning, industry, or benevolence, as the well-spring of Glory. Alas! upon our own heads be the judgment of barbarism which we pronounce upon those that have gone before! At this moment, in this period of light, while to the contented souls of many the noonday sun of civilization seems to be standing still in the heavens, as upon Gibeon, the dealings between nations are still governed by the odious rules of brute violence which once predominated between individuals. The Dark Ages have not passed away; Erebus and black Night, born of Chaos, still brood over the earth; nor can we hail the clear day, until the hearts of nations are touched, as the hearts of individual men, and all acknowledge *one and the same Law of Right.*

What has taught you, O man! thus to find glory in an act, performed by a nation, which you condemn as a crime or a barbarism, when committed by an individual?

In what vain conceit of wisdom and virtue do you find this incongruous morality? Where is it declared that God, who is no respecter of persons, is a respecter of multitudes? Whence do you draw these partial laws of an impartial God? Man is immortal; but Nations are mortal. Man has a higher destiny than Nations. Can Nations be less amenable to the supreme moral law? Each individual is an atom of the mass. Must not the mass, in its conscience, be like the individuals of which it is composed? Shall the mass, in relations with other masses, do what individuals in relations with each other may not do? As in the physical creation, so in the moral, there is but one rule for the individual and the mass. It was the lofty discovery of Newton, that the simple law which determines the fall of an apple prevails everywhere throughout the Universe, — ruling each particle in reference to every other particle, large or small, — reaching from earth to heaven, and controlling the infinite motions of the spheres. So, with equal scope, another simple law, *the Law of Right*, which binds the individual, binds also two or three when gathered together, — binds conventions and congregations of men, — binds villages, towns, and cities, — binds states, nations, and races, — clasps the whole human family in its sevenfold embrace; nay, more, beyond

> "the flaming bounds of place and time,
> The living throne, the sapphire blaze,"

it binds the angels of Heaven, Cherubim, full of knowledge, Seraphim, full of love; above all, it binds, in self-imposed bonds, a just and omnipotent God. This is the law of which the ancient poet sings, as *Queen alike of mortals and immortals.* It is of this, and not of any earthly law, that Hooker speaks in that magnificent period which sounds like an anthem: "Of Law there can be no less acknowledged than that her seat is the bosom of God, her voice the harmony of the world: all things in heaven and earth do her homage, the very least as feeling her care, and the greatest as not exempted from her power: both angels and men, and creatures of what condition soever, though each in different sort and manner, yet all with uniform consent, admiring her as the mother of their peace and joy." Often quoted, and justly admired, sometimes as the finest sentence of our English speech, this grand declaration cannot be more fitly invoked than to condemn the pretence of one law for the individual and another for the nation.

Stripped of all delusive apology, and tried by that comprehensive law under which nations are set to the bar like common men, War falls from glory into barbarous guilt, taking its place among bloody transgressions, while its flaming honors are turned into shame. Painful to existing prejudice as this may be, we must learn to abhor it, as we abhor similar transgressions by vulgar offender. Every word of reprobation which the enlightened conscience now fastens upon the savage combatant in Trial by Battle, or which it applies to the unhappy being who in murderous duel takes the life of his fellow-man, belongs also to the nation that appeals to War. Amidst the thunders of Sinai God declared, "Thou shalt not kill"; and the voice of these thunders, with this commandment, is prolonged to our own day in the echoes of Christian churches. What mortal shall restrict the application of these words? Who on earth is empowered to vary or abridge the commandments of God? Who shall presume to declare that this injunction was directed, not to nations, but to individuals only, — not to many, but to one only, — that one man shall not kill, but that many may, — that one man shall not slay in Duel, but that a nation may slay a multitude in the duel of War, — that each individual is forbidden to destroy the life of a single human being, but that a nation is not forbidden to cut off by the sword a whole people? We are struck with horror, and our hair stands on end, at the report of a single murder; we think of the soul hurried to final account; we hunt the murderer; and Government puts forth its energies to secure his punishment. Viewed in the unclouded light of Truth, what is War but organized murder, — murder of malice aforethought, — in cold blood, — under sanctions of *impious law*, — through the operation of an extensive machinery of crime, — with innumerable hands, — at incalculable cost of money, — by subtle contrivances of cunning and skill, — or amidst the fiendish atrocities of the savage, brutal assault?

By another commandment, not less solemn, it is declared, "Thou shalt not steal"; and then again there is another forbidding to covet what belongs to others: but all this is done by War, which is stealing and covetousness organized by International Law. The Scythian, undisturbed by the illusion of military glory, snatched a phrase of justice from an acknowledged criminal, when he called Alexander "the greatest robber in the world." And the Roman satirist, filled with similar truth, in pungent words touched to the quick that flagrant, unblushing injustice which dooms to condign punishment the very guilt that in another sphere and on a grander scale is hailed with acclamation: —

"Ille crucem sceleris pretium tulit, hic diadema."[1]

[1] Juvenal, Sat. XIII. 105. The same judgment is pronounced by Fénelon

While condemning the ordinary malefactor, mankind, blind to the real character of War, may yet a little longer crown the giant actor with glory; a generous posterity may pardon to unconscious barbarism the atrocities which have been waged; but the *custom*, as organized by existing law, cannot escape the unerring judgment of reason and religion. The outrages, which, under most solemn sanctions, it permits and invokes for professed purposes of justice, cannot be authorized by any human power; and they must rise in overwhelming judgment, not only against those who wield the weapons of Battle, but more still against all who uphold its monstrous Arbitrament.

When, O, when shall the St. Louis of the Nations arise, — Christian ruler or Christian people, — who, in the Spirit of True Greatness, shall proclaim, that henceforward forever the great Trial by Battle shall cease, — that "these battles" shall be *abolished* throughout the Commonwealth of Civilization, — that *a spectacle so degrading* shall never be allowed again to take place, — and that it is the duty of nations, involving the highest and wisest policy, to establish love between each other, and, in all respects, at all times, with all persons, whether their own people or the people of other lands, to be governed by the sacred *Law of Right*, as between man and man?

IV.

I am now brought to review the obstacles encountered by those who, according to the injunction of St. Augus-

in his counsels to royalty, entitled, *Examen de Conscience sur les Devoirs de la Royauté*.

tine, would *make war on War*, and slay it with the word. To some of these obstacles I alluded at the beginning, especially the warlike literature, by which the character is formed. The world has supped so full with battles, that its modes of thought and many of its rules of conduct are incarnadined with blood, as the bones of swine, feeding on madder, are said to become red. Not to be tempted by this theme, I hasten on to expose in succession those various PREJUDICES so powerful still in keeping alive the *custom* of War, including that greatest prejudice, mighty parent of an infinite brood, at whose unreasoning behest untold sums are absorbed in Preparations for War.

1. One of the most important is the prejudice from *belief in its necessity*. When War is called a necessity, it is meant, of course, that its object can be attained in no other way. Now I think it has already appeared, with distinctness approaching demonstration, that the professed object of War, which is justice between nations, is in no respect promoted by War, — that force is not justice, nor in any way conducive to justice, — that the eagles of victory are the emblems of successful force only, and not of established right. Justice is obtained solely by the exercise of reason and judgment; but these are silent in the din of arms. Justice is without passion; but War lets loose all the worst passions, while "Chance, high arbiter, more embroils the fray." The age is gone when a nation within the enchanted circle of civilization could make war upon its neighbors for any declared purpose of booty or vengeance. It does "nought in hate, but all in *honor*." Such is the present rule. Professions of tenderness mingle with

the first mutterings of strife. As if conscience-struck at the criminal abyss into which they are plunging, each of the great litigants seeks to fix upon the other some charge of hostile aggression, or to set up the excuse of defending some asserted right, some Texas, some Oregon. Each, like Pontius Pilate, vainly washes its hands of innocent blood, and straightway allows a crime at which the whole heavens are darkened, and two kindred countries are severed, as the vail of the Temple was rent in twain.

Proper modes for the determination of international disputes are Negotiation, Mediation, Arbitration, and a Congress of Nations, — all practicable, and calculated to secure peaceful justice. Under existing Law of Nations these may be employed at any time. *But the very law sanctioning War may be changed,* as regards two or more nations by treaty between them, and as regards the body of nations by general consent. If nations can agree in solemn provisions of International Law to establish War as Arbiter of Justice, they can also agree to abolish this arbitrament, and to establish peaceful substitutes, — precisely as similar substitutes are established by Municipal Law to determine controversies among individuals. A system of Arbitration may be instituted, or a Congress of Nations, charged with the high duty of organizing an *Ultimate Tribunal,* instead of "these battles." To do this, the will only is required.

Let it not be said, then, that war is a *necessity;* and may our country aspire to the glory of taking the lead in disowning the barbarous system of LYNCH LAW among nations, while it proclaims peaceful *substitutes!* Such a glory, unlike the earthly fame of battle, will be immortal as the stars, dropping perpetual light upon the souls of men.

2. Another prejudice is founded on *the practice of nations,* past and present. There is no crime or enormity in morals which may not find the support of human example, often on an extended scale. But it will not be urged in our day that we are to look for a standard of duty in the conduct of vain, fallible, mistaken man. Not by any subtile alchemy can man transmute Wrong into Right. Because War is according to the practice of the world, it does not follow that it is right. For ages the world worshipped false gods, — not less false because all bowed before them. At this moment the prevailing numbers of mankind are heathen; but heathenism is not therefore true. Once it was the practice of nations to slaughter prisoners of war; but the Spirit of War recoils now from this bloody sacrifice. By a perverse morality in Sparta, theft, instead of being a crime, was, like War, dignified into an art and accomplishment; like War, it was admitted into the system of youthful education; and, like War, it was illustrated by an instance of unconquerable firmness, barbaric counterfeit of virtue. The Spartan youth, with the stolen fox beneath his robe eating into his bowels, is an example of fortitude not unlike that so often admired in the soldier. Other illustrations crowd upon the mind; but I will not dwell upon them. We turn with disgust from Spartan cruelty and the wolves of Taygetus, — from the awful cannibalism of the Feejee Islands, — from the profane rites of innumerable savages, — from the crushing Juggernaut, — from the Hindoo widow on her funeral pyre, — from the

Indian dancing at the stake; but had not all these, like War, the sanction of established usage?

Often is it said that we need not be wiser than our fathers. Rather strive to excel our fathers. What in them was good imitate; but do not bind ourselves, as in chains of Fate, by their imperfect example. In all modesty be it said, we have lived to little purpose, if we are not wiser than the generations that have gone before. It is the exalted distinction of man that he is progressive, — that his reason is not merely the reason of a single human being, but that of the whole human race, in all ages from which knowledge has descended, in all lands from which it has been borne away. We are the heirs to an inheritance grandly accumulating from generation to generation, with the superadded products of other lands. The child at his mother's knee is now taught the orbits of the heavenly bodies,

> "Where worlds on worlds compose one Universe,"

the nature of this globe, the character of the tribes by which it is covered, and the geography of countries, to an extent far beyond the ken of the most learned in other days. It is true, therefore, that antiquity is the real infancy of man. Then is he immature, ignorant, wayward, selfish, childish, finding his chief happiness in lowest pleasures, unconscious of the higher. The animal reigns supreme, and he seeks contest, war, blood. Already he has lived through infancy and childhood. Reason and the kindlier virtues, repudiating and abhorring force, now bear sway. The time has come for temperance, moderation, peace. We are the true ancients. The single lock on the battered forehead of old Time is thinner now than when our fathers attempted to grasp it; the hour-glass has been turned often since; the scythe is heavier laden with the work of death.

Let us not, then, take for a lamp to our feet the feeble taper that glimmers from the sepulchre of the Past. Rather hail that ever-burning light above, in whose beams is the brightness of noonday.

3. There is a topic which I approach with diffidence, but in the spirit of frankness. It is the influence which War, though condemned by Christ, has derived from the *Christian Church.* When Constantine, on one of his marches, at the head of his army, beheld the luminous trophy of the cross in the sky, right above the meridian sun, inscribed with the words, *By this conquer*, had his soul been penetrated by the true spirit of Him whose precious symbol it was, he would have found no inspiration to the spear and the sword. He would have received the lesson of self-sacrifice as from the lips of the Saviour, and learned that by no earthly weapon of battle can true victory be won. The pride of conquest would have been rebuked, and the bawble sceptre have fallen from his hands. *By this conquer:* by patience, suffering, forgiveness of evil, by all those virtues of which the cross is the affecting token, *conquer*, and the victory shall be greater than any in the annals of Roman conquest; it may not yet find a place in the records of man, but it will appear in the register of everlasting life.

The Christian Church, after the early centuries, failed to discern the peculiar spiritual beauty of the faith it professed. Like Constantine, it found new incentive to War in the religion of Peace; and such is its character, even in our own day. The Pope of Rome, the asserted head of the Church, Vicegerent of Christ upon earth, whose seal is a fisherman, on whose banner is a Lamb before the Holy Cross, assumed the command of armies, mingling the thunders of Battle with the thunders of the Vatican. The dagger projecting from the sacred vestments of De Retz, while still an archbishop, was justly derided by the Parisian crowd as "the Archbishop's breviary." We read of mitred prelates in armor of proof, and seem still to catch the clink of the golden spurs of bishops in the streets of Cologne. The sword of knighthood was consecrated by the Church, and priests were expert masters in military exercises. I have seen at the gates of the Papal Palace in Rome a constant guard of Swiss soldiers; I have seen, too, in our own streets, a show as incongruous and inconsistent, — the pastor of a Christian church swelling the pomp of a military parade. And some have heard, within a few short weeks, in a Christian pulpit, from the lips of an eminent Christian divine, a sermon, where we are encouraged to *serve the God of Battles, and, as citizen soldiers, fight for Peace*:[1] a sentiment in unhappy harmony with the profane language of the British peer, who, in addressing the House of Lords, said, "*The best road to Peace, my Lords, is War*, and that in the manner we are taught to worship our Creator, namely, by carrying it on with all our souls, with all our minds, with all our hearts, and with all our strength,"[2] — but finding small support in a religion that expressly enjoins, when one cheek is smitten, to

[1] Discourse before the Ancient and Honorable Artillery Company, by A. H. Vinton.

[2] Earl of Abingdon, May 30, 1794: Hansard, Parl. Hist., XXXI. 680.

turn the other, and which we hear with pain from a minister of Christian truth, — alas! thus made inferior to that of the heathen who *preferred the unjustest peace to the justest war.*[1]

Well may we marvel that now, in an age of civilization, the God of Battles should be invoked. "*Deo imperante,* QUEM ADESSE BELLANTIBUS CREDUNT," are the appropriate words of surprise in which Tacitus describes a similar delusion of the ancient Germans.[2] The polite Roman did not think God present with fighting men. This ancient superstition must have lost something of its hold even in Germany; for, at a recent period, her most renowned captain, — whose false glory procured for him the title of Great, — Frederick of Prussia, declared, with commendable frankness, that he always found the God of Battles on the side of the strongest regiments; and when it was proposed to place on his banner, soon to flout the sky of Silesia, the inscription, *For* GOD *and Country,* he rejected the first word, declaring it not proper to introduce the name of the Deity in the quarrels of men. By this elevated sentiment the warrior monarch may be remembered, when his fame of battle has passed away.

The French priest of Mars, who proclaimed the

1 "*Vel iniquissimam pacem justissimo bello anteferrem,*" are the words of Cicero. (Epist. A. Cæcinæ: Epp. ad Diversos, VI. 6.) Only eight days after Franklin had placed his name to the treaty of peace which acknowledged the independence of his country, he wrote to a friend, "May we never see another war! for, in my opinion, there never was a good war or a bad peace." (Letter to Josiah Quincy: Works, ed. Sparks, Vol. X. p. 11.) It is with sincere regret that I seem, by a particular allusion, to depart for a moment from so great a theme; but the person and the theme here become united. I cannot refrain from the effort to tear this iron branch of War from the golden tree of Christian Truth, even though a voice come forth from the breaking bough.

2 De Moribus German., Cap. 7.

"divinity" of War, rivals the ancient Germans in faith that God is the tutelary guardian of battle, and he finds a new title, which he says "shines" on all the pages of Scripture, being none other than *God of Armies.*[1] Never was greater mistake. No theology, no theodicy, has ever attributed to God this title. God is God of Heaven, God of Hosts, the Living God, and he is God of Peace,—so called by St. Paul, saying, "Now the God of Peace be with you all,"[2] and again, "The God of Peace shall bruise Satan shortly,"[3] — but God of Armies he is not, as he is not God of Battles.[4] The title, whether of Armies or of Hosts, thus invoked for War, has an opposite import, even angelic, — the armies named being simply, according to authorities Ecclesiastical and Rabbinical, the hosts of angels standing about the throne. Who, then, is God of Battles? It is Mars, — man-slaying, blood-polluted, city-smiting Mars![5] It is not He who binds the sweet influences of the Pleiades and looses the bands of Orion, who causes the sun to shine on the evil and the good, who distils the oil of gladness upon every upright heart, who tempers the wind to the shorn lamb, — the Fountain of Mercy and Goodness, the God of Justice and Love. Mars is not the God of Christians; he is not Our Father in Heaven; to him can ascend no prayers of Christian thanksgiving, no words of Christian worship, no pealing anthem to swell the note of praise.

And yet Christ and Mars are still brought into fel-

1 Joseph de Maistre, Soirées de Saint-Pétersbourg, Tom. II. p. 27.

2 Romans, xv. 33.

3 Ibid., xvi. 20.

4 A volume so common as Cruden's Concordance shows the audacity of the martial claim.

5 Iliad, V. 31.

lowship, even interchanging pulpits. What a picture of contrasts! A national ship of the line now floats in this harbor. Many of you have pressed its deck, and observed with admiration the completeness which prevails in all its parts, — its lithe masts and complex network of ropes, — its thick wooden walls, within which are more than the soldiers of Ulysses, — its strong defences, and its numerous dread and rude-throated engines of War. There, each Sabbath, amidst this armament of blood, while the wave comes gently plashing against the frowning sides, from a pulpit supported by a cannon, in repose now, but ready to awake its dormant thunder charged with death, a Christian preacher addresses officers and crew. May his instructions carry strength and succor to their souls! But, in such a place, those highest words of the Master he professes, "Blessed are the peacemakers," "Love your enemies," "Resist not evil," must, like Macbeth's "Amen," stick in the throat.

It will not be doubted that this strange and unblessed conjunction of the Church with War has no little influence in blinding the world to the truth, too slowly recognized, that the whole custom of war *is contrary to Christianity.*

Individual interests mingle with prevailing errors, and are so far concerned in maintaining them that military men yield reluctantly to this truth. Like lawyers, as described by Voltaire, they are "conservators of ancient barbarous usages." But that these usages should obtain countenance in the Church is one of those anomalies which make us feel the weakness of our nature, if not the elevation of Christian truth. To uphold the Arbitrament of War requires no more than to uphold the Trial by Battle; for the two are identical, except in proportion. One is a giant, the other a pygmy. Long ago the Church condemned the pygmy, and this Christian judgment now awaits extension to the giant. Meanwhile it is perpetual testimony; nor should it be forgotten, that, for some time after the Apostles, when the message of peace and good-will was first received, many yielded to it so completely as to reject arms of all kinds. Such was the voice of Justin Martyr, Irenæus, Tertullian, and Origen, while Augustine pleads always for Peace. Gibbon coldly recounts, how Maximilian, a youthful recruit from Africa, refused to serve, insisting that his conscience would not permit him to embrace the profession of soldier, and then how Marcellus the Centurion, on the day of a public festival, threw away his belt, his arms, and the ensigns of command, exclaiming with a loud voice, that he would obey none but Jesus Christ, the Eternal King.[1] Martyrdom ensued, and the Church has inscribed their names on its everlasting rolls, thus forever commemorating their testimony. These are early examples, not without successors. But Mars, so potent, especially in Rome, was not easily dislodged, and down to this day holds his place at Christian altars.

"Thee to defend the Moloch priest prefers
The prayer of hate, and bellows to the herd,
That Deity, accomplice Deity,
In the fierce jealousy of wakened wrath,
Will go forth with our armies and our fleets
To scatter the red ruin on their foes!
O, blasphemy! to mingle fiendish deeds
With blessedness!"[2]

1 Gibbon, Decline and Fall of the Roman Empire, Chap. XVI. Vol. I. p. 680.

2 Coleridge, Religious Musings, written Christmas Eve, 1794.

One of the beautiful pictures adorning the dome of a church in Rome, by that master of Art, whose immortal colors speak as with the voice of a poet, the Divine Raphael, represents Mars in the attitude of War, with a drawn sword uplifted and ready to strike, while an unarmed angel from behind, with gentle, but irresistible force, arrests and holds the descending hand. Such is the true image of Christian duty; nor can I readily perceive any difference in principle between those ministers of the Gospel who themselves gird on the sword, as in the olden time, and those others, unarmed, and in customary suit of solemn black, who lend the sanction of their presence to the martial array, or to any form of preparation for War. The drummer, who pleaded that he did not fight, was held more responsible for the battle than the soldier, — as it was the sound of his drum that inflamed the flagging courage of the troops.

4. From prejudices engendered by the Church I pass to prejudices engendered by the army itself, having their immediate origin in military life, but unfortunately diffusing themselves throughout the community, in widening, though less apparent circles. I allude directly to what is called *the Point of Honor*, early child of Chivalry, living representative of its barbarism.[1] It is difficult to define what is so evanescent, so impalpable, so chimerical, so unreal, and yet which exercises such fiendish

[1] The *Point of Honor* has a literature of its own, illustrated by many volumes, some idea of which may be obtained in Brunet, " Manuel du Libraire," Tom. VI. col. 1636 - 1638, under the head of *Chevalerie au Moyen Age, comprenant les Tournois, les Combats Singuliers*, etc. One of these has a title much in advance of the age in which it appeared: " Chrestienne Confutation du Point d'Honneur sur lequel la Noblesse fonde aujourd'hui ses Querelles et Monomachies," par Christ. de Chiffontaine, Paris, 1579.

power over many men, and controls the intercourse of nations. As a little water, fallen into the crevice of a rock, under the congelation of winter, swells till it bursts the thick and stony fibres, so a word or slender act, dropping into the heart of man, under the hardening influence of this pernicious sentiment, dilates till it rends in pieces the sacred depository of human affection, and the demons Hate and Strife are left to rage. The musing Hamlet saw this sentiment in its strange and unnatural potency, when his soul pictured to his contemplations an

> "army of such mass and charge,
> Led by a delicate and tender prince, ...
> Exposing what is mortal and unsure
> To all that fortune, death, and danger dare,
> *Even for an egg-shell*";

and when, again, giving to the sentiment its strongest and most popular expression, he exclaims, —

> "Rightly to be great
> Is not to stir without great argument,
> *But greatly to find quarrel in a straw,*
> *When honor 's at the stake.*"

And when is honor at stake? This inquiry opens again the argument with which I commenced, and with which I hope to close. Honor can be at stake only where justice and beneficence are at stake; it can never depend on egg-shell or straw; it can never depend on any hasty word of anger or folly, not even if followed by vulgar violence. True honor appears in the dignity of the human soul, in that highest moral and intellectual excellence which is the nearest approach to qualities we reverence as attributes of God. Our community frowns with indignation upon the profaneness of the duel, having its rise in this irrational *point of honor.* Are you aware that you indulge the same sentiment on a gigantic scale, when you recognize this very point of honor as a proper apology for War? We have already seen that justice is in no respect promoted by War. Is True Honor promoted where justice is not?

The very word Honor, as used by the world, fails to express any elevated sentiment. How immeasurably below the sentiment of Duty! It is a word of easy virtue, that has been prostituted to the most opposite characters and transactions. From the field of Pavia, where France suffered one of the worst reverses in her annals, the defeated king writes to his mother, "All is lost, except *honor.*" At a later day, the renowned French cook, Vatel, in a paroxysm of grief and mortification at the failure of two dishes for the table, exclaims, "I have lost my *honor!*" and stabs himself to the heart.[1] Montesquieu, whose writings are constellations of epigrams, calls honor a prejudice only, which he places in direct contrast with virtue,—the former being the animating principle of monarchy, and the latter the animating principle of a republic; but he reveals the inferiority of honor, as a principle, when he adds, that, in a well-governed monarchy, almost everybody is a good

1 The death of the culinary martyr is described by Madame de Sévigné with the accustomed coldness and brilliancy of her fashionable pen (Lettres L. and LI., Tom. I. pp. 164, 165). It was attributed, she says, *to the high sense of honor he had after his own way.* Tributes multiply. A French vaudeville associates his name with that of this brilliant writer, saying, "Madame de Sévigné and Vatel are the people who *honored* the age of Louis XIV." The *Almanach des Gourmands*, in the Epistle Dedicatory of its concluding volume, addresses the venerable shade of the heroic cook: "You have proved that the *fanaticism of honor* can exist in the kitchen as well as the camp." Berchoux commemorates the dying exclamation in *La Gastronomie*, Chant III.:—

"*Je suis perdu d'honneur*, deux rôtis ont manqué."

citizen, while it is rare to meet a really good man.[1] The man of honor is not the man of virtue. By an instinct pointing to the truth, we do not apply this term to the high columnar qualities which sustain and decorate life, — parental affection, justice, benevolence, the attributes of God. He would seem to borrow a feebler phrase, showing a slight appreciation of the distinctive character to whom reverence is accorded, who should speak of father, mother, judge, angel, or finally of God, as *persons of honor*. In such sacred connections, we feel, beyond the force of any argument, the mundane character of the sentiment which plays such a part in history and even in common life.

The rule of honor is founded in the imagined necessity of resenting by force a supposed injury, whether of word or act.[2] Admit the injury received, seeming to sully the character; is it wiped away by any force, and descent to the brutal level of its author? "Could I wipe your blood from my conscience as easily as this insult from my face," said a Marshal of France, greater on this occasion than on any field of fame, "I would lay you dead at my feet." Plato, reporting the angelic wisdom of Socrates, declares, in one of those beautiful dialogues shining with stellar light across the ages,

1 Esprit des Lois, Liv. III. ch. 3 – 7.

2 This is well exposed in a comedy of Molière.

"*Don Pedre.* Souhaitez-vous quelque chose de moi?

"*Hali.* Oui, un conseil sur *un fait d'honneur*. Je sais qu'en ces matières il est mal-aisé de trouver un cavalier plus consommé que vous. . . . .

"Seigneur, *j'ai reçu un soufflet.* Vous savez ce qu'est un soufflet, lorsqu'il se donne à main ouverte sur le beau milieu de la joue. *J'ai ce soufflet fort sur le cœur; et je suis dans l'incertitude, si, pour me venger de l'affront, je dois me battre avec mon homme, ou bien le faire assassiner.*

"*Don Pedre.* Assassiner, c'est le plus sûr et le plus court chemin."

Le Sicilien, Sc. XIII.

that *to do a wrong is more shameful than to receive a wrong.*[1] And this benign sentiment commends itself alike to the Christian, who is bid to render good for evil, and to the enlightened soul of man. But who confessing its truth will resort to force on any point of *honor?*

In ancient Athens, as in unchristianized Christian lands, there were sophists who urged that *to suffer* was unbecoming a man, and would draw down incalculable evil. The following passage, which I translate with scrupulous literalness, will show the manner in which the moral cowardice of these persons of little faith was rebuked by him whom the gods of Greece pronounced Wisest of Men.

"These things being so, let us inquire what it is you reproach me with: whether it is well said, or not, that I, forsooth, am not able to assist either myself or any of my friends or my relations, or to save myself from the greatest dangers, but that, like the infamous, I am at the mercy of any one who may choose to smite me on the face (for this was your juvenile expression), or take away my property, or drive me out of the city, or (the extreme case) kill me, and that to be so situated is, as you say, the most shameful of all things. But my view is, — a view many times expressed already, but there is no objection to its being stated again, — *my view, I say, is, O Callicles, that to be struck on the face unjustly is not most shameful, nor to have my body mutilated, nor my purse cut; but that to strike and cut me and mine unjustly is more shameful and worse — and stealing, too,*

[1] This proposition is enforced by Socrates, with unanswerable reasoning and illustration, throughout the *Gorgias*, which Cicero read diligently while studying at Athens (De Oratore, I. 11).

and enslaving, and housebreaking, and, in general, doing any wrong whatever to me and mine, is more shameful and worse — for him who does the wrong than for me who suffer it. These things, which thus appeared to us in the former part of this discussion, are secured and bound (even if the expression be somewhat rustical) with iron and adamantine arguments, as indeed they would seem to be; and unless you, or some one stronger than you, can break them, it is impossible for any one, saying otherwise than as I now say, to speak correctly: since, for my part, *I always have the same thing to say, — that I know not how these things are, but that, of all whom I have ever discoursed with as now, no one is able to say otherwise without being ridiculous.*"[1]

Such is the wisdom of Socrates, as reported by Plato; and it has found beautiful expression in the verse of an English poet, who says, —

> "Dear as freedom is, and in my heart's
> Just estimation prized above all price,
> *I had much rather be myself the slave*
> *And wear the bonds than fasten them on him.*"[2]

The modern *point of honor* did not obtain a place in warlike antiquity. Themistocles at Salamis, when threatened with a blow, did not send a cartel to the Spartan commander. "Strike, but hear," was the response of that firm nature, which felt that true honor is gained only in the performance of duty. It was in the depths of modern barbarism, in the age of chivalry, that this sentiment shot up into wildest and rankest fancies. Not a step was taken without it. No act without reference to the "bewitching duel." And every stage in the combat, from the ceremonial at its

[1] Gorgias, Cap. LXIV.

[2] Cowper, The Task, Book II. vv. 33–36.

beginning to its deadly close, was measured by this fantastic law. Nobody forgets *As You Like It*, with its humorous picture of a quarrel in progress to a duel, through the seven degrees of Touchstone. Nothing more ridiculous, as nothing can be more disgusting, than the degradation in which this whole fantasy of honor had its origin, as fully appears from an authentic incident in the life of its most brilliant representative. The Chevalier Bayard, cynosure of chivalry, the good knight without fear and without reproach, battling with the Spaniard Señor Don Alonso de Soto Mayor, succeeded by a feint in striking him such a blow, that the weapon, despite the gorget, penetrated the throat four fingers deep. The wounded Spaniard grappled with his antagonist until they both rolled on the ground, when Bayard, drawing his dagger, and thrusting the point directly into the nostrils of his foe, exclaimed, "Señor Don Alonso, surrender, or you are a dead man!" — a speech which appeared superfluous, as the second of the Spaniard cried out, "Señor Bayard, he is dead already; you have conquered." The French knight "would gladly have given a hundred thousand crowns, if he had had them, to have vanquished him alive," says the Chronicle; but now falling upon his knees, he kissed the earth three times, then rose and drew his dead enemy from the field, saying to the second, "Señor Don Diego, have I done enough?" To which the other piteously replied, "Too much, Señor Bayard, for the *honor* of Spain!" when the latter very generously presented him with the corpse, it being his right, by the Law of Honor, to dispose of it as he thought proper: an act highly commended by the chivalrous Brantôme, who thinks it difficult to say which did most *honor* to the faultless knight, — not dragging the dead body by a leg ignominiously from the field, like the carcass of a dog, or condescending to fight while suffering under an ague![1]

In such a transaction, conferring honor upon the brightest son of chivalry, we learn the real character of an age whose departure has been lamented with such touching, but inappropriate eloquence. Thank God! the age of chivalry is gone; but it cannot be allowed to prolong its fanaticism of honor into our day. This must remain with the lances, swords, and daggers by which it was guarded, or appear, if it insists, only with its inseparable American companions, bowie-knife, pistol, and rifle.

A true standard of conduct is found only in the highest civilization, with those two inspirations, justice and benevolence, — never in any barbarism, though affecting the semblance of sensibility and refinement. But this standard, while governing the relations of the individual, must be recognized by nations also. Alas! alas! how long? We still wait that happy day, now beginning to dawn, harbinger of infinite happiness beyond, when nations, like men, shall confess that it is better to receive a wrong than do a wrong.

5. There is still another influence stimulating War, and interfering with the natural attractions of Peace: I refer to a selfish and exaggerated *prejudice of country*, leading to physical aggrandizement and political exaltation at the expense of other countries, and in disre-

[1] La Tresjoyeuse, Plaisante et Recreative Hystoire, composée par le Loyal Serviteur, des Faiz, Gestes, Triumphes et Prouesses du Bon Chevalier sans Paour et sans Reprouche, le Gentil Seigneur de Bayart, Chap. XXII.: Petitot, Collection Complète des Mémoires relatifs à l'Histoire de France, Tom. XV. pp. 238–244. Brantôme, Discours sur les Duels: Œuvres, Tom VIII. pp. 34, 35.

gard of justice. Nursed by the literature of antiquity, we imbibe the sentiment of heathen patriotism. Exclusive love for the land of birth belonged to the religion of Greece and Rome. This sentiment was material as well as exclusive. The Oracle directed the returning Roman to kiss his mother, and he kissed Mother Earth. Agamemnon, according to Æschylus, on regaining his home, after perilous separation for more than ten years at the siege of Troy, before addressing family, friend, or countryman, salutes Argos :—

"By your leave, lords, first Argos I salute."

The schoolboy does not forget the victim of Verres, with the memorable cry which was to stay the descending fasces of the lictor, "I am a Roman citizen,"—nor those other words echoing through the dark Past, "How sweet and becoming to die for country!" Of little avail the nobler cry, "I am a man," or the Christian ejaculation, swelling the soul, "How sweet and becoming to die for duty!" The beautiful genius of Cicero, instinct at times with truth almost divine, did not ascend to that heaven where it is taught that all mankind are neighbors and kindred. To the love of universal man may be applied those words by which the great Roman elevated his selfish patriotism to virtue, when he said that *country alone embraced all the charities of all.*[1] Attach this admired phrase to the single idea of country, and you see how contracted are its charities, compared with that world-wide circle where our neighbor is the suffering

[1] "Cari sunt parentes, cari liberi, propinqui, familiares ; sed *omnes omnium caritates patria una complexa est.*" (De Offic., Lib. I. cap. 17.) It is curious to observe how Cicero puts aside that expression of true humanity which fell from Terence, "*Humani nihil a me alienum puto.*" He says, "*Est enim difficilis cura rerum alienarum.*" Ibid., Lib. I. cap. 9.

man, though at the farthest pole. Such a sentiment would dry up those precious fountains now diffusing themselves in distant unenlightened lands, from the icy mountains of Greenland to the coral islands of the Pacific Sea.

It is the policy of rulers to encourage this exclusive patriotism, and here they are aided by the examples of antiquity. I do not know that any one nation is permitted to reproach another with this selfishness. All are selfish. Men are taught to live, not for mankind, but only for a small portion of mankind. The pride, vanity, ambition, brutality even, which all rebuke in the individual, are accounted virtues, if displayed in the name of country. Among us the sentiment is active, while it derives new force from the point with which it has been expressed. An officer of our navy, one of the heroes nurtured by War, whose name has been praised in churches, going beyond all Greek, all Roman example, exclaimed, "Our country, *right or wrong*," — a sentiment dethroning God and enthroning the Devil, whose flagitious character must be rebuked by every honest heart. How different was virtuous Andrew Fletcher, whose heroical uprightness, amidst the trials of his time, has become immortal in the saying, that he "would readily lose his life to *serve* his country, but would not do a base thing to *save* it."[1] Better words, or more truly patriotic, were never uttered. "Our country, our whole country, and *nothing but our country*," are other delusive sounds, which, first falling from the lips of an eminent American orator, are often painted on banners, and echoed by innumerable multitudes. Cold and dreary, narrow and selfish would be

1 Character, prefixed to Political Works, p. viii.

this life, if *nothing but our country* occupied the soul,—if the thoughts that wander through eternity, if the infinite affections of our nature, were restrained to that place where we find ourselves by the accident of birth.

By a natural sentiment we incline to the spot where we were born, to the fields that witnessed the sports of childhood, to the seat of youthful studies, and to the institutions under which we have been trained. The finger of God writes all these things indelibly upon the heart of man, so that even in death he reverts with fondness to early associations, and longs for a draught of cold water from the bucket in his father's well. This sentiment is independent of reflection: for it begins before reflection, grows with our growth, and strengthens with our strength. It is the same in all countries having the same degree of enlightenment, differing only according to enlightenment, under whose genial influence it softens and refines. It is the strongest with those least enlightened. The wretched Hottentot never travels away from his melting sun; the wretched Esquimau never travels away from his freezing cold; nor does either know or care for other lands. This is his patriotism. The same instinct belongs to animals. There is no beast not instinctively a patriot, cherishing his own country with all its traditions, which he guards instinctively against all comers. Thus again, in considering the origin of War, do we encounter the animal in man. But as human nature is elevated, as the animal is subdued, that patriotism which is without reason shares the generous change and gradually loses its barbarous egotism. To the enlarged vision a new world is disclosed, and we begin to discern the distant mountain-peaks, all gilded by the beams of morning, revealing that God has not placed us alone on this earth, but that others, equally with ourselves, are children of his care.

The curious spirit goes further, and, while recognizing an inborn attachment to the place of birth, searches into the nature of the allegiance required. According to the old idea, still too prevalent, man is made for the State, not the State for man. Far otherwise is the truth. The State is an artificial body, for the security of the people. How constantly do we find in human history that the people are sacrificed for the State, — to build the Roman name, to secure for England the trident of the sea, to carry abroad the conquering eagles of France! This is to barter the greater for the less, — to sacrifice humanity, embracing more even than country *all the charities of all*, for the sake of a mistaken grandeur.

Not that I love country less, but Humanity more, do I now and here plead the cause of a higher and truer patriotism. I cannot forget that we are men by a more sacred bond than we are citizens, — that we are children of a common Father more than we are Americans.

Thus do seeming diversities of nations — separated by accident of language, mountain, river, or sea — all disappear, and the multitudinous tribes of the globe stand forth as members of one vast Human Family, where strife is treason to Heaven, and all war is nothing else than *civil* war. In vain restrict this odious term, importing so much of horror, to the dissensions of a single community. It belongs also to feuds between nations. The soul trembles aghast in the contemplation of fields drenched with fraternal gore, where the happiness of homes is shivered by neighbors, and kinsman sinks beneath the steel nerved by a kinsman's hand. This is civil war, accursed forever in the calendar of Time. In the faithful record of the future, recognizing the True Grandeur of Nations, the Muse of History, inspired by a loftier justice and touched to finer sensibilities, will extend to Universal Man the sympathy now confined to country, and no war will be waged without arousing everlasting judgment.

6. I might here pause, feeling that those who have accompanied me to this stage will be ready to join in condemnation of War, and to hail Peace as the only condition becoming the dignity of human nature, while it opens vistas of all kinds abundant with the most fruitful promises. But there is one other consideration, yielding to none in importance, — perhaps more important than all, being at once cause and effect, — the cause of strong prejudice in favor of War, and the effect of this prejudice. I refer to *Preparations for War* in time of Peace. Here is an immense practical evil, requiring remedy. In exposing its character too much care cannot be taken.

I shall not dwell upon the fearful cost of War itself. That is present in the mountainous accumulations of debt, piled like Ossa upon Pelion, with which civilization is pressed to earth. According to the most recent tables, the public debt of European nations, so far as known, amounts to the terrific sum of $7,777,521,840, — all the growth of War! It is said that there are throughout these nations 17,000,000 paupers, or persons subsisting at the public expense, without contributing to its resources. If these millions of public debt, forming only a part of what has been wasted in War, could be apportioned among these poor, it would give to each $450, — a sum placing all above want, and about equal to the average wealth of an inhabitant of Massachusetts.

The public debt of Great Britain in 1842 reached to $3,827,833,102, the growth of War since 1688. This amount is equal to two thirds of all the harvest of gold and silver yielded by Spanish America, including Mexico and Peru, from the discovery of our hemisphere by Christopher Columbus to the beginning of the present century, as calculated by Humboldt.[1] It is much larger than the mass of all the precious metals constituting at this moment the circulating medium of the world. Sometimes it is rashly said, by those who have given little attention to the subject, that all this expenditure has been widely distributed, and therefore beneficial to the people; but this apology forgets that it has not been bestowed on any productive industry or useful object. The magnitude of this waste appears by contrast. For instance, the aggregate capital of all the joint-stock companies in England of which there was any known record in 1842, embracing canals, docks, bridges, insurance, banks, gas-lights, water, mines, railways, and other miscellaneous objects, was about $800,000,000, — all devoted to the welfare of the people, but how much less in amount than the War Debt! For the six years preceding 1842, the average payment for interest on this debt was $141,645,157 annually. If we add to this sum the further annual outlay of $66,780,817 for the army, navy, and ordnance, we shall have $208,425,974 as the annual tax of the English people, to pay for for-

[1] New Spain, Vol. III. p. 431.

mer wars and prepare for new. During this same period, an annual appropriation of $24,858,442 was sufficient for the entire civil service. Thus War consumed ninety cents of every dollar pressed by heavy taxation from the English people. What fabulous monster, what chimæra dire, ever raged with a maw so ravenous? The remaining ten cents sufficed to maintain the splendor of the throne, the administration of justice, and diplomatic relations with foreign powers, — in short, all the more legitimate objects of a nation.[1]

Thus much for the general cost of War. Let us now look exclusively at the *Preparations for War in time of Peace.* It is one of the miseries of War, that even in Peace its evils continue to be felt beyond any other by which suffering humanity is oppressed. If Bellona withdraws from the field, we only lose sight of her flaming torches; the baying of her dogs is heard on the mountains, and civilized man thinks to find protection from their sudden fury only by inclosing himself in the barbarous armor of battle. At this moment, the Christian nations, worshipping a symbol of common brotherhood, occupy intrenched camps, with armed watch, to prevent surprise from each other. Recognizing War as Arbiter of Justice, they hold themselves perpetually ready for the bloody umpirage.

It is difficult, if not impossible, to arrive at any exact estimate of these Preparations, ranging under four different heads, — Standing Army, Navy, Fortifications, and Militia, or irregular troops.

[1] Here and in subsequent pages I have relied upon the Encyclopædia Britannica, the Annual Register, McCulloch's Commercial Dictionary, Laurie's Universal Geography, founded on the works of Malte-Brun and Balbi, and the calculations of Hon. William Jay, in War and Peace, p. 16, and in his Address before the Peace Society, pp. 28, 29.

The number of soldiers now affecting to keep the peace of European Christendom, as a *Standing Army*, without counting the Navy, is upwards of two millions: some estimates place it as high as three millions. The army of Great Britain, including the forces in India, exceeds 300,000 men; that of France, 350,000; that of Russia, 730,000, and is reckoned by some as high as 1,000,000; that of Austria, 275,000; that of Prussia, 150,000. Taking the smaller number, and supposing these two millions to require for their support an average annual sum of only $150 each, the result would be $300,000,000 for sustenance alone; and reckoning one officer to ten soldiers, and allowing to each of the latter an English shilling a day, or $88.33 a year, for wages, and to the former an average annual salary of $500, we have for the pay of the whole no less than $258,994,000, or an appalling sum-total, for both sustenance and pay, of $558,994,000 a year. If the same calculation be made, supposing the force three millions, the sum-total will be $838,491,000! But to this enormous sum must be added another still more enormous, on account of loss sustained by the withdrawal of these hardy, healthy millions, in the bloom of life, from useful, productive labor. It is supposed that it costs an average sum of $500 to rear a soldier, and that the value of his labor, if devoted to useful objects, would be $150 a year. Therefore, in setting apart two millions of men as soldiers, the Christian powers sustain a loss of $1,000,000,000 on account of training, and $300,000,000 on account of labor, in addition to the millions annually expended for sustenance and pay. So much for the Standing Army of Christian Europe in time of Peace.

Glance now at the *Navy*. The Royal Navy of Great Britain consists at present of 557 ships; but deducting such as are used for convict ships, floating chapels, and coal depots, the efficient Navy comprises 88 ships of the line, 109 frigates, 190 small frigates, corvettes, brigs, and cutters, including packets, 65 steamers of various sizes, 3 troop-ships and yachts: in all, 455 ships. Of these, in 1839, 190 were in commission, carrying in all 4,202 guns, with crews numbering 34,465 men. The Navy of France, though not comparable with that of England, is of vast force. By royal ordinance of 1st January, 1837, it was fixed in time of peace at 40 ships of the line, 50 frigates, 40 steamers, and 19 smaller vessels, with crews numbering, in 1839, 20,317 men. The Russian Navy is composed of two large fleets, — one in the Gulf of Finland, and the other in the Black Sea; but the exact amount of their force is a subject of dispute among naval men and publicists. Some idea of the Navy may be derived from the number of hands. The crews of the Baltic amounted, in 1837, to not less than 30,800 men, and those of the Black Sea to 19,800, or altogether 50,600, — being nearly equal to those of England and France combined. The Austrian Navy comprised, in 1837, 8 ships of the line, 8 frigates, 4 sloops, 6 brigs, 7 schooners or galleys, and smaller vessels: the number of men in its service, in 1839, was 4,547. The Navy of Denmark comprised, at the close of 1837, 7 ships of the line, 7 frigates, 5 sloops, 6 brigs, 3 schooners, 5 cutters, 58 gunboats, 6 gun-rafts, and 3 bomb-vessels, requiring about 6,500 men. The Navy of Sweden and Norway consisted recently of 238 gunboats, 11 ships of the line, 8 frigates, 4 corvettes, and 6 brigs, with several smaller vessels. The Navy of

Greece has 32 ships of war, carrying 190 guns, with 2,400 men. The Navy of Holland, in 1839, had 8 ships of the line, 21 frigates, 15 corvettes, 21 brigs, and 95 gunboats. Of the untold cost absorbed in these mighty Preparations it is impossible to form an accurate idea. But we may lament that means so gigantic are applied by Christian Europe, in time of Peace, to the construction and maintenance of such superfluous wooden walls.

In the *Fortifications and Arsenals* of Europe, crowning every height, commanding every valley, frowning over every plain and every sea, wealth beyond calculation has been sunk. Who can tell the immense sums expended in hollowing out the living rock of Gibraltar? Who can calculate the cost of all the Preparations at Woolwich, its 27,000 cannon, and its small arms counted by hundreds of thousands? France alone contains more than one hundred and twenty fortified places; and it is supposed that the yet unfinished fortifications of Paris have cost upward of *fifty millions of dollars.*

The cost of the *Militia,* or irregular troops, the Yeomanry of England, the National Guard of Paris, and the *Landwehr* and *Landsturm* of Prussia, must add other incalculable sums to these enormous amounts.

Turn now to the United States, separated by a broad ocean from immediate contact with the Great Powers of Christendom, bound by treaties of amity and commerce with all the nations of the earth, connected with all by strong ties of mutual interest, and professing a devotion to the principles of Peace. Are Treaties of Amity mere words? Are relations of Commerce and mutual interest mere things of a day? Are professions of Peace vain? Else why not repose in quiet, unvexed by Preparations for War?

Colossal as are European expenditures for these purposes, they are still greater among us in proportion to other expenses of the National Government.

It appears that the average *annual* expenses of the National Government, for the six years ending 1840, exclusive of payments on account of debt, were $26,474,892. Of this sum, the average appropriation each year for military and naval purposes amounted to $21,328,903, being eighty per cent. Yes, — of all the annual appropriations by the National Government, eighty cents in every dollar were applied in this unproductive manner. The remaining twenty cents sufficed to maintain the Government in all its branches, Executive, Legislative, and Judicial, — the administration of justice, our relations with foreign nations, the post-office, and all the lighthouses, which, in happy, useful contrast with the forts, shed their cheerful signals over the rough waves beating upon our long and indented coast, from the Bay of Fundy to the mouth of the Mississippi. The relative expenditures of nations for Military Preparations in time of Peace, exclusive of payments on account of debts, when accurately understood, must surprise the advocates of economy in our country. In proportion to the whole expenditure of Government, they are, in Austria, as 33 per cent; in France, as 38 per cent; in Prussia, as 44 per cent; in Great Britain, as 74 per cent; in the UNITED STATES, as 80 per cent![1]

[1] I have verified these results, but do little more than follow Judge Jay, who has illustrated this important point with his accustomed accuracy. — *Address before the American Peace Society*, p. 30.

To this stupendous waste may be added the still larger and equally superfluous expenses of the Militia throughout the country, placed recently by a candid and able writer at $50,000,000 a year![1]

By a table of the National expenditures,[2] exclusive of payments on account of the Public Debt, it appears, that, *in fifty-four years from the formation of our present Government*, that is, from 1789 down to 1843, $155,282,217 were expended for civil purposes, comprehending the executive, the legislative, the judiciary, the post-office, light-houses, and intercourse with foreign governments. During this same period, $370,981,521 were devoted to the Military establishment, and $169,707,214 to the Naval establishment, — the two forming an aggregate of $540,688,735. Deducting from this amount appropriations during three years of War, and we find that more than *four hundred and sixty millions* were absorbed by vain Preparations for War in time of Peace. Add to this amount a moderate sum for the expenses of the Militia during the same period, which, as we have seen, are placed at $50,000,000 a year, — for the past years we may take an average of $25,000,000, — and we have the enormous sum-total of $1,350,000,000 piled upon the $460,000,000, the whole amounting to *eighteen hundred and ten millions* of dollars, a sum not easily conceived by the human faculties, sunk, under the sanction of the National Government, in mere *peaceful Preparations for War*: almost *twelve times* as much as was dedicated by the National Government, during the same period, to all other purposes whatsoever.

[1] Jay, War and Peace, p. 13.

[2] Executive Document No. 15, Twenty-Eighth Congress, First Session, pp 1018-19.

From this serried array of figures the mind instinctively recoils. If we examine them from a nearer point of view, and, selecting some particular item, compare it with the figures representing other interests in the community, they will present a front still more dread.

Within cannon-range of this city stands an institution of learning which was one of the earliest cares of our forefathers, the conscientious Puritans. Favored child in an age of trial and struggle, — carefully nursed through a period of hardship and anxiety, — endowed at that time by the oblations of men like Harvard, — sustained from its first foundation by the parental arm of the Commonwealth, by a constant succession of munificent bequests, and by the prayers of good men, — the University at Cambridge now invites our homage, as the most ancient, most interesting, and most important seat of learning in the land, — possessing the oldest and most valuable library, — one of the largest museums of mineralogy and natural history, — with a School of Law which annually receives into its bosom more than one hundred and fifty sons from all parts of the Union, where they listen to instruction from professors whose names are among the most valuable possessions of the land, — also a School of Divinity, fount of true learning and piety, — also one of the largest and most flourishing Schools of Medicine in the country, — and besides these, a general body of teachers, twenty-seven in number, many of whose names help to keep the name of the country respectable in every part of the globe, where science, learning, and taste are cherished, — the whole presided over at this moment by a gentleman early distinguished in public life by unconquerable energy and masculine eloquence, at a later period by the unsurpassed ability with which he administered the affairs of our city, and now, in a green old age, full of years and honors, preparing to lay down his present high trust.[1] Such is Harvard University; and as one of the humblest of her children, happy in the memories of a youth nurtured in her classic retreats, I cannot allude to her without an expression of filial affection and respect.

It appears from the last Report of the Treasurer, that the whole available property of the University, the various accumulation of more than two centuries of generosity, amounts to $703,175.

Change the scene, and cast your eyes upon another object. There now swings idly at her moorings in this harbor a ship of the line, the Ohio, carrying ninety guns, finished as late as 1836 at an expense of $547,888, — repaired only two years afterwards, in 1838, for $233,012, — with an armament which has cost $53,945, — making an aggregate of $834,845, as the actual outlay at this moment for that single ship,[2] — more than $100,000 beyond all the available wealth of the richest and most ancient seat of learning in the land! Choose ye, my fellow-citizens of a Christian state, between the two caskets, — that wherein is the loveliness of truth, or that which contains the carrion death.

I refer to the Ohio because this ship happens to be in our waters; but I do not take the strongest case afforded by our Navy. Other ships have absorbed larger sums. The expense of the Delaware, in 1842, had reached $1,051,000.

1 Hon. Josiah Quincy.

2 Executive Document No. 132, Twenty-Seventh Congress, Third Session.

Pursue the comparison still further. The expenditures of the University during the last year, for the general purposes of the College, the instruction of the Undergraduates, and for the Schools of Law and Divinity, amounted to $47,935. The cost of the Ohio for one year of service, in salaries, wages, and provisions, is $220,000,—being $172,000 above the annual expenditures of the University, and more than *four times* as much as those expenditures. In other words, for the annual sum lavished on a single ship of the line, *four* institutions like Harvard University might be supported.

Furthermore, the pay of the Captain of a ship like the Ohio is $4,500, when in service,—$3,500, when on leave of absence, or off duty. The salary of the President of Harvard University is $2,235, without leave of absence, and never off duty.

If the large endowments of Harvard University are dwarfed by comparison with a single ship of the line, how must it be with other institutions of learning and beneficence, less favored by the bounty of many generations? The average cost of a sloop of war is $315,000,—more, probably, than all the endowments of those twin stars of learning in the Western part of Massachusetts, the Colleges at Williamstown and Amherst, and of that single star in the East, the guide to many ingenuous youth, the Seminary at Andover. The yearly expense of a sloop of war in service is about $50,000,—more than the annual expenditures of these three institutions combined.

I might press the comparison with other institutions of beneficence,—with our annual appropriations for the Blind, that noble and successful charity which sheds true lustre upon the Commonwealth, amounting to $12,000, and for the Insane, another charity dear to humanity, amounting to $27,844.

Take all the institutions of Learning and Beneficence, the crown jewels of the Commonwealth, schools, colleges, hospitals, asylums, and the sums by which they have been purchased and preserved are trivial and beggarly, compared with the treasures squandered within the borders of Massachusetts in vain Preparations for War, — upon the Navy Yard at Charlestown, with its stores on hand, costing $4,741,000, — the fortifications in the harbors of Massachusetts, where untold sums are already sunk, and it is now proposed to sink $3,875,000 more,[1] — and the Arsenal at Springfield, containing, in 1842, 175,118 muskets, valued at $2,099,998,[2] and maintained by an annual appropriation of $200,000, whose highest value will ever be, in the judgment of all lovers of truth, that it inspired a poem which in influence will be mightier than a battle, and will endure when arsenals and fortifications have crumbled to earth. Some of the verses of this Psalm of Peace may relieve the detail of statistics, while they happily blend with my argument.

"Were half the power that fills the world with terror,
Were half the wealth bestowed on camps and courts,
Given to redeem the human mind from error,
There were no need of arsenals or forts:

"The warrior's name would be a name abhorred,
And every nation that should lift again
Its hand against a brother on its forehead
Would wear forevermore the curse of Cain." [3]

[1] Report of Secretary of War, Senate Document No. 2, Twenty-Seventh Congress, Second Session, — where we are asked to invest in a general system of land defences $51,677,929.

[2] Executive Document No. 3, Twenty-Seventh Congress, Third Session.

[3] Longfellow, The Arsenal at Springfield.

Turn now to a high and peculiar interest of the nation, the administration of justice. Perhaps no part of our system is regarded with more pride and confidence, especially by the enlightened sense of the country. To this, indeed, all other concerns of Government, with all its complications of machinery, are in a manner subordinate, since it is for the sake of justice that men come together in communities and establish laws. What part of the Government can compare in importance with the National Judiciary, that great balance-wheel of the Constitution, controlling the relations of the several States to each other, the legislation of Congress and of the States, besides private interests to an incalculable amount? Nor can the citizen who discerns the true glory of his country fail to recognize in the immortal judgments of MARSHALL, now departed, and of STORY, who is still spared to us — *serus in cœlum redeat!* — a higher claim to admiration and gratitude than can be found in any triumph of battle. The expenses of this great department under the National Government, in 1842, embracing the cost of court-houses, the salaries of judges, the pay of juries, and of all the law officers throughout the United States, in short, all the outlay by which justice, according to the requirement of Magna Charta, is carried to every man's door, amounted to $560,990, — a larger sum than is usually appropriated for this purpose, but how insignificant, compared with the cormorant demands of Army and Navy!

Let me allude to one more curiosity of waste. By a calculation founded on the expenses of the Navy it appears that the average cost of each gun carried over the ocean for one year amounts to about fifteen thousand dollars, — a sum sufficient to maintain ten or even twenty professors of Colleges, and equal to the salaries of all the Judges of the Supreme Court of Massachusetts and the Governor combined!

Such are illustrations of that tax which nations constituting the great Federation of Civilization, including our own country, impose on the people, in time of profound peace, for no permanent productive work, for no institution of learning, for no gentle charity, for no purpose of good. Wearily climbing from expenditure to expenditure, from waste to waste, we seem to pass beyond the region of ordinary measurement; Alps on Alps arise, on whose crowning heights of everlasting cold, far above the habitations of man, where no green thing lives, where no creature draws breath, we behold the sharp, icy, flashing glacier of War.

In the contemplation of this spectacle the soul swells with alternate despair and hope: with despair, at the thought of such wealth, capable of such service to Humanity, not merely wasted, but bestowed to perpetuate Hate; with hope, as the blessed vision arises of all these incalculable means secured to purposes of Peace. The whole world labors with poverty and distress; and the painful question occurs in Europe more than here, What shall become of the poor, — the increasing Standing Army of the poor? Could the voice that now addresses you penetrate those distant councils, or councils nearer home, it would say, Disband your Standing Armies of soldiers, employ your Navies in peaceful and enriching commerce, abandon Fortifications and Arsenals, or dedicate them to works of Beneficence, as the statue of Jupiter Capitolinus was changed to the image of a Christian saint; in fine, utterly renounce the present incongruous system of *Armed Peace.*

That I may not seem to accept this conclusion too hastily, at least as regards our own country, I shall consider the asserted usefulness of the national armaments, — and then expose the fallacy, at least in the present age and among Christian nations, of the maxim, that in time of Peace we must prepare for War.

For what use is the Standing Army of the United States? For many generations it has been a principle of freedom to avoid a standing army; and one of the complaints in the Declaration of Independence was, that George the Third had quartered large bodies of troops in the Colonies. For the first years after the adoption of the National Constitution, during our period of weakness, before our power was assured, before our name had become respected in the family of nations, under the administration of Washington, a small sum was ample for the military establishment of the United States. It was at a later day that the country, touched by martial insanity, abandoned the true economy of a Republic, and, in imitation of monarchical powers, lavished means, grudged to Peace, in vain preparation for War. It may now be said of our Army, as Dunning said of the influence of the Crown, it has increased, is increasing, and ought to be diminished. At this moment there are in the country more than sixty military posts. For any of these it would be difficult to present a reasonable apology, — unless, perhaps, on some distant Indian frontier. Of what use is the detachment of the Second Artillery at the quiet town of New London, in Connecticut? Of what use is the detachment of the First Artillery in that pleasant resort of fashion, Newport? By exhilarating music and showy parade they may amuse an idle hour; but is it not equally true that emotions of a different character will be aroused in thoughtful bosoms? He must have lost something of sensibility to the dignity of human nature who can observe, without at least a passing regret, all the details of discipline — drill, marching, countermarching — which fill the life of the soldier, and prepare him to become the rude, inanimate part of that *machine* to which an army is likened by the great living master of the Art of War.[1] And this sensibility may be more disturbed by the spectacle of ingenuous youth, in chosen numbers, under the auspices of the Government, amidst the bewitching scenery of West Point, painfully trained to these same exercises, — at a cost to the country, since the establishment of this Academy, of above four millions of dollars.

In Europe, Standing Armies are supposed to be needed in support of Government; but this excuse cannot prevail here. The monarchs of the Old World, like the chiefs of the ancient German tribes, are upborne on the shields of the soldiery. Happily, with us, Government needs no janizaries. The hearts of the people are a sufficient support.

I hear a voice from some defender of this abuse, some upholder of this "rotten borough," crying, The Army is needed for defence! As well might you say that the shadow is needed for defence. For what is the Army of the United States, but the feeble shadow of the American people? *In placing the Army on its present footing, so small in numbers, compared with the forces of great*

[1] The Duke of Wellington.

European States, our Government tacitly admits its superfluousness for defence. It only remains to declare that the country will repose in the consciousness of right, without the extravagance of soldiers, unproductive consumers of the fruits of the earth, who might do the country good service in the various departments of useful industry.

For what use is the Navy of the United States? The annual expense of our Navy, during recent years, has been upwards of six millions of dollars. For what purpose? Not for the apprehension of pirates, since frigates and ships of the line are of too great bulk for this service. Not for the suppression of the Slave Trade; for, under the stipulations with Great Britain, we employ only eighty guns in this holy alliance. Not to protect our coasts; for all agree that our few ships would form an unavailing defence against any serious attack. Not for these purposes, you admit; *but for the protection of our Navigation.* This is not the occasion for minute estimates. Suffice it to say, that an intelligent merchant, extensively engaged in commerce for the last twenty years, and who speaks, therefore, with the authority of knowledge, has demonstrated, in a tract of perfect clearness,[1] that the annual profits of the whole mercantile marine of the country do not equal the annual expenditure of our Navy. Admitting the profit of a merchant ship to be four thousand dollars a year, which is a large allowance, it will take the earnings of one hundred ships to build and employ for one year a single sloop of war, of one hundred and fifty ships to build and employ a frigate, and of nearly three hundred

[1] I refer to the pamphlet of S. E. Coues, "United States Navy: What is its Use?"

ships to build and employ a ship of the line. Thus more than five hundred ships must do a profitable business to earn a sufficient sum for the support of this little fleet. Still further, taking a received estimate putting the mercantile marine of the United States at forty millions of dollars, we find that it is only a little more than six times the annual cost of the Navy; so that this interest is protected at a charge of more than *fifteen per cent* of its whole value! Protection at such price is not less ruinous than one of Pyrrhus's victories.

It is to the Navy as an unnecessary arm of national defence, and part of the War establishment, that I confine my objection. So far as it is required for science, or for the *police* of the seas, — to scour them of pirates, and, above all, to defeat the hateful traffic in human flesh, — it is a fit engine of Government, and cannot be obnoxious as a portion of the machinery of War. But, surely, a most costly navy to protect navigation in time of Peace against assaults from civilized nations is absurdly superfluous. The free cities of Hamburg and Bremen, survivors of the powerful Hanseatic League, with a commerce whitening the most distant seas, are without a single ship of war. Following this prudent example, the United States might be willing to abandon an institution already become a vain and expensive toy.

For what use are the Fortifications of the United States? We have already seen the enormous sums locked in the odious mortmain of their everlasting masonry. Like the Pyramids, they seem by mass and solidity to defy Time. Nor can I doubt that hereafter, like these same monuments, they will be looked upon with wonder, as the types of an extinct superstition, not less degrading than that of Ancient Egypt. Under the pretence of saving the country from conquest and bloodshed they are reared. But whence the danger ? On what side ? What people to fear ? No civilized nation threatens our borders with rapine or trespass. None will. Nor, in the existing state of civilization, and under existing International Law, is it possible to suppose any war with such a nation, unless, renouncing the peaceful Tribunal of Arbitration, we voluntarily appeal to Trial by Battle. The fortifications might be of service then. But perhaps they would invite the attack they might be inadequate to defeat. According to a modern rule, illustrated with admirable ability in the diplomatic correspondence of Mr. Webster, non-combatants and their property on land are not molested. So firmly did the Duke of Wellington act upon this rule, that, throughout the revengeful campaigns of Spain, and afterwards entering France, flushed with the victory of Waterloo, he directed his army to pay for all provisions, even the forage of their horses. War is carried on against *public* property, — against *fortifications, navy-yards, and arsenals.* If these do not exist, where is its aliment, where the fuel for the flame ? Paradoxical as it seems, and disparaging to the whole trade of War, it may be proper to inquire, whether, according to acknowledged laws, now governing this bloody arbitrament, every new fortification and every additional gun in our harbor is not less a safeguard than a danger. Do they not draw the lightning of battle upon our homes, without, alas ! any conductor to hurry its terrors innocently beneath the concealing bosom of the earth ?

For what use is the Militia of the United States ?

This immense system spreads, with innumerable suckers, over the whole country, draining its best life-blood, the unbought energies of our youth. The same painful discipline which we observe in the soldier absorbs their time, though to a less degree than in the Regular Army. Theirs also is the savage pomp of War. We read with astonishment of the painted flesh and uncouth vestments of our progenitors, the ancient Britons. But the generation will come, that must regard with equal wonder the pictures of their ancestors closely dressed in padded and well-buttoned coats of blue "besmeared with gold," surmounted by a huge mountain-cap of shaggy bear-skin, and with a barbarous device, typical of brute force, *a tiger*, painted on oil-skin tied with leather to their backs! In the streets of Pisa the galley-slaves are compelled to wear dresses stamped with the name of the crime for which they are suffering punishment, — as theft, robbery, murder. Is it not a little strange that Christians, living in a land "where bells have tolled to church," should voluntarily adopt devices which, if they have any meaning, recognize the example of beasts as worthy of imitation by man?

The general considerations belonging to Preparations for War illustrate the inanity of the Militia for purposes of *national defence.* I do not know, indeed, that it is now strongly urged on this ground. It is oftener approved as an important part of the *police.* I would not undervalue the advantage of an active, efficient, ever-wakeful police; and I believe that such a police has been long required. But the Militia, where youth and character are without the strength of experience, is inadequate for this purpose. No person who has seen this arm of the police in an actual riot can hesitate in this judgment. A very small portion of the means absorbed by the Militia would provide a substantial police, competent to all the domestic emergencies of disorder and violence. The city of Boston has discarded a Fire Department composed of *accidental volunteers.* Why not do the same with the police, and set another example to the country?

I am well aware that efforts to reduce the Militia are encountered by some of the dearest prejudices of the common mind, — not only by the War Spirit, but by that other, which first animates childhood, and, at a later day, "children of a larger growth," inviting to finery of dress and parade, — the same which fantastically bedecks the dusky feather-cinctured chief of the soft regions warmed by the tropical sun, — which inserts a ring in the nose of the North American Indian, — which slits the ears of the Australian savage, and tattoos the New Zealand cannibal.

Such are the national armaments, in their true character and value. Thus far I have regarded them in the plainest light of ordinary worldly economy, without reference to those higher considerations, drawn from the nature and history of man and the truths of Christianity, which pronounce them vain. It is grateful to know, that, though having yet the support of what Jeremy Taylor calls "popular noises," the other more economical, more humane, more wise, more Christian system is daily commending itself to good people. On its side are all the virtues that truly elevate a state. Economy, sick of pygmy efforts to stanch the smallest fountain and rill of exuberant expenditure, pleads that here is a measureless, fathomless, endless river, an

Amazon of waste, rolling its prodigal waters turbidly, ruinously, hatefully, to the sea. It chides us with unnatural inconsistency, when we strain at a little twine and paper, and swallow the monstrous cables and armaments of War. Humanity pleads for the surpassing interests of Knowledge and Benevolence, from which such mighty means are withdrawn. Wisdom frowns on these Preparations, as nursing sentiments inconsistent with Peace; Christianity calmly rebukes the spirit in which they have their origin, as of little faith, and treacherous to her high behests; while History, exhibiting the sure, though gradual, Progress of Man, points with unerring finger to that destiny of True Grandeur, when nations, like individuals, disowning War as a proper Arbiter of Justice, shall abandon the oppressive apparatus of Armies, Navies, and Fortifications, by which it is waged.

Before considering the familiar injunction, *In time of Peace prepare for War*, I hope I shall not seem to descend from the proper sphere of this discussion, if I refer to the parade of *barbarous mottoes*, and of *emblems from beasts*, as another impediment to the proper appreciation of these Preparations. These mottoes and emblems, prompting to War, are obtruded on the very ensigns of power and honor, and, careless of their discreditable import, men learn to regard them with patriotic pride. In the armorial bearings of nations and individuals, beasts and birds of prey are the exemplars of True Grandeur. The lion appears on the flag of England; the leopard on the flag of Scotland; a double-headed eagle spreads its wings on the imperial standard of Austria, and again on that of Russia; while a single-headed eagle was adopted on the Napoleonic seal, and thus far the same single-headed bird is enough for Prussia. The pennons of knights, after exhausting the known kingdom of Nature, were disfigured by imaginary and impossible monsters, griffins, hippogriffs, unicorns, all intended to represent the exaggeration of brute force. The people of Massachusetts unconsciously adopt this early standard. The escutcheon used as the seal of the State has an unfortunate combination, to which I refer briefly by way of example. On that part in the language of heraldry termed the *shield* stands an Indian with a bow in his hand, — certainly no agreeable memento, except to those who find honor in the disgraceful wars where our fathers robbed and murdered King Philip of Pokanoket, and his tribe, rightful possessors of the soil. The *crest* is a raised arm *holding a drawn sabre in a threatening attitude,* — being precisely the emblem once borne on the flag of Algiers. The *scroll,* or legend, is the latter of two favorite verses, in modern Latin, which are not traced to any origin more remote than Algernon Sidney, by whom they were inscribed in an album at Copenhagen: —

> "Manus hæc inimica tyrannis
> *Ense petit placidam sub libertate quietem.*"[1]

1 The Earl of Leicester, father of Sidney, in an anxious letter, August 30, 1660, writes his son: "It is said that the University of Copenhagen brought their Album unto you, desiring you to write something therein, and that you did *scribere in Albo* these words [setting forth the verses], and put your name to it"; and then he adds, "This cannot but be publicly known, if it be true. . . . . Either you must live in exile or very privately here, and perhaps not safely." The restoration of Charles the Second had just taken place. (Meadley, Memoirs of Algernon Sidney, pp. 84, 323 – 325.) Lord Molesworth, in a work which first appeared in 1694, mentions the verses as written by Sidney in "the Book of Mottoes in the King's Library," and then tells the story, that the French Ambassador, who did not know a word of

With singular unanimity, the Legislature of Massachusetts has expressed an earnest desire for the establishment of a High Court of Nations to adjudge international controversies, and thus supersede the Arbitrament of War. It would be an act of moral dignity consistent with these professions, and becoming the character it vaunts before the world, if it abandoned the bellicose escutcheon, — at least, that *Algerine* emblem, fit only for corsairs, if not also the Latin motto with its menace of the sword. If a Latin substitute for the latter be needed, it might be those words of Virgil, "*Pacisque* imponere morem,"[1] or that sentence of noble truth from Cicero, "Sine SUMMA JUSTITIA rempublicam geri nullo modo posse":[2] the first a homage to Peace, and the second a consecration to Justice. Where such a spirit prevailed, there would be little occasion to consider the question of War Preparations.

Massachusetts is not alone in the bellicose anachronism of her banner. The nation is in the same category. Our fathers would have hesitated long before accepting the eagle for the national escutcheon, had they recalled the pungent words of Erasmus on this most unrepublican bird. "Let any physiognomist, not a blunderer in his trade," says this most learned scholar, "consider the look and features of an eagle, those rapacious and wicked eyes, that menacing curve of the beak, those cruel cheeks, that stern front, — will he

Latin, on learning their meaning, tore them from the book, as a libel on the French government, and its influence in Denmark. (Molesworth, Account of Denmark, Preface.) The inference from this narrative would seem to be that the verses were by Sidney himself.

[1] Æneid, VI. 852.

[2] De Republica, Lib. II. cap. 43.

not at once recognize *the image of a king*, a magnificent and majestic king? Add to these a dark, ill-omened color, an unpleasing, dreadful, appalling voice, and that threatening scream at which every kind of animal trembles." Proceeding with his indictment, he describes the eagle in old age as satisfied with nothing but blood, with which he prolongs his hateful life, the upper mandible growing so that he cannot feed on flesh, while the natural rapacity continues, — all of which typifies the wicked prince. But the scholar becomes orator, when, after mentioning that there are innumerable species of birds, some admirable for richness of plumage, some remarkable for snowy whiteness, some shining with befitting blackness, some pre-eminent in bodily stature, some notable for fecundity, some grateful at the rich banquet, some pleasant from loquacity, some captivating in song, some distinguished for courage, some created for the entertainment of man, — he proceeds to say: "Of all birds, the eagle alone has seemed to wise men *the apt type of royalty:* not beautiful, not musical, not fit for food, — but carnivorous, ravenous, plundering, destroying, fighting, solitary, hateful to all, the curse of all, and though able to do the greatest harm, yet wishing to do more than he can."[1] Erasmus, who says this and much more, is no mean authority. Brightest and best among the scholars who illustrated the modern revival of letters, loving peace, and detesting kings, he acquired a contemporary power and fame such as letters never bestowed before, if since, — at least until Voltaire, kindred in versatile genius, mounted the throne. In all the homage profusely offered to the latter there was

[1] Erasmi Adagia, Chil. III. Cent. VII. Prov. 1: *Scarabæus aquilam quærit*, Hallam, Literature of Europe, Part I. ch. 4. sec. 43, 44.

nothing stronger than that of Luther to Erasmus, when the great Reformer asked, "Who is the man whose soul Erasmus does not occupy, whom Erasmus does not instruct, over whom Erasmus does not reign?" His face is still familiar from the devotion of two great artists, Albert Dürer and Hans Holbein, each of whom has left to us his portrait,—while he is commemorated by a bronze statue in Rotterdam, his birthplace, and by a monument in the ancient cathedral at Basel, where he died. It is this renowned scholar who castigates our eagle. Doubtless for fighting qualities this royal bird was transferred to the coin and seal of a Republic. His presence there shows the spirit which unconsciously prevailed; and this same presence, beyond all question, exercises a certain influence, especially with the young, nursing a pride in that beak and those pounces which are the menace of War.

The maxim, *In time of Peace prepare for War,*[1] is transmitted from distant ages, when brute force was the general law. It is the terrible inheritance which painfully reminds present generations of their connection with the Past. It belongs to the dogmas of barbarism. It is the companion of harsh, tyrannical rules by which the happiness of the many is offered up to the few. It is the child of suspicion, and the forerun-

[1] If countenance were needed in thus exposing a pernicious maxim, I might find it in the German philosopher Kant, whose work on Perpetual Peace treats it with very little respect. (Kant, Sämmtliche Werke, Band VII., *Zum Ewigen Frieden*, § 1.) Since this Oration, Sir Robert Peel and the Earl of Aberdeen, each Prime Minister of England, and practically conversant with the question, have given their valuable testimony in the same direction. Life has its surprises; and I confess one in my own, when the latter, in conversation on this maxim, most kindly thanked me for what I had said against it.

ner of violence. Having in its favor almost uninterrupted usage, it possesses a hold on popular opinion not easily unloosed. And yet no conscientious man can fail, on careful observation, to detect its mischievous fallacy, — *at least among Christian nations in the present age,* — a fallacy the most costly the world has witnessed, dooming nations to annual tribute in comparison with which the extortions of conquest are as the widow's mite. So true is what Rousseau said, and Guizot has since repeated, that "a bad principle is far worse than a bad fact"; for the operations of the latter are finite, while those of the former are infinite.

I speak of this principle with earnestness; for I believe it erroneous and false, founded in ignorance and wrong, unworthy of civilization, and disgraceful to Christians. I call it a principle; but it is a mere *prejudice,* — sustained by vulgar example only, and not by enlightened truth, — obeying which, we imitate the early mariners, who, steering from headland to headland, hugged the shore, unwilling to venture upon the broad ocean, with the luminaries of heaven for their guide. If not yet discerned in its true character, it is because the clear light of truth is discolored and refracted by an atmosphere where the cloud of War covers all.

Dismissing the actual usage on the one side, and considerations of economy on the other, I would regard these Preparations in the simple light of reason, in a just appreciation of the nature of man, and in the injunctions of the highest truth. Our conclusion will be very easy. They are twice pernicious, and whoso would vindicate them must satisfactorily answer these two objections: *first,* that they inflame the people, exciting to deeds of violence, otherwise alien to the mind; and, *secondly*, that, having their origin in the low motives of distrust and hate, inevitably, by a sure law of the human mind, they excite to corresponding action in other nations. Thus, in fact, are they *promoters of War*, rather than *preservers of Peace.*

In illustration of the *first* objection, it will occur at once to every inquirer that the possession of power is in itself dangerous, tempting the purest and highest, and too rarely enjoyed without abuse. Nor is the power to employ force in War an exception. Nations possessing the greatest armaments are the most belligerent. It is the feebler powers which enjoy eras of Peace. Throughout more than seven hundred years of Roman history resounds the din of War, with only two short lulls of Peace; and in modern times this din has been echoed from France. But Switzerland has had no din. Less prepared, this Republic had less incentive to War. Not only in nations do we find this law. It applies to individuals also. The same din which resounded in Rome and was echoed from France has filled common life, and from the same cause. The *wearing of arms* has been a provocative, too often exciting, as it furnished the weapon of strife. The odious system of private quarrels, with altercation and hostile meetings even in the street, disgracing the social life of modern Europe, continued with this habit. This was its origin. But who can measure the extent of its influence? Dead bodies stretched on the pavements, and vacant chairs at home, were the contemporary witnesses. If death was hasty and unpremeditated, it was only according to the law of such encounter. Poets and authors, wearing arms, were exposed to the rude chances. The dramatist Marlowe, in some respects almost Shakespearian, "renowned for his rare art and wit," perished ignominiously under the weapon of a vulgar adversary; and Savage, whose genius and misfortune inspired the friendship and praise of Samuel Johnson, was tried at the Old Bailey for murder committed in a sudden broil. Nothing of this could have occurred without the habit of wearing arms, which was a fashion. Out of this came the *Dance of Death.*

This pernicious influence is illustrated by Judge Jay with admirable plainness. He shows the individual as an example to nations. Listen, a moment, to what he says so well. "The expert swordsman, the practised marksman, is ever more ready to engage in personal combats than the man who is unaccustomed to the use of deadly weapons. In those portions of our country where it is supposed essential to personal safety to go armed with pistols and bowie-knives mortal affrays are so frequent as to excite but little attention, and to secure, with exceedingly rare exceptions, perfect impunity to the murderer; whereas at the North and East, where we are unprovided with such facilities for taking life, comparatively few murders of the kind are perpetrated. We might, indeed, safely submit the decision of the principle we are discussing to the calculations of pecuniary interest. Let two men, equal in age and health, apply for an insurance on their lives, — one known to be ever armed to defend his honor and his life against every assailant, and the other a meek, unresisting Quaker: can we doubt for a moment which of these men would be deemed by an Insurance Company most likely to reach a good old age?"[1]

[1] Address before the American Peace Society, pp. 23, 24.

With this practical statement and its strong sense I leave this objection to War Preparations, adding a single supplementary remark, — What is good for the individual is good for nations.

The *second* objection, though different in character, is not less operative. It is founded on that law of human nature according to which the very hate or distrust to which these Preparations testify excites in others a corresponding sentiment. This law is general and fundamental. Though rarely recognized by nations as a rule of conduct, it was never without its influence on individuals. Indeed, it is little more than a practical illustration of the Horatian adage, *Si vis me flere, dolendum est primum ipsi tibi:* If you wish me to weep, you must yourself first grieve. Nobody questions its truth or applicability. But does it not proclaim that War Preparations in a period of professed Peace must naturally prompt adverse Preparations, and everywhere within the circle of their influence quicken the Spirit of War? So are we all knit together that the feelings in our own bosoms awaken corresponding feelings in the bosoms of others, — as harp answers to harp in its softest vibration, as deep responds to deep in the might of its power. What in us is good invites the good in our brother; generosity begets generosity; love wins love; Peace secures Peace; — while all in us that is bad challenges the bad in our brother; distrust engenders distrust; hate provokes hate; War arouses War. Therefore are we admonished to avoid such appeal, and this is the voice of Nature itself.

This beautiful law is everywhere. The wretched maniac, in whose mind the common principles of conduct are overthrown, confesses its overruling power;

and the vacant stare of madness is illumined by a word of love. The wild beasts confess it: and what is the story of Orpheus, whose music drew in listening rapture the lions and panthers of the forest, or of St. Jerome, whose kindness soothed the lion to lie down at his feet, but expressions of its prevailing power?[1]

Even a fable may testify. I would not be tempted too far, but, at the risk of protracting this discussion, I cannot forget illustrations which show how poetry at least, if not history, has interpreted the heart of man.

Looking back to the historic dawn, one of the most touching scenes illumined by that auroral light is the peaceful visit of the aged Priam to the tent of Achilles, entreating the body of his son. The fierce combat ended in the death of Hector, whose unhonored corse the bloody Greek has trailed behind his chariot. After twelve days of grief, the venerable father is moved to seek the remains of the son he has so dearly loved. He leaves his lofty cedarn chamber, and with a single aged attendant, unarmed, repairs to the Grecian camp beside the distant sounding sea. Entering alone, he finds Achilles in his tent, with two of his chiefs. Grasping his knees, the father kisses those terrible homicidal hands which had taken the life of his son. Touched by the sight which he beholds, the heart of the inflamed, the angry, the inflexible Achilles responds to the feelings

[1] Scholars will remember the incident recorded by Homer in the Odyssey (XIV. 30, 31), where Ulysses, on reaching his loved Ithaca, is beset by dogs, described as wild beasts in ferocity, who rush towards him barking; but he, with *craft* (that is the word of Homer), seats himself upon the ground *and lets his staff fall from his hand.* A similar incident is noticed by Mr. Mure, in his entertaining travels in Greece, and also by Mr. Borrow, in his "Bible in Spain." Pliny remarks, that all dogs may be appeased in the same way: "*Impetus eorum et sævitia mitigatur ab homine considente humi.*" Nat. Hist., Lib. VIII. cap. 40.

of Priam. He takes the suppliant by the hand, seats him by his side, consoles his grief, refreshes his weary body, and concedes to the prayers of a weak, unarmed old man what all Troy in arms could not win. In this scene, which fills a large space in the Iliad,[1] the master poet, with unconscious power, has presented a picture of the omnipotence of that law, making all mankind of kin, in obedience to which no word of kindness, no act of confidence, falls idly to the earth.

Among the early passages of Roman history, perhaps none makes a deeper impression than that scene, after the Roman youth were consumed at the Allia, and the invading Gauls under Brennus had entered the city, where in a temple were seated the venerable Senators of the Republic, too old to flee, and careless of surviving the Roman name, each on his curule chair, unarmed, looking, as Livy says, more august than mortal, and with the majesty of the gods. The Gauls gaze as upon sacred images; and the hand of slaughter, which had raged through the streets of Rome, is stayed by the sight of an unarmed assembly. This continued until one of the invaders standing nearest reached his hand to stroke gently the silver beard of a Senator, who, indignant at the license, smote the barbarian with his ivory staff, which was the signal for general vengeance. Think you that a band of savages could have slain these Senators, if the *appeal to Force* had not been made first by one of their own number? This story, though recounted by Livy, and also by Plutarch,[2] is repudiated by Niebuhr; but it is none the less interesting as a legend, attesting the law by which hostile feelings are aroused or subdued.

[1] Book XXIV. [2] Liv., Lib. V. cap. 41. Plutarch, Life of Camillus.

This great scene, in its essential parts, has been repeated in another age and country. The theatre was an African wilderness, with Christian converts for Roman Senators. The little band, with their pastor, who was a local chief, assembled on a Sabbath morning for prayer, when suddenly robbers came upon them, as the Gauls upon Rome, and demanded cattle. The pastor, asking his people to sit still, calmly pointed to the cattle, and then turned back to unite with the rest in prayer. The robbers, like the Gauls, looked on in silence, awed into forbearance, until they quietly withdrew, injuring nobody and touching nothing. Such an instance, which is derived from the report of missionaries,[1] testifies again to the might of meekness, and proves that the Roman story, though reduced to the condition of a legend, is in harmony with actual life.

An admired picture by Virgil, in his melodious epic, furnishes similar testimony. The Trojan fleet, beaten by tempest on the raging waves, is about to succumb, when the God of the Sea, suddenly appearing in tranquil power, stills the hostile elements, as a man venerable for piety and deserts by a gentle word assuages a furious populace just breaking into sedition and outrage.[2] The sea and the populace were equally appeased. Alike in the god and the man was the same peaceful presence. Elsewhere is this same influence. Guizot, illustrates this same influence, when, describing the development of mediæval civilization, he exhibits an angry multitude subdued by an unarmed man, em-

[1] Moffat, Missionary Labors and Scenes in Southern Africa, Ch. 32.

[2] "Ille regit dictis animos et pectora mulcet."

Æneid, I. 146 – 154.

ploying the *word* instead of the *sword.*[1] And surely no reader of that noble historical romance, the *Promessi Sposi,* can forget that finest scene, where Frà Cristoforo, in an age of violence, after slaying his comrade in a broil, presents himself unarmed and penitent before the family and retainers of his victim, and by dignified gentleness awakens the admiration of men raging against him. Both hemispheres are at this moment occupied with the popular romance, *Le Juif Errant,* by Eugène Sue, where is an interesting picture of Christian courage superior to the trained violence of the soldier. Another example, made familiar by recent translations of *Frithiof's Saga,* the Swedish epic,[2] is more emphatic. The scene is a battle. Frithiof is in deadly combat with Atlé, when the falchion of the latter breaks. Throwing away his own weapon, Frithiof says, —

> "*Swordless foeman's life*
> *Ne'er dyed this gallant blade.*"

The two champions now close in mutual clutch; they hug like bears, says the poet.

> "'T is o'er; for Frithiof's matchless strength
> Has felled his ponderous size,
> And 'neath that knee, a giant length,
> Supine the Viking lies.
> 'But fails my sword, thou Berserk swart,'
> The voice rang far and wide,
> 'Its point should pierce thy inmost heart,
> Its hilt should drink the tide.'
> 'Be free to lift the weaponed hand,'
> Undaunted Atlé spoke;
> Hence, fearless, quest thy distant brand:
> Thus I abide the stroke.'"

Frithiof regains his sword, intent to close the dread de-

1 Guizot, Histoire de la Civilisation en France, Tom. II. p. 36.
2 Longfellow, Poets and Poetry of Europe, p. 161: Tegnér.

bate, while his adversary awaits the stroke; but his heart responds to the generous courage of his foe; he cannot injure one who has shown such confidence in him.

> "*This quelled his ire, this checked his arm,*
> *Outstretched the hand of peace.*"

I cannot leave these illustrations without alluding again to the treatment of the insane, teaching, by conclusive example, how strong in Nature must be the responsive principle. On proposing to remove the heavy chains from the raving maniacs of the Paris hospitals, the benevolent Pinel was regarded as one who saw visions or dreamed dreams. At last his wishes were gratified. The change in the patients was immediate; the wrinkled front of warring passion was smoothed into the serene countenance of Peace. The treatment by Force is now universally abandoned; the law of kindness takes its place; and these unfortunates mingle together, unvexed by restraints implying suspicion, and therefore arousing opposition. What an example to nations, who are little better than insane! The ancient hospitals, with their violent madness, making confusion and strife, are a dark, but feeble, type of the Christian nations, obliged to wear the intolerable chains of War, assimilating the world to one great madhouse; while the peace and good-will now abounding in these retreats are the happy emblems of what awaits mankind when at last we practically recognize the supremacy of those higher sentiments which are at once a strength and a charm,—

> "making their future might
> Magnetic o'er the fixed, untrembling heart."

I might dwell also on recent experience, so full of delightful wisdom, in the treatment of the distant, degraded convict of New South Wales, showing how confidence and kindness on the part of overseers awaken a corresponding sentiment even in outcasts, from whose souls virtue seems blotted out.

Thus, from all quarters and sources — the far-off Past, the far-away Pacific, the verse of the poet, the legend of history, the cell of the mad-house, the congregation of transported criminals, the experience of daily life, the universal heart of man — ascends spontaneous tribute to that law according to which we respond to the sentiments by which we are addressed, whether of love or hate, of confidence or distrust.

If it be urged that these instances are exceptional, I reply at once, that it is not so. They are indubitable evidence of the real man, revealing the divinity of Humanity, out of which goodness, happiness, true greatness can alone proceed. They disclose susceptibilities confined to no particular race, no special period of time, no narrow circle of knowledge or refinement, but present wherever two or more human beings come together, and strong in proportion to their virtue and intelligence. Therefore on the nature of man, as impregnable ground, do I place the fallacy of this most costly and pernicious prejudice.

Nor is Human Nature the only witness: Christianity testifies in familiar texts, and then again by holiest lips. Augustine, in one of his persuasive letters, protests, with proverbial heart of flame, *against turning Peace into a Preparation for War*, and then tells the soldier whom he addresses to be *pacific even in war.*[1] From

1 "Non enim pax quæritur ut bellum excitetur. . . . Esto ergo etiam bellando pacificus." — Augustini Epistola CCV., ad Bonifacium Comitem: Opera, Tom. II. p. 318.

the religion of his Master the great Christian saint had learned that Love is more puissant than Force. To the reflecting mind, the Omnipotence of God himself is less discernible in earthquake and storm than in the gentle, but quickening, rays of the sun, and the sweet descending dews. He is a careless observer who does not recognize the superiority of gentleness and kindness in exercising influence or securing rights among men. As the storms of violence beat upon us, we hug mantles gladly thrown aside under the warmth of a genial sun.

Christianity not only teaches the superiority of Love to Force, it positively enjoins the practice of the former, as a constant, primal duty. It says, "Love your neighbors"; but it does not say, "In time of Peace rear the massive fortification, build the man-of-war, enlist standing armies, train militia, and accumulate military stores, to overawe and menace your neighbor." It directs that we should do to others as we would have them do to us, — a golden rule for all; but how inconsistent is that distrust in obedience to which nations professing peace sleep like soldiers on their arms! Nor is this all. Its precepts inculcate patience, forbearance, forgiveness of evil, even the duty of benefiting a destroyer, "as the sandal-wood, in the instant of its overthrow, sheds perfume on the axe which fells it." Can a people in whom this faith is more than an idle word authorize such enormous sacrifices to pamper the Spirit of War? Thus far nations have drawn their weapons from earthly armories, unmindful that there are others of celestial temper.

The injunction, "Love one another," is as applicable to nations as to individuals. It is one of the great laws of Heaven. And nations, like individuals, may well measure their nearness to God and to his glory by the conformity of their conduct to this duty.

In response to arguments founded on economy, the true nature of man, and Christianity, I hear the skeptical note of some advocate of the transmitted order of things, some one among the "fire-worshippers" of War, saying, All this is beautiful, but visionary; it is in advance of the age, which is not yet prepared for the great change. To such I answer: Nothing can be beautiful that is not true; but all this is true, and the time has come for its acceptance. Now is the dawning day, and now the fitting hour.

The name of Washington is invoked as authority for a prejudice which Economy, Human Nature, and Christianity repudiate. Mighty and reverend as is his name, more mighty and more reverend is Truth. The words of counsel which he gave were in accordance with the spirit of his age, — which was not shocked by the slave-trade. But his great soul, which loved virtue and inculcated justice and benevolence, frowns upon those who would use his authority as an incentive to War. God forbid that his sacred character should be profanely stretched, like the skin of John Ziska, on a militia-drum, to arouse the martial ardor of the American people!

The practice of Washington, during the eight years of his administration, compared with that of the last eight years for which we have the returns, may explain his real opinions. His condemnation of the present wasteful system speaks to us from the following table.[1]

[1] Executive Document No. 15, Twenty-eighth Congress, First Session.

Years.	Military Establishment.	Naval Establishment.
1789 – 91	$ 835,618	$ 570
1792	1,223,594	53 !
1793	1,237,620	
1794	2,733,539	61,409
1795	2,573,059	410,562
1796	1,474,672	274,784
Total, during eight years of Washington,	$ 10,078,102	$ 747,378
1835	$ 9,420,313	$ 3,864,939
1836	19,667,166	5,807,718
1837	20,702,929	6,646,915
1838	20,557,473	6,131,581
1839	14,588,664	6,182,294
1840	12,030,624	6,113,897
1841	13,704,882	6,001,077
1842	9,188,469	8,397,243
Total, during eight recent years,	$ 119,860,520	$ 49,145,664

Thus the expenditures for the national armaments under the sanction of Washington were less than *eleven million* dollars, while during a recent similar period of eight years they amounted to upwards of *one hundred and sixty-nine millions,*—an increase of nearly *fifteen hundred per cent!* To him who quotes the precept of Washington I commend the example. He must be strongly possessed by the martial mania who will not confess, that, in this age, when the whole world is at peace, and our national power is assured, *there is less need* of these Preparations than in an age convulsed with War, when our national power was little respected. The only semblance of argument in their favor is the increased wealth of the country; but the capacity to endure taxation is no criterion of its justice, or even of its expediency.

Another fallacy is also invoked, that *whatever is is right.* A barbarous practice is elevated above all those authorities by which these Preparations are condemned. We are made to count principles as nothing, because not yet recognized by nations. But they are practically applied in the relations of individuals, towns, counties, and states in our Union. *All these have disarmed.* It remains only that they should be extended to the grander sphere of nations. Be it our duty to proclaim the principles, whatever the practice. Through us let Truth speak.

From the past and the present auspicious omens cheer us for the future. The terrible wars of the French Revolution were the violent rending of the body preceding the exorcism of the fiend. Since the morning stars first sang together, the world has not witnessed a peace so harmonious and enduring as that which now blesses the Christian nations. Great questions, fraught with strife, and in another age heralds of War, are now determined by Mediation or Arbitration. Great political movements, which a few short years ago must have led to bloody encounter, are now conducted by peaceful discussion. Literature, the press, and innumerable societies, all join in the work of inculcating good-will to man. The Spirit of Humanity pervades the best writings, whether the elevated philosophical inquiries of the "Vestiges of the Creation," the ingenious, but melancholy, moralizings of the "Story of a Feather," or the overflowing raillery of "Punch." Nor can the breathing thought and burning word of poet or orator have a higher inspiration. Genius is never so Promethean as when it bears the heavenly fire to the hearths of men.

In the last age, Dr. Johnson uttered the detestable

sentiment, that he liked "a good Hater." The man of this age will say that he likes "a good Lover." Thus reversing the objects of regard, he follows a higher wisdom and a purer religion than the renowned moralist knew. He recognizes that peculiar Heaven-born sentiment, the Brotherhood of Man, soon to become the decisive touchstone of human institutions. He confesses the power of Love, destined to enter more and more into the concerns of life. And as Love is more heavenly than Hate, so must its influence redound more to the true glory of man and the approval of God. A Christian poet — whose few verses bear him with unflagging wing in immortal flight — has joined this sentiment with Prayer. Thus he speaks, in words of uncommon pathos and power: —

> "He prayeth well who loveth well
> Both man and bird and beast.
>
> "He prayeth best who loveth best
> All things, both great and small;
> For the dear God who loveth us,
> He made and loveth all."[1]

The ancient Law of Hate is yielding to the Law of Love. It is seen in manifold labors of philanthropy and in missions of charity. It is seen in institutions for the insane, the blind, the deaf, the dumb, the poor, the outcast, — in generous efforts to relieve those who are in prison, — in public schools, opening the gates of knowledge to all the children of the land. It is seen in the diffusive amenities of social life, and in the increasing fellowship of nations; also in the rising opposition to Slavery and to War.

There are yet other special auguries of this great

[1] Coleridge, Rime of the Ancient Mariner, Part VII.

change, auspicating, in the natural progress of man, the abandonment of all international Preparations for War. To these I allude briefly, but with a deep conviction of their significance.

Look at the Past, and see how War itself is changed, so that its oldest "fire-worshipper" would hardly know it. At first nothing but savagery, with disgusting rites, whether in the North American Indian with Powhatan as chief, or the earlier Assyrian with Nebuchadnezzar as king, but yielding gradually to the influence of civilization. With the Greeks it was less savage, but always barbarous, — also with Rome always barbarous. Too slowly Christianity exerted a humanizing power. Rabelais relates how the friar Jean des Entommeures clubbed twelve thousand and more enemies, "without mentioning women and children, which is understood always." But this was War, as seen by that great genius in his day. This can be no longer. Women and children are safe now. The divine metamorphosis has begun.

Look again at the Past, and observe the *change in dress*. Down to a period quite recent the sword was the indispensable companion of the gentleman, wherever he appeared, whether in street or society; but he would be deemed madman or bully who should wear it now. At an earlier period the armor of complete steel was the habiliment of the knight. From the picturesque sketch by Sir Walter Scott, in the "Lay of the Last Minstrel," we learn the barbarous constraint of this custom.

> "Ten of them were sheathed in steel,
> With belted sword, and spur on heel;
> They quitted not their harness bright,
> Neither by day nor yet by night:

They lay down to rest
With corslet laced,
Pillowed on buckler cold and hard;
They carved at the meal
With gloves of steel,
And they drank the red wine through the helmet barred."

But all this is changed now.

Observe the *change in architecture and in domestic life.* Places once chosen for castles or houses were savage, inaccessible retreats, where the massive structure was reared to repel attack and to enclose its inhabitants. Even monasteries and churches were fortified, and girdled by towers, ramparts, and ditches,— while a child was stationed as watchman, to observe what passed at a distance, and announce the approach of an enemy. Homes of peaceful citizens in towns were castellated, often without so much as an aperture for light near the ground, but with loopholes through which the shafts of the crossbow were aimed. The colored plates now so common, from mediæval illustrations, especially of Froissart, exhibit these *belligerent armaments,* always so burdensome. From a letter of Margaret Paston, in the time of Henry the Sixth, of England, I draw supplementary testimony. Addressing in dutiful phrase her "right worshipful husband," she asks him to procure for her "some crossbows, and wyndacs [grappling-irons] to bind them with, and quarrels [arrows with square heads]," also "two or three short pole-axes to keep within doors"; and she tells her absent lord of apparent preparations by a neighbor,— "great ordnance within the house," "bars to bar the door crosswise," and "wickets on every quarter of the house to shoot out at, both with bows and with hand-guns."[1]

[1] Paston Letters, CXIII. (LXXVII. Vol. III. p. 315.)

Savages could hardly live in greater distrust. Let now the Poet of Chivalry describe another scene: —

"Ten squires, ten yeomen, mail-clad men,
Waited the beck of the warders ten;
Thirty steeds, both fleet and wight,
Stood saddled in stable day and night,
Barbed with frontlet of steel, I trow,
And with Jedwood axe at saddle-bow;
A hundred more fed free in stall:
Such was the custom of Branksome Hall."

This also is all changed now.

The principles causing this change are not only active still, but increasing in activity; nor can they be confined to individuals. Nations must soon declare them, and, abandoning martial habiliments and fortifications, enter upon peaceful, *unarmed life.* With shame let it be said, that they continue to live in the very relations of distrust towards neighbors which shock us in the knights of Branksome Hall, and in the house of Margaret Paston. They pillow themselves on "buckler cold and hard," while their highest anxiety and largest expenditure are for the accumulation of new munitions of War. The barbarism which individuals have renounced nations still cherish. So doing, they take counsel of the wild-boar in the fable, who whetted his tusks on a tree of the forest when no enemy was near, saying, that in time of Peace he must prepare for War. Has not the time come, when man, whom God created in his own image, and to whom he gave the Heaven-directed countenance, shall cease to look down to the beast for an example of conduct? Nay, let me not dishonor the beasts by the comparison. The superior animals, at least, prey not, like men, upon their own species. The kingly lion turns from his brother lion;

the ferocious tiger will not raven upon his kindred tiger; the wild-boar of the forest does not glut his sharpened tusks upon a kindred boar.

> "Sed jam serpentum major concordia: parcit
> Cognatis maculis similis fera: quando leoni
> Fortior eripuit vitam leo? quo nemore unquam
> Exspiravit aper majoris dentibus apri?
> Indica tigris agit rabida cum tigride *pacem*
> *Perpetuam*."[1]

To an early monarch of France just homage has been offered for effort in the cause of Peace, particularly in abolishing the Trial by Battle. To another monarch of France, in our own day, descendant of St. Louis, and lover of Peace worthy of the illustrious lineage, Louis Philippe, belongs the honest fame of first from the throne publishing the truth that Peace is endangered by Preparations for War. "The sentiment, or rather the principle," he says, in reply to an address from the London Peace Convention in 1843, "that in Peace you must prepare for War, *is one of difficulty and danger; for while we keep armies on land to preserve peace, they are at the same time incentives and instruments of war.* He rejoiced in all efforts to preserve peace, for that was what all needed. He thought the time was coming when we should get rid entirely of war in all civilized countries." This time has been hailed by a generous voice from the Army itself, by a Marshal of France, — Bugeaud, the Governor of Algiers, — who, at a public dinner in Paris, gave as a toast these words of salutation to a new and approaching era of happiness: "To the pacific union of the great human family, by the association of individuals, nations, and races! To the annihilation of War! To the transformation of destructive armies into

[1] Juvenal, Sat. XV. 159-164.

corps of industrious laborers, who will consecrate their lives to the cultivation and embellishment of the world!" Be it our duty to speed this consummation! And may other soldiers emulate the pacific aspiration of this veteran chief, until *the trade of War* ceases from the earth![1]

To William Penn belongs the distinction, destined to brighten as men advance in virtue, of first in human history establishing the *Law of Love* as a rule of conduct in the intercourse of nations. While recognizing the duty "to support power in reverence with the people, and to secure the people from the abuse of power,"[2] as a great end of government, he declined the superfluous protection of arms against foreign force, and aimed to "reduce the savage nations by just and gentle manners to the love of civil society and the Christian religion." His serene countenance, as he stands with his followers in what he called the sweet and clear air of Pennsylvania, all unarmed, beneath the spreading elm, forming the great treaty of friendship with the untutored Indians, — whose savage display fills the surrounding forest as far as the eye can reach, — not to wrest their lands by violence, but to obtain them by peaceful purchase, — is to my mind the proudest picture in the history of

[1] There was a moment when the aspiration of the French marshal seemed fulfilled even in France, if we may credit the early Madame de Lafayette, who, in the first sentence of her Memoirs, announces perfect tranquillity, where "no other arms were known than instruments for the cultivation of the earth and for building, and the troops were employed on these things." Part of their work was to divert the waters of the Eure, so that the fountains at Versailles should have a perpetual supply: but this was better than War. — MADAME DE LAFAYETTE, *Mémoires de la Cour de France pour les Années* 1688 *et* 1689, p. 1.

[2] Preface to Penn's Frame of Government of the Province of Pennsylvania: Hazard's Register of Pennsylvania, Vol. I. p. 338. See also Clarkson's Memoirs of Penn, Vol. I. p. 238, Philadelphia, 1814.

our country. "The great God," said the illustrious Quaker, in words of sincerity and truth addressed to the Sachems, "hath written his law in our hearts, by which we are taught and commanded to love and help and do good to one another. It is not our custom to use hostile weapons against our fellow-creatures, for which reason we come unarmed. Our object is not to do injury, but to do good. We are now met on the broad pathway of good faith and good will, so that no advantage is to be taken on either side, but all is to be openness, brotherhood, and love, while all are to be treated as of the same flesh and blood."[1] These are words of True Greatness. "Without any carnal weapons," says one of his companions, "we entered the land, and inhabited therein, as safe as if there had been thousands of garrisons." What a sublime attestation! "This little State," says Oldmixon, "subsisted in the midst of six Indian nations without so much as a militia for its defence." A great man worthy of the mantle of Penn, the venerable philanthropist, Clarkson, in his life of the founder, pictures the people of Pennsylvania as armed, though without arms, — strong, though without strength, — safe, without the ordinary means of safety. According to him, the constable's staff was the only instrument of authority for the greater part of a century; and never, during the administration of Penn, or that of his proper successors, was there a quarrel or a war.[2]

Greater than the divinity that doth hedge a king is the divinity that encompasses the righteous man and the righteous people. The flowers of prosperity smiled

1 Clarkson's Memoirs of Penn, Vol. I. Ch. 18.

2 Ibid., Vol. II. Ch. 23.

in the footprints of William Penn. His people were unmolested and happy, while (sad, but true contrast!) other colonies, acting upon the policy of the world, building forts, and showing themselves in arms, were harassed by perpetual alarm, and pierced by the sharp arrows of savage war.

This pattern of a Christian commonwealth never fails to arrest the admiration of all who contemplate its beauties. It drew an epigram of eulogy from the caustic pen of Voltaire, and has been fondly painted by sympathetic historians. Every ingenuous soul in our day offers willing tribute to those graces of justice and humanity, by the side of which contemporary life on this continent seems coarse and earthy.

Not to barren words can we confine ourselves in recognition of virtue. While we see the right, and approve it too, we must dare to pursue it. Now, in this age of civilization, surrounded by Christian nations, it is easy to follow the successful example of William Penn encompassed by savages. Recognizing those two transcendent ordinances of God, the *Law of Right* and the *Law of Love,* — twin suns which illumine the moral universe, — why not aspire to the true glory, and, what is higher than glory, the great good, of taking the lead in *the disarming of the nations?* Let us abandon the system of Preparations for War in time of Peace, as irrational, unchristian, vainly prodigal of expense, and having a direct tendency to excite the evil against which it professes to guard. Let the enormous means thus released from iron hands be devoted to labors of beneficence. Our battlements shall be schools, hospitals, colleges, and churches; our arsenals shall be libraries; our navy shall be peaceful ships, on errands of perpetual commerce;

our army shall be the teachers of youth and the ministers of religion. This is the cheap defence of nations. In such intrenchments what Christian soul can be touched with fear? Angels of the Lord will throw over the land an invisible, but impenetrable panoply: —

> "Or if Virtue feeble were,
> Heaven itself would stoop to her."[1]

At the thought of such a change, the imagination loses itself in vain effort to follow the multitudinous streams of happiness which gush forth from a thousand hills. Then shall the naked be clothed and the hungry fed; institutions of science and learning shall crown every hill-top; hospitals for the sick, and other retreats for the unfortunate children of the world, for all who suffer in any way, in mind, body, or estate, shall nestle in every valley; while the spires of new churches leap exulting to the skies. The whole land shall testify to the change. Art shall confess it in the new inspiration of the canvas and the marble. The

[1] These are the concluding words of that most exquisite creation of early genius, the "Comus." Beyond their intrinsic value, they have authority from the circumstance that they were adopted by Milton as a motto, and inscribed by him in an album at Geneva, while on his foreign travels. This album is now in my hands. The truth thus embalmed by the grandest poet of modern times is also illustrated in familiar words by the most graceful poet of antiquity: —

> "Integer vitæ scelerisque purus
> Non eget Mauris jaculis, neque arcu,
> Nec venenatis gravida sagittis,
> Fusce, pharetra."
> Hor., *Carm.* I. xxii. 1-4.

Dryden pictures the same in some of his most magical lines: —

> "A milk-white hind, immortal and unchanged,
> Fed on the lawns, and in the forest ranged;
> Without unspotted, innocent within,
> *She feared no danger, for she knew no sin.*"
> *The Hind and the Panther*, Part I. 1-4.

harp of the poet shall proclaim it in a loftier rhyme. Above all, the heart of man shall bear witness to it, in the elevation of his sentiments, in the expansion of his affections, in his devotion to the highest truth, in his appreciation of true greatness. The eagle of our country, without the terror of his beak, and dropping the forceful thunderbolt from his pounces, shall soar, with the olive of Peace, into untried realms of ether, nearer to the sun.

I pause to review the field over which we have passed. We have beheld War, sanctioned by International Law as a mode of determining *justice* between nations, elevated into an *established custom,* defined and guarded by a complex code known as the Laws of War; we have detected its origin in an appeal, not to the moral and intellectual part of man's nature, in which alone is Justice, but to that low part which he has in common with the beast; we have contemplated its infinite miseries to the human race; we have weighed its sufficiency as a mode of determining justice between nations, and found that it is a rude invocation to force, or a gigantic game of chance, in which God's children are profanely treated as a pack of cards, while, in unnatural wickedness, it is justly likened to the monstrous and impious custom of Trial by Battle, which disgraced the Dark Ages, — thus showing, that, in this day of boastful civilization, justice between nations is determined by the same rules of barbarous, brutal violence which once controlled the relations between individuals. We have next considered the various prejudices by which War is sustained, founded on a false belief in its necessity, — the practice of nations, past and present, —

the infidelity of the Christian Church, — a mistaken sentiment of honor, — an exaggerated idea of the duties of patriotism, — and finally, that monster prejudice which draws its vampire life from the vast Preparations for War in time of Peace; — especially dwelling, at this stage, upon the thriftless, irrational, and unchristian character of these Preparations, — hailing also the auguries of their overthrow, — and catching a vision of the surpassing good that will be achieved, when the boundless means thus barbarously employed are dedicated to works of Peace, opening the serene path to that righteousness which exalteth a nation.

And now, if it be asked why, in considering the TRUE GRANDEUR OF NATIONS, I dwell thus singly and exclusively on War, it is because War is utterly and irreconcilably inconsistent with True Greatness. Thus far, man has worshipped in Military Glory a phantom idol, compared with which the colossal images of ancient Babylon or modern Hindostan are but toys; and we, in this favored land of freedom, in this blessed day of light, are among the idolaters. The Heaven-descended injunction, *Know thyself*, still speaks to an unheeding world from the far-off letters of gold at Delphi: *Know thyself; know that the moral is the noblest part of man*, transcending far that which is the seat of passion, strife, and War, — nobler than the intellect itself. And the human heart, in its untutored, spontaneous homage to the virtues of Peace, declares the same truth, — admonishing the military idolater that it is not the bloody combats, even of bravest chiefs, even of gods themselves, as they echo from the resounding lines of the great Poet of War, which receive the warmest admiration, but those two scenes where are painted the gentle, unwarlike affections of our nature, the Parting of Hector from Andromache, and the Supplication of Priam. In the definitive election of these peaceful pictures, the soul of man, inspired by a better wisdom than that of books, and drawn unconsciously by the heavenly attraction of what is truly great, acknowledges, in touching instances, the vanity of Military Glory. The Beatitudes of Christ, which shrink from saying, "Blessed are the War-makers," inculcate the same lesson. Reason affirms and repeats what the heart has prompted and Christianity proclaimed. Suppose War decided by *Force*, where is the glory? Suppose it decided by *Chance*, where is the glory? Surely, in other ways True Greatness lies. Nor is it difficult to tell where.

True Greatness consists in imitating, as nearly as possible for finite man, the perfections of an Infinite Creator, — above all, in cultivating those highest perfections, Justice and Love: Justice, which, like that of St. Louis, does not swerve to the right hand or to the left; Love, which, like that of William Penn, regards all mankind as of kin. "God is angry," says Plato, "when any one censures a man like Himself, *or praises a man of an opposite character:* and the godlike man is the good man."[1] Again, in another of those lovely dialogues precious with immortal truth: "Nothing resembles God more than that man among us who has attained to the highest degree of justice."[2] The True Greatness of Nations is in those qualities which constitute the true greatness of the individual. It is not in extent of territory, or vastness of population, or accumulation of

[1] Minos, § 12.

[2] Theætetus, § 85.

wealth, — not in fortifications, or armies, or navies, — not in the sulphurous blaze of battle, — not in Golgothas, though covered by monuments that kiss the clouds; for all these are creatures and representatives of those qualities in our nature which are unlike anything in God's nature. Nor is it in triumphs of the intellect alone, — in literature, learning, science, or art. The polished Greeks, our masters in the delights of art, and the commanding Romans, overawing the earth with their power, were little more than splendid savages. And the age of Louis the Fourteenth, of France, spanning so long a period of ordinary worldly magnificence, thronged by marshals bending under military laurels, enlivened by the unsurpassed comedy of Molière, dignified by the tragic genius of Corneille, illumined by the splendors of Bossuet, is degraded by immoralities that cannot be mentioned without a blush, by a heartlessness in comparison with which the ice of Nova Zembla is warm, and by a succession of deeds of injustice not to be washed out by the tears of all the recording angels of Heaven.

The True Greatness of a Nation cannot be in triumphs of the intellect alone. Literature and art may enlarge the sphere of its influence; they may adorn it; but in their nature they are but accessaries. *The True Grandeur of Humanity is in moral elevation, sustained, enlightened, and decorated by the intellect of man.* The surest tokens of this grandeur in a nation are that Christian Beneficence which diffuses the greatest happiness among all, and that passionless, godlike Justice which controls the relations of the nation to other nations, and to all the people committed to its charge.

But War crushes with bloody heel all beneficence, all happiness, all justice, all that is godlike in man, — suspending every commandment of the Decalogue, setting at naught every principle of the Gospel, and silencing all law, human as well as divine, except only that impious code of its own, the *Laws of War*. If in its dismal annals there is any cheerful passage, be assured it is not inspired by a martial Fury. Let it not be forgotten, let it be ever borne in mind, as you ponder this theme, that the virtues which shed their charm over its horrors are all borrowed of Peace, — that they are emanations from the Spirit of Love, which is so strong in the heart of man that it survives the rudest assault. The flowers of gentleness, kindliness, fidelity, humanity, which flourish unregarded in the rich meadows of Peace, receive unwonted admiration when we discern them in War, — like violets shedding their perfume on the perilous edge of the precipice, beyond the smiling borders of civilization. God be praised for all the examples of magnanimous virtue which he has vouchsafed to mankind! God be praised, that the Roman Emperor, about to start on a distant expedition of War, encompassed by squadrons of cavalry, and by golden eagles swaying in the wind, stooped from his saddle to hear the prayer of a humble widow, demanding justice for the death of her son![1] God be praised, that Sidney, on the field of battle, gave with dying hand the cup of cold water to the dying soldier! That single act of

[1] According to the legends of the Catholic Church, this most admired instance of justice opened to Trajan, although a heathen, the gates of salvation. Dante found the scene and the "visible speech" of the widow and Emperor storied on the walls of Purgatory, and has transmitted them in a passage which commends itself hardly less than any in the divine poem. — See *Purgatorio*, Canto X.

self-forgetful sacrifice has consecrated the deadly field of Zutphen, far, oh, far beyond its battle; it has consecrated thy name, gallant Sidney, beyond any feat of thy sword, beyond any triumph of thy pen! But there are lowly suppliants in other places than the camp; there are hands outstretched elsewhere than on fields of blood. Everywhere is opportunity for deeds of like charity. Know well that these are not the product of War. They do not spring from enmity, hatred, and strife, but from those benign sentiments whose natural and ripened fruit of joy and blessing are found only in Peace. If at any time they appear in the soldier, it is less *because* than *notwithstanding* he is the hireling of battle. Let me not be told, then, of the virtues of War. Let not the acts of generosity and sacrifice sometimes blossoming on its fields be invoked in its defence. From such a giant root of bitterness no true good can spring. The poisonous tree, in Oriental imagery, though watered by nectar and covered with roses, produces only the fruit of death.

Casting our eyes over the history of nations, with horror we discern the succession of murderous slaughters by which their progress is marked. Even as the hunter follows the wild beast to his lair by the drops of blood on the ground, so we follow Man, faint, weary, staggering with wounds, through the Black Forest of the Past, which he has reddened with his gore. Oh, let it not be in the future ages as in those we now contemplate! Let the grandeur of man be discerned, not in bloody victory or ravenous conquest, but in the blessings he has secured, in the good he has accomplished, in the triumphs of Justice and Beneficence, in the establishment of Perpetual Peace!

As ocean washes every shore, and with all-embracing arms clasps every land, while on its heaving bosom it bears the products of various climes, so Peace surrounds, protects, and upholds all other blessings. Without it, commerce is vain, the ardor of industry is restrained, justice is arrested, happiness is blasted, virtue sickens and dies.

Peace, too, has its own peculiar victories, in comparison with which Marathon and Bannockburn and Bunker Hill, fields sacred in the history of human freedom, lose their lustre. Our own Washington rises to a truly heavenly stature, not when we follow him through the ice of the Delaware to the capture of Trenton, not when we behold him victorious over Cornwallis at Yorktown, but when we regard him, in noble deference to Justice, refusing the kingly crown which a faithless soldiery proffered, and at a later day upholding the peaceful neutrality of the country, while he met unmoved the clamor of the people wickedly crying for War. What glory of battle in England's annals will not fade by the side of that great act of justice, when her Parliament, at a cost of one hundred million dollars, gave freedom to eight hundred thousand slaves? And when the day shall come (may these eyes be gladdened by its beams!) that shall witness an act of larger justice still, — the peaceful emancipation of three million fellow-men "guilty of a skin not colored as our own," now, in this land of jubilant freedom, bound in gloomy bondage, — then will there be a victory by the side of which that of Bunker Hill will be as the farthing candle held up to the sun. That victory will need no monument of stone. It will be written on the grateful hearts of countless multitudes that shall proclaim it to the latest generation. It will be one of the famed landmarks of civilization, — or, better still, a link in the golden chain by which Humanity connects itself with the throne of God.

As man is higher than the beasts of the field, as the angels are higher than man, as Christ is higher than Mars, as he that ruleth his spirit is higher than he that taketh a city, — so are the victories of Peace higher than the victories of War.

Far be from us, fellow-citizens, on this festival, the pride of national victory, and the illusion of national freedom, in which we are too prone to indulge! None of you make rude boast of individual prosperity or prowess. And here I end as I began. Our country cannot do what an individual cannot do. Therefore it must not vaunt or be puffed up. Rather bend to unperformed duties. Independence is not all. We have but half done, when we have made ourselves free. The scornful taunt wrung from bitter experience of the great Revolution in France must not be levelled at us: "They wish to be *free*, but know not how to be *just*."[1] Nor is priceless Freedom an end in itself, but rather the means of Justice and Beneficence, where alone is enduring concord, with that attendant happiness which is the final end and aim of Nations, as of every human heart. It is not enough to be free. There must be Peace which cannot fail, and other nations must share the great possession. For this good must we labor, bearing ever in mind two special objects, complements of each other: first, the Arbitrament of War must end; and,

1 "*Ils veulent être libres, et ne savent pas être justes*," was the famous exclamation of Sieyès.

secondly, Disarmament must begin. With this ending and this beginning the great gates of the Future will be opened, and the guardian virtues will assert a new empire. Alas! until this is done, National Honor and National Glory will yet longer flaunt in blood, and there can be no True Grandeur of Nations.

To this great work let me summon you. That Future, which filled the lofty vision of sages and bards in Greece and Rome, which was foretold by Prophets and heralded by Evangelists, when man, in Happy Isles, or in a new Paradise, shall confess the loveliness of Peace, may you secure, if not for yourselves, at least for your children! *Believe* that you can do it, and you *can* do it. The true Golden Age is before, not behind. If man has once been driven from Paradise, while an angel with flaming sword forbade his return, there is another Paradise, even on earth, which he may make for himself, by the cultivation of knowledge, religion, and the kindly virtues of life, — where the confusion of tongues shall be dissolved in the union of hearts, and joyous Nature, borrowing prolific charms from prevailing Harmony, shall spread her lap with unimagined bounty, and there shall be perpetual jocund Spring, and sweet strains borne on "the odoriferous wing of gentle gales," through valleys of delight more pleasant than the Vale of Tempe, richer than the Garden of the Hesperides, with no dragon to guard its golden fruit.

Is it said that the age does not demand this work? The robber conqueror of the Past, from fiery sepulchre, demands it; the precious blood of millions unjustly shed in War, crying from the ground, demands it; the heart of the good man demands it; the conscience, even of the soldier, whispers, "Peace!" There are considerations springing from our situation and condition which fervently invite us to take the lead. Here should join the patriotic ardor of the land, the ambition of the statesman, the effort of the scholar, the pervasive influence of the press, the mild persuasion of the sanctuary, the early teaching of the school. Here, in ampler ether and diviner air, are untried fields for exalted triumph, more truly worthy the American name than any snatched from rivers of blood. War is known as the *Last Reason of Kings.* Let it be no reason of our Republic. Let us renounce and throw off forever the yoke of a tyranny most oppressive of all in the world's annals. As those standing on the mountain-top first discern the coming beams of morning, so may we, from the vantage-ground of liberal institutions, first recognize the ascending sun of a new era! Lift high the gates, and let the King of Glory in, — the King of True Glory, — of Peace! I catch the last words of music from the lips of innocence and beauty,[1] —

"And let the whole earth be filled with His Glory!"

It is a beautiful picture in Grecian story, that there was at least one spot, the small island of Delos, dedicated to the gods, and kept at all times sacred from War. No hostile foot ever pressed this kindly soil, and citizens of all countries met here, in common worship, beneath the ægis of inviolable Peace. So let us dedicate our beloved country; and may the blessed consecration be felt in all its parts, everywhere throughout its ample domain! The Temple of Honor shall

[1] The services of the choir on this occasion were performed by the youthful daughters of the public schools of Boston.

be enclosed by the Temple of Concord, that it may never more be entered through any portal of War; the horn of Abundance shall overflow at its gates; the angel of Religion shall be the guide over its steps of flashing adamant; while within its happy courts, purged of Violence and Wrong, JUSTICE, returned to the earth from long exile in the skies, with equal scales for nations as for men, shall rear her serene and majestic front; and by her side, greatest of all, CHARITY, sublime in meekness, hoping all and enduring all, shall divinely temper every righteous decree, and with words of infinite cheer inspire to those deeds that cannot vanish away. And the future chief of the Republic, destined to uphold the glories of a new era, unspotted by human blood, shall be first in Peace, first in the hearts of his countrymen.

While seeking these fruitful glories for ourselves, let us strive for their extension to other lands. Let the bugles sound the *Truce of God* to the whole world forever. Not to one people, but to every people, let the glad tidings go. The selfish boast of the Spartan women, that they never saw the smoke of an enemy's camp, must become the universal chorus of mankind, while the iron belt of War, now encompassing the globe, is exchanged for the golden cestus of Peace, clothing all with celestial beauty. History dwells with fondness on the reverent homage bestowed by massacring soldiers upon the spot occupied by the sepulchre of the Lord. Vain man! why confine regard to a few feet of sacred mould? The whole earth is the sepulchre of the Lord; nor can any righteous man profane any part thereof. Confessing this truth, let us now, on this Sabbath of the Nation, lay a new and living stone in the grand Temple of Universal Peace, whose dome shall be lofty as the firmament of heaven, broad and comprehensive as earth itself.

WAR SYSTEM OF THE COMMONWEALTH OF NATIONS.

Address before the American Peace Society, at its Anniversary Meeting in the Park Street Church, Boston, May 28, 1849.

That it may please Thee to give to all nations unity, peace, and concord. — The Litany.

What angel shall descend to reconcile
The Christian states, and end their guilty toil?
Waller.

Quæ harmonia a musicis dicitur in cantu, ea est in civitate concordia. — CICERO, *De Republica*, Lib. II. Cap. 42.

Una dies Fabios ad bellum miserat omnes,
Ad bellum missos perdidit una dies.
OVID, *Fasti*, Lib. II. 235, 236.

Cum hac persuasione vivendum est: Non sum uni angulo natus; patria mea totus hic mundus est. — SENECA, *Epistola* XXVIII.

Illi enim exorsi sunt non ab observandis telis aut armis aut tubis; id enim invisum illis est propter Deum quem in conscientia sua gestant. — MARCUS AURELIUS, *Epistola ad Senatum:* S. Justini *Apologia I. pro Christianis*, Cap. 71.

War is one of the greatest plagues that can afflict humanity: it destroys religion, it destroys states, it destroys families. Any scourge, in fact, is preferable to it. Famine and pestilence become as nothing in comparison with it. . . . . Cannons and fire-arms are cruel and damnable machines. I believe them to have been the direct suggestion of the Devil. . . . . If Adam had seen in a vision the horrible instruments his children were to invent, he would have died of grief. — MARTIN LUTHER, *Table-Talk*, tr. Hazlitt, pp. 331 - 332.

Mulei Abdelummi, assaulted by his brother and wounded in the church, 1577, would not stirre till *sala*, or prayer, was done. — PURCHAS, *Pilgrims*, Part II. Book IX. Chap. 12, § 6, p. 1564.

A duel may still be granted in some cases by the law of England, and only there. That the Church allowed it anciently appears by this: In their public liturgies there were prayers appointed for the duellists to say; the judge used to bid them go to such a church and pray, etc. But whether is this lawful? If you grant any war lawful, I make no doubt but to convince it. — SELDEN, *Table-Talk: Duel.*

I look upon the way of Treaties as a retiring from fighting like beasts to arguing like men, whose strength should be more in their understandings than in their limbs. — *Eikon Basilike*, XVIII.

Se peut-il rien de plus plaisant qu'un homme ait droit de me tuer parce qu'il demeure au delà de l'eau, et que son prince a querelle avec le mien, quoique je n'en aie aucune avec lui? — PASCAL, *Pensées*, Part. I. Art. VI. 9.

Pourquoi me tuez-vous? Eh quoi! ne demeurez-vous pas de l'autre côté de l'eau? Mon ami, si vous demeuriez de ce côté, je serais un assassin; cela serait injuste de vous tuer de la sorte: mais puisque vous demeurez de l'autre côté, je suis un brave, et cela est juste. — *Ibid.*, Part. I. Art. IX. 3.

De tout temps les hommes, pour quelque morceau de terre de plus ou de moins, *sont convenus* entre eux de se dépouiller, se brûler, se tuer, s'égorger les uns les autres; et pour le faire plus ingénieusement et avec plus de sûreté, ils ont inventé de belles règles qu'on appelle l'art militaire: ils ont attaché à la pratique de ces règles *la gloire*, ou la plus solide réputation; et ils ont depuis enchéri de siècle en siècle sur la manière de se détruire réciproquement. — La Bruyère, *Du Souverain ou de la République*.

La calamita esser innamorata del ferro. — Vico, *Scienza Nuova*, Lib. I., *Degli Elementi*, XXXII.

Unlistening, barbarous Force, to whom the sword
Is reason, honor, law.

Thomson, *Liberty*, Part IV. 45, 46.

Enfin, tandis que les deux rois faisaient chanter des *Te Deum*, chacun dans son camp, il prit le parti d'aller raisonner ailleurs des effets et des causes. Il passa par-dessus des tas de morts et de mourants, et gagna d'abord un village voisin; il était en cendres : c'était un village Abare, que les Bulgares avaient brûlé, *selon les lois du droit public.* — Voltaire, *Candide ou l'Optimiste*, Chap. III.

The rage and violence of public war, what is it but a suspension of justice among the warring parties? — Hume, *Essays: Inquiry concerning the Principles of Morals*, Section III., *Of Justice*, Part I.

A single robber or a few associates are branded with their genuine name; but the exploits of a numerous band assume the character of lawful and honorable war. — Gibbon, *Decline and Fall of the Roman Empire*, Chap. 50.

The glory of a warrior prince can only be written in letters of blood, and he can only be immortalized by the remembrance of the devastation of provinces and the desolation of nations. A warrior king depends for his reputation on the vulgar crowd, and must address himself to prejudice and ignorance to obtain the applause of a day, which the pen of the philosopher, the page of the historian, often annul, even before death comes to enshroud the mortal faculties in the nothingness from which they came. Consult, Sire, the laws of the King of Kings, and acknowledge that the God of the Universe is a God of Peace. — Right Hon. Hugh Elliot, *British Minister in Sweden, to Gustavus III., November* 10, 1788: *Memoir*, by the Countess of Minto, p. 324.

C'est un usage reçu en Europe, qu'un gentilhomme vende, à une querelle étrangère, le sang qui appartient à sa patrie; qu'il s'engage à assassiner, en bataille rangée, qui il plaira au prince qui le soudoie; et ce métier est regardé comme honorable. — Condorcet, *Note* 109 *aux Pensées de Pascal.*

C'était un affreux spectacle que cette déroute. Les blessés, qui ne pouvaient se traîner, se couchaient sur le chemin; on les foulait aux pieds; les femmes poussaient des cris, les enfans pleuraient, les officiers frappaient les fuyards. Au milieu de tout ce désordre, ma mère avait passé sans que je la reconnusse. Un enfant avait voulu l'arrêter et la tuer, parce qu'elle fuyait. — Madame de la Rochejaquelein, *Mémoires*, Chap. XVII. p. 301.

Let the soldier be abroad, if he will; he can do nothing in this age. There is another personage, a personage less imposing in the eyes of some, perhaps insignificant. The schoolmaster is abroad, and I trust to him, armed with his primer, against the soldier in full military array. — BROUGHAM, *Speech in the House of Commons, January* 29, 1828.

Was it possible for me to avoid the reflections which crowded into my mind, ... when I reflected that this peaceful and guiltless and useful triumph over the elements and over Nature herself had cost a million only of money, whilst fifteen hundred millions had been squandered on cruelty and crime, in naturalizing barbarism over the world, shrouding the nations in darkness, making bloodshed tinge the earth of every country under the sun, — in one horrid and comprehensive word, squandered on WAR, the greatest curse of the human race, and the greatest crime, because it involves every other crime within its execrable name? .... I look backwards with shame, with regret unspeakable, with indignation to which I should in vain attempt to give utterance, ... when I think, that, if one hundred, and but one hundred, of those fifteen hundred millions, had been employed in promoting the arts of peace and the progress of civilization and of wealth and prosperity amongst us, instead of that other employment which is too hateful to think of, and almost nowadays too disgusting to speak of (and I hope to live to see the day when such things will be incredible, when, looking back, we shall find it impossible to believe they ever happened), instead of being burdened with eight hundred millions of debt, borrowed after spending seven hundred millions, borrowed when we had no more to spend, we should have seen the whole country covered with such works as now unite Manchester and Liverpool, and should have enjoyed peace uninterrupted during the last forty years, with all the blessings which an industrious and a virtuous people deserve, and which peace profusely sheds upon their lot. — IBID., *Speech at Liverpool, July* 20, 1835.

Who can read these, and such passages as these [from Plato], without wishing that some who call themselves Christians, some Christian Principalities and Powers, had taken a lesson from the Heathen sage, and, if their nature forbade them to abstain from massacres and injustice, at least had not committed the scandalous impiety, as he calls it, of singing in places of Christian worship, and for the accomplishment of their enormous crimes, *Te Deums*, which in Plato's Republic would have been punished as blasphemy? Who, indeed, can refrain from lamenting another pernicious kind of sacrilege, an anthropomorphism, yet more frequent, — that of making Christian temples resound with prayers for victory over our enemies, and thanksgiving for their defeat? Assuredly such a ritual as this is not taken from the New Testament. — IBID., *Discourse of Natural Theology*, Note VIII.

War is on its last legs; and a universal peace is as sure as is the prevalence of civilization over barbarism, of liberal governments over feudal forms. The question for us is only, *How soon?* — EMERSON, *War: Æsthetic Papers*, ed. E. P. Peabody, p. 42.

A day will come when the only battle-field will be the market open to commerce and the mind opening to new ideas. A day will come when bullets and bomb-shells will be replaced by votes, by the universal suffrage of nations, by the venerable arbitration of a great Sovereign Senate, which will be to Europe what the Parliament is to England, what the Diet is to Germany, what the Legislative Assembly is to France. A day will come when a cannon will be exhibited in public museums, just as an instrument of torture is now, and people will be astonished how such a thing could have been. A day will come when those two immense groups, the United States of America and the United States of Europe, shall be seen placed in presence of each other, extending the hand of fellowship across the ocean. — VICTOR HUGO, *Inaugural Address at the Peace Congress of Paris, August* 22, 1849.

Clearly, beyond question, whatsoever be our theories about human nature and its capabilities and outcomes, the less war and cutting of throats we have among us, it will be better for us all. One rejoices much to see that immeasurable tendencies of this time are already pointing towards the results you aim at, — that, to all appearance, as men no longer wear swords in the streets, so neither by-and-by will nations. — CARLYLE, *Letter to the Peace Congress at London, July*, 1851.

The longer I live, the more I am convinced of the necessity of a powerful association to plead the cause of Universal Peace and International Arbitration; and I feel confident that the time is not far distant when war will be as impossible among civilized nations as duelling is among civilized men. — SIR DAVID BREWSTER, *Letter to the Peace Conference at Edinburgh, October*, 1853.

Aujourd'hui encore on bénit les drapeaux qui conduisent les hommes à de mutuels égorgements. En donnant à un Dieu de paix le nom de *Dieu des Armées*, on fait de l'Être infini en bonté le complice de ceux qui s'abreuvent des larmes de leurs semblables. Aujourd'hui encore on chante d'impies *Te Deum* pour le remercier de ces victoires obtenues au prix d'épouvantables massacres, victoires qu'il faudrait ou expier comme des crimes lorsqu'elles ont été remportées dans des guerres offensives ou déplorer comme la plus triste des nécessités quand elles ont été obtenues dans des guerres défensives. — LARROQUE, *De la Guerre et des Armées Permanentes*, Part. III. § 4.

La monarchie, sous les formes mêmes les plus tempérées, tiendra toujours à avoir à sa dévotion des armées permanentes. Or avec les armées en permanence l'abolition de la guerre est impossible. Par conséquent la grande fédération des peuples, au moins de tous les peuples Européens, dans le but d'arriver à l'abolition de la guerre par l'institution d'un droit international et d'un tribunal supérieur chargé de le faire observer, ne sera réalisable que le jour où ces peuples seront organisés sous la forme républicaine. Quand luira ce jour? — IBID., Avant-propos, p. 6.

Sir J. Lubbock quotes the case of a tribe in Baffin's Bay who "could not be made to understand what was meant by war, nor had they any warlike weapons." No wonder, poor people! They had been driven into regions where no stronger race could desire to follow them. — DUKE OF ARGYLL, *Primeval Man*, p. 177.

ADDRESS.

MR. PRESIDENT AND GENTLEMEN, — We are assembled in what may be called the Holy Week of our community, — not occupied by pomps of a complex ceremonial, swelling in tides of music, beneath time-honored arches, but set apart, with the unadorned simplicity of early custom, to anniversary meetings of those charitable and religious associations from whose good works our country derives such true honor. Each association is distinct. Gathered within the folds of each are its own members, devoted to its chosen objects: and yet all are harmonious together; for all are inspired by one sentiment, — the welfare of the united Human Family. Each has its own separate orbit, a pathway of light; while all together constitute a system which moves in a still grander orbit.

Among all these associations, none is so truly comprehensive as ours. The prisoner in his cell, the slave in his chains, the sailor on ocean wanderings, the Pagan on far off continent or island, and the ignorant here at home, will all be commended by eloquent voices. I need not say that you should listen to these voices, and answer to their appeal. But, while mindful of these interests, justly claiming your care, it is my present and most grateful duty to commend that other cause, the great cause of Peace, which in its wider embrace enfolds prisoner, slave, sailor, the ignorant, all mankind, — which to each of these charities is the source of strength and light, I may say of life itself, as the sun in the heavens.

Peace is the grand Christian charity, fountain and parent of all other charities. Let Peace be removed, and all other charities sicken and die. Let Peace exert her gladsome sway, and all other charities quicken into life. Peace is the distinctive promise and possession of Christianity, — so much so, that, where Peace is not, Christianity cannot be. It is also the promise of Heaven, being the beautiful consummation of that rest and felicity which the saints above are said to enjoy. There is nothing elevated which is not exalted by Peace. There is nothing valuable which does not gain from Peace. Of Wisdom herself it is said, that all her ways are pleasantness, and all her paths are Peace. And these golden words are refined by the saying of the Christian Father, that the perfection of joy is Peace. Naturally Peace is the longing and aspiration of the noblest souls, whether for themselves or for country. In the bitterness of exile, away from the Florence immortalized by his divine poem, and pacing the cloisters of a convent, where a sympathetic monk inquired, "What do you seek?" Dante answered, in accents distilled from the heart, "*Peace!*"[1] In the memorable English struggles, while King and Parliament were rending the land, a gallant supporter of monarchy, the chivalrous Falkland, touched by the intolerable woes of

[1] Longfellow's Poets and Poetry of Europe, p. 513.

War, cried, in words which consecrate his memory more than any feat of arms, "*Peace! peace!*"[1] Not in aspiration only, but in benediction, is this word uttered. As the Apostle went forth on his errand, as the son forsook his father's roof, the choicest blessing was, "*Peace be with you!*" When the Saviour was born, angels from heaven, amidst choiring melodies, let fall that supreme benediction, never before vouchsafed to the children of the Human Family, "*Peace on earth, and good-will towards men!*"

To maintain this charity, to promote these aspirations, to welcome these benedictions, is the object of our Society. To fill men in private with all those sentiments which make for Peace, to lead men in public to the recognition of those paramount principles which are the safeguard of Peace, above all, to teach the True Grandeur of Peace, and to unfold the folly and wickedness of the Institution of War and of the War System, now recognized and established by the Commonwealth of Nations as the mode of determining international controversies, — such is the object of our Society.

There are persons who allow themselves sometimes to speak of associations like ours, if not with disapprobation, at least with levity and distrust. A writer so humane and genial as Robert Southey left on record a gibe at the "Society for the Abolition of War," saying that it had "not obtained sufficient notice even to be in disrepute."[2] It is not uncommon to hear our aims characterized as visionary, impracticable, Utopian. Sometimes it is hastily said that they are contrary to

1 Clarendon, History of the Rebellion, Book VII. Vol. IV. p. 255.

2 Colloquies on the Progress and Prospects of Society, Vol. I. p. 224.

the nature of man, that they require for success a complete reconstruction of human character, and that they necessarily assume in man qualities, capacities, and virtues which do not belong to his nature. This mistaken idea was once strongly expressed in the taunt, that "an Anti-War Society is as little practicable as an Anti-Thunder-and-Lightning Society."[1]

Never a moment when this beautiful cause was not the occasion of jest, varying with the character of the objector. More than a century ago there was something of this kind, which arrested the attention of no less a person than Leibnitz, and afterwards of Fontenelle. It was where an elegant Dutch trifler, as described by Leibnitz, following the custom of his country, placed as a sign over his door the motto, *To Perpetual Peace*, with the picture of a cemetery, — meaning to suggest that only with the dead could this desire of good men be fulfilled. Not with the living, so the elegant Dutch trifler proclaimed over his door. A different person, also of Holland, who was both diplomatist and historian, the scholarly Aitzema, caught the jest, and illustrated it by a Latin couplet: —

> "Qui pacem quæris libertatemque, viator,
> Aut nusquam aut isto sub tumulo invenies"; —

which, being translated, means, "Traveller, who seekest Peace and Liberty, either nowhere or under that mound thou wilt find them."[2] Do not fail to observe that Liberty is here doomed to the same grave as Peace. Alas, that there should be such despair! At length Liberty is rising. May not Peace rise also?

[1] Hon. Jeremiah Mason, of Boston, to Mr. Sumner.

[2] Leibnitz, Codex Juris Gentium Diplomaticus, Dissert. I. § 1: Opera (ed. Dutens), Tom. IV. Pars 3, pp. 287, 288. Fontenelle, Éloge de Leibnitz: Œuvres, Tom. V. p. 456.

Doubtless objections, to say nothing of jests, striking at the heart of our cause, exert a certain influence over the public mind. They often proceed from persons of sincerity and goodness, who would rejoice to see the truth as we see it. But, plausible as they appear to those who have not properly meditated this subject, I cannot but regard them — I believe that all who candidly listen to me must hereafter regard them — as prejudices, without foundation in sense or reason, which must yield to a plain and careful examination of the precise objects proposed.

Let me not content myself, in response to these critics, with the easy answer, that, if our aims are visionary, impracticable, Utopian, then the unfulfilled promises of the Scriptures are vain, — then the Lord's Prayer, in which we ask that God's kingdom may come on earth, is a mockery, — then Christianity is no better than the statutes of Utopia. Let me not content myself with reminding you that all the great reforms by which mankind have been advanced encountered similar objections, — that the abolition of the punishment of death for theft, so long delayed, was first suggested in the "Utopia" of Sir Thomas More, — that the efforts to abolish the slave-trade were opposed, almost in our day, as visionary, — in short, that all endeavors for human improvement, for knowledge, for freedom, for virtue, all the great causes which dignify human history, and save it from being a mere protracted War Bulletin, a common sewer, a *Cloaca Maxima*, flooded with perpetual uncleanness, have been pronounced Utopian, — while, in spite of distrust, prejudice, and enmity, all these causes gradually found acceptance, as they gradually came to be understood, and the aspirations of one age became the acquisitions of the next.

Satisfactory to some as this answer might be, I cannot content myself with leaving our cause in this way. I shall meet all assaults, and show, by careful exposition, that our objects are in no respect visionary, — that the cause of Peace does not depend upon any reconstruction of the human character, or upon holding in check the general laws of man's being, — but that it deals with man as he is, according to the experience of history, — and, above all, that our immediate and particular aim, the abolition of the Institution of War, and of the whole War System, as *established* Arbiter of Right in the Commonwealth of Nations, is as practicable as it would be beneficent.

I begin by putting aside questions, often pushed forward, which an accurate analysis shows to be independent of the true issue. Their introduction has perplexed the discussion, by transferring to the great cause of International Peace doubts which do not belong to it.

One of these is the declared right, inherent in each individual, to take the life of an assailant in order to save his own life, — compendiously called the *Right of Self-Defence,* usually recognized by philosophers and publicists as founded in Nature and the instincts of men. The exercise of this right is carefully restricted to cases where life itself is in actual jeopardy. No defence of property, no vindication of what is called *personal honor,* justifies this extreme resort. Nor does this right imply the right of attack; for, instead of attacking one another, on account of injuries past or impending, men need only resort to the proper tribunals of justice. There are, however, many most respectable persons, particularly of the denomination of Friends, some of whom I may now have the honor of addressing, who believe that the exercise of this right, even thus limited, is in direct contravention of Christian precepts. Their views find faithful utterance in the writings of Jonathan Dymond, of which at least this may be said, that they strengthen and elevate, even if they do not always satisfy, the understanding. "We shall be asked," says Dymond, "'Suppose a ruffian breaks into your house, and rushes into your room with his arm lifted to murder you; do you not believe that Christianity allows you to kill him?' This is the last refuge of the cause. Our answer to it is explicit, — *We do not believe it.*"[1] While thus candidly and openly avowing an extreme sentiment of non-resistance, this excellent person is careful to remind the reader that the case of the ruffian does not practically illustrate the true character of War, unless it appears that war is undertaken simply for the preservation of life, when no other alternative remains to a people than to kill or be killed. According to this view, the robber on land who places his pistol at the breast of the traveller, the pirate who threatens life on the high seas, and the riotous disturber of the public peace who puts life in jeopardy at home, cannot be opposed by the sacrifice of life. Of course all who subscribe to this renunciation of self-defence must join in efforts to abolish the Arbitrament of War. Our appeal is to the larger number who make no such application of Christian precepts, who recognize the right of self-defence as belonging to each individual, and who believe in the necessity at times of

1 On the Applicability of the Pacific Principles of the New Testament to the Conduct of States, p. 10.

exercising this right, whether against a robber, a pirate, or a mob.

Another question, closely connected with that of self-defence, is the asserted *Right of Revolt or Revolution.* Shall a people endure political oppression, or the denial of freedom, without resistance? The answer to this question will necessarily affect the rights of three million fellow-citizens held in slavery among us. If such a right unqualifiedly exists, — and sympathy with our fathers, and with the struggles for freedom now agitating Europe, must make us hesitate to question its existence, — then these three millions of fellow-men, into whose souls we thrust the iron of the deadliest bondage the world has yet witnessed, must be justified in resisting to death the power that holds them. A popular writer on ethics, Dr. Paley, has said: "It may be as much a duty at one time to resist Government as it is at another to obey it, — to wit, whenever more advantage will in our opinion accrue to the community from resistance than mischief. The lawfulness of resistance, or the lawfulness of a revolt, does not depend alone upon the grievance which is sustained or feared, but also upon the probable expense and event of the contest."[1] This view distinctly recognizes the right of resistance, but limits it by the chance of success, founding it on no higher ground than expediency. A right thus vaguely defined and bounded must be invoked with reluctance and distrust. The lover of Peace, while admitting, that, unhappily, in the present state of the world, an exigency for its exercise may arise, must confess the inherent barbarism of such an agency, and admire, even

[1] Principles of Moral and Political Philosophy, Book VI. ch. 3.

if he cannot entirely adopt, the sentiment of Daniel O'Connell: "Remember that no political change is worth a single crime, or, above all, a single drop of human blood."

These questions I put aside, not as unimportant, not as unworthy of careful consideration, but as unessential to the cause which I now present. If I am asked — as advocates of Peace are often asked — whether a robber, a pirate, a mob, may be resisted by the sacrifice of life, I answer, that they may be so resisted, — mournfully, necessarily. If I am asked to sympathize with the efforts for freedom now finding vent in rebellion and revolution, I cannot hesitate to say, that, wherever Freedom struggles, wherever Right is, there my sympathies must be. And I believe I speak not only for myself, but for our Society, when I add, that, while it is our constant aim to diffuse those sentiments which promote good-will in all the relations of life, which exhibit the beauty of Peace everywhere, in *national* affairs as well as *international*, and while especially recognizing that central truth, the Brotherhood of Man, in whose noonday light all violence among men is dismal and abhorred as among brothers, it is nevertheless no part of our purpose to impeach the right to take life in self-defence or when the public necessity requires, nor to question the justifiableness of resistance to outrage and oppression. On these points there are diversities of opinion among the friends of Peace, which this Society, confining itself to efforts for the overthrow of War, is not constrained to determine.

Waiving, then, these matters, with their perplexities and difficulties, which do not in any respect belong to the cause, I come now to the precise object we hope to accomplish, — *The Abolition of the Institution of War, and of the whole War System, as an established Arbiter of Justice in the Commonwealth of Nations.* In the accurate statement of our aims you will at once perceive the strength of our position. Much is always gained by a clear understanding of the question in issue; and the cause of Peace unquestionably suffers often because it is misrepresented or not fully comprehended. In the hope of removing this difficulty, I shall *first* unfold the true character of War and the War System, involving the question of Preparations for War, and the question of a Militia. The way will then be open, in the *second* branch of this Address, for a consideration of the means by which this system can be overthrown. Here I shall exhibit the examples of nations, and the efforts of individuals, constituting the Peace Movement, with the auguries of its triumph, briefly touching, at the close, on our duties to this great cause, and the vanity of Military Glory. In all that I say I cannot forget that I am addressing a Christian association, for a Christian charity, in a Christian church.

I.

AND, first, of *War and the War System in the Commonwealth of Nations.* By the Commonwealth of Nations I understand the Fraternity of Christian Nations recognizing a Common Law in their relations with each other, usually called the Law of Nations. This law, being established by the consent of nations, is not necessarily the law of all nations, but only of such as recognize it. The Europeans and the Orientals often differ with regard to its provisions; nor would it be proper to say, that, at this time, the Ottomans, or the Mahometans in general, or the Chinese, have become parties to it.[1] The prevailing elements of this law are the Law of Nature, the truths of Christianity, the usages of nations, the opinions of publicists, and the written texts or enactments found in diplomatic acts or treaties. In origin and growth it is not unlike the various systems of municipal jurisprudence, all of which are referred to kindred sources.

It is often said, in excuse for the allowance of War, that nations are independent, and acknowledge no *common superior*. True, indeed, they are politically independent, and acknowledge no common political sovereign, with power to enforce the law. But they do acknowledge a common superior, of unquestioned influence and authority, whose rules they are bound to obey. This common superior, acknowledged by all, is none other than the Law of Nations, with the Law of Nature as a controlling element. It were superfluous to dwell at length upon opinions of publicists and jurists declaring this supremacy. "The Law of Nature," says Vattel, a classic in this department, "is not less *obligatory* with respect to states, or to men united in political society, than to individuals."[2] An eminent English authority, Lord Stowell, so famous as Sir William Scott, says, "The *Conventional Law of Mankind*, which is evidenced in their practice, *allows* some and *prohibits* other modes of destruction."[3] A recent German jurist says, "A nation associating itself with the general so-

1 Since the delivery of this Address, Turkey and China have accepted our Law of Nations.

2 Law of Nations, Preface.

3 Robinson's, Chr., Admiralty Reports, Vol. I. p. 140.

ciety of nations *thereby recognizes a law common to all nations,* by which its international relations are to be regulated."[1] Lastly, a popular English moralist, whom I have already quoted, and to whom I refer because his name is so familiar, Dr. Paley, says, that the principal part of what is called the Law of Nations derives its obligatory character "*simply from the fact of its being established, and the general duty of conforming to established rules* upon questions and between parties where nothing but *positive regulations* can prevent disputes, and where disputes are followed by such destructive consequences."[2]

The Law of Nations is, then, the Supreme Law of the Commonwealth of Nations, governing their relations with each other, determining their reciprocal rights, and sanctioning all remedies for the violation of these rights. To the Commonwealth of Nations this law is what the Constitution and Municipal Law of Massachusetts are to the associate towns and counties composing the State, or what, by apter illustration, the National Constitution of our Union is to the thirty several States which now recognize it as the supreme law.

But the Law of Nations, — and here is a point of infinite importance to the clear understanding of the subject, — while anticipating and providing for controversies between nations, recognizes and establishes War as final Arbiter. It distinctly says to nations, "If you cannot agree together, then stake your cause upon *Trial by Battle.*" The mode of trial thus recognized and established has its own procedure, with rules and regulations,

1 Heffter, Das Europäische Völkerrecht der Gegenwart, § 2.

2 Principles of Moral and Political Philosophy, Book VI. ch. 12.

under the name of Laws of War, constituting a branch of International Law. "The Laws of War," says Dr. Paley, "are part of the Law of Nations, and founded, as to their authority, upon the same principle with the rest of that code, namely, upon the fact of their being *established*, no matter when or by whom." [1] Nobody doubts that the Laws of War are established by nations.

It is not uncommon to speak of the *practice* of War, or the *custom* of War, — a term adopted by that devoted friend of Peace, the late Noah Worcester. Its apologists and expounders have called it "a judicial trial," — "one of the highest trials of right," — "a process of justice," — "an appeal for justice," — "a mode of obtaining rights," — "a prosecution of rights by force," — "a mode of condign punishment." I prefer to characterize it as an INSTITUTION, established by the Commonwealth of Nations as Arbiter of Justice. As Slavery is an Institution, growing out of local custom, sanctioned, defined, and established by Municipal Law, so War is an Institution, growing out of general custom, sanctioned, defined, and established by the Law of Nations.

Only when we contemplate War in this light can we fully perceive its combined folly and wickedness. Let me bring this home to your minds. Boston and Cambridge are adjoining towns, separated by the River Charles. In the event of controversy between these different jurisdictions, the Municipal Law establishes a judicial tribunal, and not War, as arbiter. Ascending higher, in the event of controversy between two different counties, as between Essex and Middlesex, the same Municipal Law establishes a judicial tribunal,

1 Principles of Moral and Political Philosophy, Book VI. ch. 12.

and not War, as arbiter. Ascending yet higher, in the event of controversy between two different States of our Union, the Constitution establishes a judicial tribunal, the Supreme Court of the United States, and not War, as arbiter. But now mark: at the next stage there is a change of arbiter. In the event of controversy between two different States of the Commonwealth of Nations, the supreme law establishes, not a judicial tribunal, but War, as arbiter. War is the institution *established* for the determination of justice between nations.

Provisions of the Municipal Law of Massachusetts, and of the National Constitution, are not vain words. To all familiar with our courts it is well known that suits between towns, and likewise between counties, are often entertained and satisfactorily adjudicated. The records of the Supreme Court of the United States show also that States of the Union habitually refer important controversies to this tribunal. Before this high court is now pending an action of the State of Missouri against the State of Iowa, founded on a question of boundary, where the former claims a section of territory — larger than many German principalities — extending along the whole northern border of Missouri, with several miles of breadth, and comprising more than two thousand square miles. Within a short period this same tribunal has decided a similar question between our own State of Massachusetts and our neighbor, Rhode Island, — the latter pertinaciously claiming a section of territory, about three miles broad, on a portion of our southern frontier.

Suppose that in these different cases between towns counties, states, War had been *established* by the supreme law as arbiter; imagine the disastrous consequences; picture the imperfect justice which must have been the end and fruit of such a contest; and while rejoicing that in these cases we are happily relieved from an alternative so wretched and deplorable, reflect that on a larger theatre, where grander interests are staked, in the relations between nations, under the solemn sanction of the Law of Nations, War is *established* as Arbiter of Justice. Reflect also that a complex and subtile code, known as Laws of War, is established to regulate the resort to this arbiter.

Recognizing the irrational and unchristian character of War as established arbiter between towns, counties, and states, we learn to condemn it as established arbiter between nations. If wrong in one case, it must be wrong in the other. But there is another parallel supplied by history, from which we may form a yet clearer idea: I refer to the system of *Private Wars*, or, more properly, *Petty Wars*, which darkened even the Dark Ages. This must not be confounded with the *Trial by Battle*, although the two were alike in recognizing the sword as Arbiter of Justice. The *right to wage war* (*le droit de guerroyer*) was accorded by the early Municipal Law of European States, particularly of the Continent, to all independent chiefs, however petty, but not to vassals; precisely as the *right to wage war* is now accorded by International Law to all independent states and principalities, however petty, but not to subjects. It was mentioned often among the "liberties" to which independent chiefs were entitled; as it is still recognized by International Law among the "liberties" of independent nations. In proportion as any sovereignty was absorbed in some larger lordship, this offensive *right* or "liberty" gradually disappeared. In France it prevailed extensively, till at last King John, by an ordinance dated 1361, expressly forbade Petty Wars throughout his kingdom, saying, in excellent words, "We by these presents ordain that all challenges and wars, and all acts of violence against all persons, in all parts whatsoever of our kingdom, shall henceforth cease; and all assemblies, musters, and raids of men-at-arms or archers; and also all pillages, seizures of goods and persons illegally, *vengeances and counter-vengeances,* surprisals and ambuscades. . . . . All which things we will to be kept and observed everywhere without infringement, on pain of incurring our indignation, and of being reputed and held disobedient and rebellious towards us and the crown, and at our mercy in body and goods."[1] It was reserved for that indefatigable king, Louis the Eleventh, while Dauphin, as late as 1451, to make another effort in the same direction, by expressly abrogating one of the "liberties" of Dauphiné, being none other than the *right of war,* immemorially secured to the inhabitants of this province.[2] From these royal ordinances the Commonwealth of Nations might borrow appropriate words, in abrogating forever the Public Wars, or, more properly, the Grand Wars, with their *vengeances and counter-vengeances,* which are yet sanctioned by International Law among the "liberties" of Christian nations.

At a later day, in Germany, effective measures were taken against the same prevailing evil. Contests there

[1] Cauchy, Du Duel considéré dans ses Origines, Liv. I. Seconde Époque, Ch. V. Tom. I. pp. 91, 92.

[2] Du Cange, Dissertations sur l'Histoire de St. Louis, Diss. XXVII. (XXIX.): *Des Guerres Privées.*

were not confined to feudal lords. Associations of tradesmen, and even of domestics, sent defiance to each other, and even to whole cities, on pretences trivial as those sometimes the occasion of the Grand Wars between nations. There are still extant *Declarations of War* by a Lord of Frauenstein against the free city of Frankfort, because a young lady of the city refused to dance with the uncle of the belligerent, — by the baker and other domestics of the Margrave of Baden against Esslingen, Reutlingen, and other imperial cities, — by the baker of the Count Palatine Louis against the cities of Augsburg, Ulm, and Rottweil, — by the shoeblacks of the University of Leipsic against the provost and other members, — and, in 1477, by the cook of Eppenstein, with his scullions, dairy-maids, and dish-washers, against Otho, Count of Solms. Finally, in 1495, at the Diet of Worms, so memorable in German annals, the Emperor Maximilian sanctioned an ordinance which proclaimed a permanent Peace throughout Germany, abolished the *right* or "liberty" of Private War, and instituted a Supreme Tribunal, under the ancient name of Imperial Chamber, to which recourse might be had, even by nobles, princes, and states, for the determination of disputes without appeal to the sword.[1]

Trial by Battle, or "judicial combat," furnishes the most vivid picture of the Arbitrament of War, beyond even what is found in the system of *Petty Wars*. It was at one period, particularly in France, the universal umpire between private individuals. All causes, criminal and civil, with all the questions incident thereto, were referred to this senseless trial. Not bodily in-

[1] Coxe, History of the House of Austria, Ch. XIX. and XXI.

firmity or old age could exempt a litigant from the hazard of the Battle, even to determine differences of the most trivial import. At last substitutes were allowed, and, as in War, bravoes or champions were hired for wages to enter the lists. The proceedings were conducted gravely according to prescribed forms, which were digested into a system of peculiar subtilty and minuteness, — as War in our day is according to an established code, the Laws of War. Thus do violence, lawlessness, and absurdity shelter themselves beneath the Rule of Law! Religion also lent her sanctions. With presence and prayer the priest cheered the insensate combatant, and appealed for aid to Jesus Christ, the Prince of Peace.

The Church, to its honor, early perceived the wickedness of this system. By voices of pious bishops, by ordinances of solemn councils, by anathemas of popes, it condemned whosoever should slay another in a battle so impious and inimical to Christian peace, as "a most wicked homicide and bloody robber"[1]; while it treated the unhappy victim as a volunteer, guilty of his own death, and handed his remains to unhonored burial without psalm or prayer. With sacerdotal supplication it vainly sought the withdrawal of all countenance from this great evil, and the support of the civil power in ecclesiastical censures. To these just efforts let praise and gratitude be offered! But, alas! authentic incidents, and the forms still on record in ancient missals, attest the unhappy sanction which Trial by

[1] "Statuimus, juxta antiquum ecclesiasticæ observationis morem, ut quicumque tam impia et Christianæ paci inimica pugna alterum occiderit seu vulneribus debilem reddiderit, *velut homicida nequissimus et latro cruentus*, ab Ecclesiæ et omnium fidelium cœtu reddatur separatus," etc. — Canon XII. Concil. Valent., — quoted by Cauchy, Du Duel, Liv. I. Première Époque, Ch. III., Tom. I. p. 43, note.

Battle succeeded in obtaining even from the Church, — as in our day the English Liturgy, and the conduct of the Christian clergy in all countries, attest the unhappy sanction which the Institution of War yet enjoys. Admonitions of the Church and labors of good men slowly prevailed. Proofs by witnesses and by titles were gradually adopted, though opposed by the selfishness of camp-followers, subaltern officers, and even of lords, greedy for the fees or wages of combat. In England Trial by Battle was attacked by Henry the Second, striving to substitute Trial by Jury. In France it was expressly forbidden by that illustrious monarch, St. Louis, in an immortal ordinance. At last, this system, so wasteful of life, so barbarous in character, so vain and inefficient as Arbiter of Justice, yielded to judicial tribunals.

The Trial by Battle is not Roman in origin. It may be traced to the forests of Germany, where the rule prevailed of referring to the sword what at Rome was referred to the prætor; so that a judicial tribunal, when urged upon these barbarians, was regarded as an innovation.[1] The very words of surprise at the German custom are yet applicable to the Arbitrament of War.

The absurdity of Trial by Battle may be learned from the instances where it was invoked. Though originally permitted to determine questions of personal character, it was extended so as to embrace criminal cases, and even questions of property. In 961 the title to a church was submitted to this ordeal.[2] Some time later a grave point of law was submitted. The question was, "Whether the sons of a son ought to be reckoned

1 "Nunc agentes gratias, quod ea Romana justitia finiret, feritasque sua novitate incognitæ disciplinæ mitesceret, et solita armis decerni jure terminarentur." — Velleius Paterculus, Lib. II. c. 118.

2 Robertson, History of Charles V., Vol. I. Note 22.

among the children of the family, and succeed equally with their uncles, if their father happened to die while their grandfather was alive." The general opinion at first was for reference of the question to the adjudication of arbiters; but we are informed by a contemporary ecclesiastic, who reports the case, that the Emperor, Otho the First, "taking better counsel, and unwilling that nobles and elders of the people should be treated *dishonorably*, ordered the matter to be decided by champions with the sword." The champion of the grandchildren prevailed, and they were enabled to share with their uncles in the inheritance.[1] Human folly did not end here. A question of theology was surrendered to the same arbitrament, being nothing less than whether the Musarabic Liturgy, used in the churches of Spain, or the Liturgy approved at Rome, contained the form of worship most acceptable to the Deity. The Spaniards contended zealously for the liturgy of their ancestors. The Pope urged the liturgy having his own infallible sanction. The controversy was submitted to Trial by Battle. Two knights in complete armor entered the lists. The champion of the Musarabic Liturgy was victorious. But there was an appeal to the ordeal of fire. A copy of each liturgy was cast into the flames. The Musarabic Liturgy remained unhurt, while the other vanished into ashes. And yet this judgment, first by battle and then by fire, was eluded or overthrown, showing how, as with War, the final conclusion is uncertain, and testifying against any appeal, except to human reason.[2]

[1] Widukindii, Res Gestæ Saxonicæ, Lib. II. c. 10: Monumenta Germaniæ Historica, ed. Pertz, Scriptorum Tom. III. p. 440.

[2] Robertson, History of Charles V., Vol. I. Note 22. — The Duel has a liter-

An early king of the Lombards, in a formal decree, condemned the Trial by Battle as "impious"[1]; Montesquieu, at a later time, branded it as "monstrous"[2]; and Sir William Blackstone characterized it as "clearly an unchristian, as well as most uncertain, method of trial."[3] In the light of our day all unite in this condemnation. No man hesitates. No man undertakes its apology; nor does any man count as "glory" the feats of arms which it prompted and displayed. But the laws of morals are general, and not special. They apply to communities and to nations, as well as to individuals; nor is it possible, by any cunning of logic, or any device of human wit, to distinguish between that domestic institution, the Trial by Battle, established by Municipal Law as arbiter between individuals, and that international institution, the grander Trial by Battle, established by the Christian Commonwealth as arbiter between nations. If the judicial combat was impious, monstrous, and unchristian, then is War impious, monstrous, and unchristian.

It has been pointedly said in England, that the whole object of king, lords, and commons, and of the complex British Constitution, is "to get twelve men into

ature of its own, which is not neglected by Brunet in his *Manuel du Libraire*, where, under the head of *Les Combats Singuliers*, Tom. VI. col. 1636 - 1638, *Table Méthodique*, 28717 - 28749, will be found titles in various languages, from which I select the following: Joan. de Lignano, Tractatus de Bello, de Repressaliis, et de Duello, Papiæ, 1487; Tractatus de Duello, en Lat. y en Castellano, por D. Castillo, Taurini, 1525; Alciat, De Singulari Certamine, Lugd., 1543. In the development of civilization how can the literature of War expect more honor than that of the Duel?

1 Liutprandi Leges, Lib. VI. cap. 65: Muratori, Rerum Italic. Script., Tom. I. Pars 2, p. 74.

2 Esprit des Lois, Liv. XXVIII. ch. 23.

3 Commentaries, Book IV. ch. 33, Vol. IV. p. 418.

a jury-box"; and Mr. Hume repeats the idea, when he declares that the *administration of justice* is the grand aim of government. If this be true of individual nations in municipal affairs, it is equally true of the Commonwealth of Nations. The whole complex system of the Law of Nations, overarching all the Christian nations, has but one distinct object,—*the administration of justice* between nations. Would that with tongue or pen I could adequately expose the enormity of this system, involving, as it does, the precepts of religion, the dictates of common sense, the suggestions of economy, and the most precious sympathies of humanity! Would that now I could impart to all who hear me something of my own conviction!

I need not dwell on the waste and cruelty thus authorized. Travelling the page of history, these stare us wildly in the face at every turn. We see the desolation and death keeping step with the bloody track; we look upon sacked towns, ravaged territories, violated homes; we behold all the sweet charities of life changed to wormwood and gall. The soul is penetrated by the sharp moan of mothers, sisters, and daughters, of fathers, brothers, and sons, who, in the bitterness of bereavement, refuse to be comforted. The eye rests at last upon one of those fair fields, where Nature, in her abundance, spreads her cloth of gold, spacious and apt for the entertainment of mighty multitudes,—or, perhaps, from curious subtilty of position, like the carpet in Arabian tale, contracting for the accommodation of a few only, or dilating for an innumerable host. Here, under a bright sun, such as shone at Austerlitz or Buena Vista, amidst the peaceful harmonies of Nature, on the Sabbath of Peace, are bands of brothers, children of a common Father, heirs to a common happiness, struggling together in deadly fight, — with madness of fallen spirits, murderously seeking the lives of brothers who never injured them or their kindred. The havoc rages; the ground is soaked with commingling blood; the air is rent by commingling cries; horse and rider are stretched together on the earth. More revolting than mangled victims, gashed limbs, lifeless trunks, spattering brains, are the lawless passions which sweep, tempest-like, through the fiendish tumult.

"'Nearer comes the storm and nearer, rolling fast and frightful on.
Speak, Ximena, speak, and tell us, who has lost and who has won?'
'Alas! alas! I know not, sister; friend and foe together fall;
O'er the dying rush the living; pray, my sister, for them all!'"

Horror-struck, we ask, wherefore this hateful contest? The melancholy, but truthful, answer comes, that this is the *established* method of determining justice between nations!

The scene changes. Far away on some distant pathway of the ocean, two ships approach each other, with white canvas broadly spread to receive the flying gale. They are proudly built. All of human art has been lavished in their graceful proportions and compacted sides, while in dimensions they look like floating happy islands of the sea. A numerous crew, with costly appliances of comfort, hives in their secure shelter. Surely these two travellers must meet in joy and friendship; the flag at mast-head will give the signal of fellowship; the delighted sailors will cluster in rigging and on yardarms to look each other in the face, while exhilarating voices mingle in accents of gladness uncontrollable. Alas! alas! it is not so. Not as brothers, not as friends, not as wayfarers of the common ocean, do they come together, but as enemies. The closing vessels now bristle fiercely with death-dealing implements. On their spacious decks, aloft on all their masts, flashes the deadly musketry. From their sides spout cataracts of flame, amidst the pealing thunders of a fatal artillery. They who had escaped "the dreadful touch of merchant-marring rocks," who on their long and solitary way had sped unharmed by wind or wave, whom the hurricane had spared, in whose favor storms and seas had intermitted their immitigable war, now at last fall by the hand of each other. From both ships the same spectacle of horror greets us. On decks reddened with blood, the murders of the Sicilian Vespers and of St. Bartholomew, with the fires of Smithfield, break forth anew, and concentrate their rage. Each is a swimming Golgotha. At length these vessels — such pageants of the sea, such marvels of art, once so stately, but now rudely shattered by cannon-ball, with shivered masts and ragged sails — exist only as unmanageable wrecks, weltering on the uncertain wave, whose transient lull of peace is their sole safety. In amazement at this strange, unnatural contest, away from country and home, where there is no country or home to defend, we ask again, Wherefore this dismal scene? Again the melancholy, but truthful, answer promptly comes, that this is the *established* method of determining justice between nations.

Yes! the barbarous, brutal relations which once prevailed between individuals, which prevailed still longer between communities composing nations, are not yet banished from the great Christian Commonwealth. Religion, reason, humanity, first penetrate the individual, next larger bodies, and, widening in influence, slowly leaven nations. Thus, while condemning the bloody contests of individuals, also of towns, counties, principalities, provinces, and denying to all these the right of *waging war*, or of appeal to *Trial by Battle*, we continue to uphold an atrocious *System* of folly and crime, which is to nations what the System of Petty Wars was to towns, counties, principalities, provinces, also what the Duel was to individuals: for *War is the Duel of Nations.*[1] As from Pluto's throne flowed those terrible rivers, Styx, Acheron, Cocytus, and Phlegethon, with lamenting waters and currents of flame, so from this established System flow the direful tides of War. "Give them Hell," was the language written on a slate by an American officer, speechless from approaching death. "Ours is a damnable profession," was the confession of a veteran British general. "War is the trade of barbarians," exclaimed Napoleon, in a moment of truthful remorse, prompted by his bloodiest field. Alas! these words are not too strong. The business of War cannot be other than the trade of barbarians, cannot be other than a damnable profession; and War itself is certainly Hell on earth. But forget not, bear always in mind, and let the idea sink deep into your souls, animating you to constant endeavor, that this trade of barbarians, this damnable profession, is part of the War System, sanctioned by International Law, — and that War itself is Hell, recognized, legalized, established, organized, by

[1] Plautus speaks in the *Epidicus* (Act III. Sc. iv. 14, 15) of one who obtained great riches by the *Duelling Art*, meaning the Art of War: —

"*Arte duellica*
Divitias magnas indeptum."

And Horace, in his Odes (Lib. IV. Carm. xv. 4–9), hails the age of Augustus, as at peace, or *free from Duels*, and with the Temple of Janus closed: —

"Tua, Cæsar, ætas
. . . . . vacuum *duellis*
Janum Quirini clausit."

the Commonwealth of Nations, for the determination of international questions!

"Put together," says Voltaire, "all the vices of all ages and places, and they will not come up to the mischiefs of one campaign."[1] This strong speech is supported by the story of ancient mythology, that Juno confided the infant Mars to Priapus. Another of nearer truth might be made. Put together all the ills and calamities from the visitations of God, whether in convulsions of Nature, or in pestilence and famine, and they will not equal the ills and calamities inflicted by man upon his brother-man, through the visitation of War, — while, alas! the sufferings of War are too often without the alleviation of those gentle virtues which ever attend the involuntary misfortunes of the race. Where the horse of Attila had been a blade of grass would not grow; but in the footprints of pestilence, famine, and earthquake the kindly charities spring into life.

The last hundred years have witnessed three peculiar visitations of God: first, the earthquake at Lisbon; next, the Asiatic cholera, as it moved slow and ghastly, with scythe of death, from the Delta of the Ganges over Bengal, Persia, Arabia, Syria, Russia, till Europe and America shuddered before the spectral reaper; and, lastly, the recent famine in Ireland, consuming with remorseless rage the population of that ill-starred land. It is impossible to estimate precisely the deadly work of cholera or famine, nor can we picture the miseries which they entailed; but the single brief event of the earthquake may be portrayed in authentic colors.

Lisbon, whose ancient origin is referred by fable to

1 Dictionnaire Philosophique, Art. *Guerre*.

the wanderings of Ulysses, was one of the fairest cities of Europe. From the summit of seven hills it looked down upon the sea, and the bay bordered with cheerful villages,—upon the broad Tagus, expanding into a harbor ample for all the navies of Europe,—and upon a country of rare beauty, smiling with the olive and the orange, amidst grateful shadows of the cypress and the elm. A climate offering flowers in winter enhanced the peculiar advantages of position; and a numerous population thronged its narrow and irregular streets. Its forty churches, its palaces, its public edifices, its warehouses, its convents, its fortresses, its citadel, had become a boast. Not by War, not by the hand of man, were these solid structures levelled, and all these delights changed to desolation.

Lisbon, on the morning of November 1, 1755, was taken and sacked by an earthquake. The spacious warehouses were destroyed; the lordly palaces, the massive convents, the impregnable fortresses, with the lofty citadel, were toppled to the ground; and as the affrighted people sought shelter in the churches, they were crushed beneath the falling masses. Twenty thousand persons perished. Fire and robbery mingled with earthquake, and the beautiful city seemed to be obliterated. The nations of Europe were touched by this terrible catastrophe, and succor from all sides was soon offered. Within three months, English vessels appeared in the Tagus, loaded with generous contributions,—twenty thousand pounds in gold, a similar sum in silver, six thousand barrels of salted meat, four thousand barrels of butter, one thousand bags of biscuit, twelve hundred barrels of rice, ten thousand quintals of corn, besides hats, stockings, and shoes.

Such was the desolation, and such the charity, sown by the earthquake at Lisbon, — an event which, after the lapse of nearly a century, still stands without a parallel. But War shakes from its terrible folds all this desolation, without its attendant charity. Nay, more ; the Commonwealth of Nations *voluntarily agrees, each with the others.* under the grave sanctions of International Law, to invoke this desolation, in the settlement of controversies among its members, while it expressly declares that all nations, not already parties to the controversy, must abstain from any succor to the unhappy victim. High tribunals are established expressly to uphold this arbitrament, and, with unrelenting severity, to enforce its ancillary injunctions, to the end that no aid, no charity, shall come to revive the sufferer or alleviate the calamity. Vera Cruz has been bombarded and wasted by American arms. Its citadel, churches, houses, were shattered, and peaceful families at the fireside torn in mutilated fragments by the murderous bursting shell; but the English, the universal charities, which helped to restore Lisbon, were not offered to the ruined Mexican city. They could not have been offered, without offending against the *Laws of War!*

It is because men see War, in the darkness of prejudice, only as an agency of attack or defence, or as a desperate sally of wickedness, that they fail to recognize it as a form of judgment, sanctioned and *legalized* by Public Authority. Regarding it in its true character, as an *establishment* of the Commonwealth of Nations, and one of the " liberties " accorded to independent nations, it is no longer the expression merely of lawless or hasty passion, no longer the necessary incident of imperfect human nature, no longer an unavoidable, uncontrollable volcanic eruption of rage, of *vengeances and counter-vengeances*, knowing no bound; but it becomes a gigantic and monstrous Institution for the adjudication of international rights, — as if an earthquake, or other visitation of God, with its uncounted woes, and without its attendant charities, were legally invoked as Arbiter of Justice.

Surely all must unite in condemning the Arbitrament of War. The simplest may read and comprehend its enormity. Can we yet hesitate? But if War be thus odious, if it be the Duel of Nations, if it be the old surviving Trial by Battle, then must its unquestionable barbarism affect all its incidents, all its machinery, all its enginery, together with all who sanction it, and all who have any part or lot in it, — in fine, the whole vast System. It is impossible, by any discrimination, to separate the component parts. We must regard it as a whole, in its entirety. But half our work is done, if we confine ourselves to a condemnation of the Institution merely. There are all its instruments and agencies, all its adjuncts and accessaries, all its furniture and equipage, all its armaments and operations, the whole apparatus of forts, navies, armies, military display, military chaplains, and military sermons, — all together constituting, in connection with the Institution of War, what may be called the WAR SYSTEM. This System we would abolish, believing that religion, humanity, and policy require the establishment of some peaceful means for the administration of international justice, and also *the general disarming of the Christian nations*, to the end that the prodigious expenditures now absorbed by the War System may be applied to purposes of usefulness and beneficence, and that the *business* of the soldier may cease forever.

While earnestly professing this object, I desire again to exclude all question of self-defence, and to affirm the duty of upholding government, and maintaining the supremacy of the law, whether on land or sea. Admitting the necessity of Force for such purpose, *Christianity revolts at Force as the substitute for a judicial tribunal.* The example of the Great Teacher, the practice of the early disciples, the injunctions of self-denial, love, non-resistance to evil, — sometimes supposed to forbid Force in any exigency, even of self-defence, — all these must apply with unquestionable certainty to the established System of War. *Here, at least, there can be no doubt.* If the sword, in the hand of an assaulted individual, may become the instrument of sincere self-defence, if, under the sanction of a judicial tribunal, it may become the instrument of Justice also, *surely it can never be the Arbiter of Justice.* Here is a distinction vital to the cause of Peace, and never to be forgotten in presenting its claims. The cautious sword of the magistrate is unlike — oh, how unlike! — the ruthless sword of War.

The component parts of the War System may all be resolved into PREPARATIONS FOR WAR, — as court-house, jail, judges, sheriffs, constables, and *posse comitatus* are *preparations* for the administration of municipal justice. If justice were not to be administered, these would not exist. If War were not sanctioned by the Commonwealth of Nations, as the means of determining international controversies, then forts, navies, armies, military display, military chaplains, and military sermons would not exist. They would be useless and irrational, except for the rare occasions of a police,—as similar preparations would now be in Boston, for defence against our learned neighbor, Cambridge,—or in the County of Essex, for defence against its populous neighbor, the County of Middlesex,—or in the State of Massachusetts, for defence against its conterminous States, Rhode Island and New York. Only recently have men learned to question these preparations; for it is only recently that they have opened their eyes to the true character of the system, in which they are a part. *It will yet be seen, that, sustaining these, we sustain the system.* Still further, it will yet be seen, that, sustaining these, we wastefully offend against economy, and violate also the most precious sentiments of Human Brotherhood,—taking counsel of distrust, instead of love, and provoking to rivalry and enmity, instead of association and peace.

Time does not allow me to discuss the nature of these preparations; and I am the more willing to abridge what I am tempted to say, because, on another occasion, I have treated this part of the subject. But I cannot forbear to expose their inconsistency with the spirit of Christianity. From a general comprehension of the War System, we perceive the unchristian character of the preparations it encourages and requires, nay, which are the synonyms of the system, or at least its representatives. I might exhibit this character by an examination of the Laws of War, drawn from no celestial fount, but from a dark profound of Heathenism. This is unnecessary. The Constitution of our own country furnishes an illustration remarkable as a touchstone of the whole system. No town, county, or state has the "liberty" to "declare War." The exercise of any proper self-defence, arising from actual necessity, requires no such "liberty." Congress is expressly authorized to "declare War," — that is, to invoke the Arbitrament of Arms. And the Constitution proceeds to state, that all "giving aid and comfort" to the enemy shall be deemed traitors. Mark now what is said by a higher authority. "Love your enemies"; "If thine enemy hunger, feed him; if he thirst, give him drink." Under the War System, obedience to these positive injunctions may expose a person to the penalty of the highest crime known to the law. Can this be a Christian system? But so long as War exists as an Institution this terrible inconsistency must appear.

The character of these preparations is distinctly, though unconsciously, attested by the names of vessels in the British Navy. From the latest official list I select an illustrative catalogue. Most are steam-ships of recent construction. Therefore they represent the spirit of the British Navy in our day, — nay, of those War Preparations in which they play so conspicuous a part. Here are the champions: Acheron, Adder, Alecto, Avenger, Basilisk, Bloodhound, Bulldog, Crocodile, Erebus, Firebrand, Fury, Gladiator, Goliah, Gorgon, Harpy, Hecate, Hound, Jackal, Mastiff, Pluto, Rattlesnake, Revenge, Salamander, Savage, Scorpion, Scourge, Serpent, Spider, Spiteful, Spitfire, Styx, Sulphur, Tartar, Tartarus, Teazer, Terrible, Terror, Vengeance, Viper, Vixen, Virago, Volcano, Vulture, Warspite, Wildfire, Wolf, Wolverine!

Such is the Christian array of Victoria, Defender of the Faith! It may remind us of the companions of

King John, at another period of English history,—"Falkes the Merciless," "Mauleon the Bloody," "Walter Buck, the Assassin,"[1]—or of that Pagan swarm, the savage warriors of our own continent, with the names of Black-Hawk, Man-Killer, and Wild-Boar. Well might they seem to be

> "all the grisly legions that troop
> Under the sooty flag of Acheron!"

As a people is known by its laws, as a man is known by the company he keeps, as a tree is known by its fruits, so is the War System fully and unequivocally known by the Laws of War, by its diabolical ministers, typical of its preparations, and by all the accursed fruits of War. Controlled by such a code, employing such representatives, sustained by such agencies, animated by such Furies, and producing such fruits of tears and bitterness, it must be open to question. Tell me not that it is sanctioned by any religion except of Mars; do not enroll the Saviour and his disciples in its Satanic squadron; do not invoke the Gospel of Peace, in profane vindication of an *Institution,* which, by its own too palpable confession, exists in defiance of the most cherished Christian sentiments; do not dishonor the Divine Spirit of gentleness, forbearance, love, by supposing that it can ever enter into this System, except to change its whole nature and name, to cast out the devils which possess it, and fill its gigantic energies with the inspiration of Beneficence.

I need say little of military chaplains or military sermons. Like the steamships of the Navy, they come under the head of Preparations. They are part of the War System. They belong to the same school with priests of former times, who held the picture of the

1 Matthew Paris, Historia Major, p. 274.

Prince of Peace before the barbarous champion of the Duel, saying, "Sir Knight, behold here the remembrance of our Lord and Redeemer, Jesus Christ, who willingly gave his most precious body to death in order to save us. Now ask of him mercy, and pray that on this day he may be willing to aid you, if you have right, for he is the sovereign judge."[1] They belong to the same school with English prelates, who, in the name of the Prince of Peace, consecrate banners to flaunt in remote war, saying, "Be thou in the midst of our hosts, as thou wast in the plains of India and in the field of Waterloo; and may these banners, which we bless and consecrate this day, lead them ever on to glorious victory." No judgment of such appeals can be more severe than that of Plato, who called men "most impious," who by prayer and sacrifice thought to propitiate the Gods towards slaughter and outrages upon justice, — thus, says the heathen philosopher, making those pure beings the accomplices of their crimes by sharing with them the spoil, as the wolves leave something to the dogs, that these may allow them to ravage the sheepfold.[2] Consenting to degrade the "blessedness" of the Gospel to the "impiety" of the War System, our clergy follow long established custom, without considering the true character of the system whose ministers they become. Their apology will be, that "they know not what they do."

Again I repeat, so long as the War System prevails under the sanction of International Law, these painful incongruities will be apparent. They belong to a system so essentially irrational, that all the admitted virtues of many of its agents cannot save it from judgment.

1 Cauchy, Du Duel, Liv. I. Seconde Époque, Ch. III. Tom. I. p. 74.
2 Plato, Laws, Book X. ch. 13, 14.

Here the question occurs, Is the *Militia* obnoxious to the same condemnation? So far as the militia constitutes part of the War System, it is impossible to distinguish it from the rest of the system. It is a portion of the extensive apparatus provided for the determination of international disputes. From this character it borrows the unwholesome attractions of War, while disporting itself, like the North American Indian, in finery and parade. Of the latter feature I shall speak only incidentally. If War be a Christian institution, those who act as its agents should shroud themselves in colors congenial with their dreadful trade. With sorrow and solemnity, not with gladness and pomp, they should proceed to their melancholy office. The Jew Shylock exposes the mockery of street-shows in Venice with a sarcasm not without echo here:—

> "When you hear the drum,
> And the vile squeaking of the wry-necked fife,
> Clamber not you up to the casements then,
> Nor thrust your head into the public street,
> To gaze on Christian fools with varnished faces;
> But stop my house's ears,—I mean my casements:
> Let not the sound of shallow foppery enter
> My sober house."

Not as part of the War System, but only as an agent for preserving domestic peace, and for sustaining the law, is the militia entitled to support. And here arises the important practical question,—interesting to opponents of the War System as to lovers of order,—whether the same good object may not be accomplished by an agent less expensive, less cumbersome, and less tardy, forming no part of the War System, and therefore in no respect liable to the doubts encountered by the militia. Supporters of the militia do not disguise its growing unpopularity. The eminent Military Commissioners of Massachusetts, to whom in 1847 was referred the duty of arranging a system for its organization and discipline, confess that there is "either a defect of power in the State government to an efficient and salutary militia organization, or *the absence of a public sentiment in its favor,* and a consequent unwillingness to submit to the requirements of service which alone can sustain it"; and they add, that they "have been met, in the performance of their task, with information, from all quarters, of its general neglect, and of the certain and rapid declension of the militia in numbers and efficiency."[1] And the Adjutant-General of Massachusetts, after alluding to the different systems which have fallen into disuse, remarks, that "the fate of each system is indicative of public sentiment; and until public sentiment changes, *no military system whatever can be sustained in the State.*"[2] Nor is this condition of public sentiment for the first time noticed. It was remarked by the Commissioners charged by the Legislature with this subject as long ago as 1839. In their Report they say, "It is enough to know that all attempts, hitherto, to uphold the system, in its original design of organization, discipline, and subordination, *are at last brought to an unsuccessful issue.*"[3]

None familiar with public opinion in our country, and particularly in Massachusetts, will question the accuracy of these official statements. It is true that there is an indisposition to assume the burdens of the militia. Its offices and dignities have ceased to be an object of general regard. This, certainly, must be founded in the con-

1 Mass. Senate Documents, 1848: Doc. No. 13, pp. 4, 5.

2 Ibid., Doc. No. 15, p. 23.

3 Mass. House Documents, 1839: Doc. No. 6, p. 14.

viction that it is no longer necessary or useful; for it is not customary with the people of Massachusetts to decline occasions of service necessary or useful to the community. The interest in military celebrations has decayed. Nor should it be concealed that there are large numbers whose honest sentiments are not of mere indifference, who regard with aversion the fanfaronade of a militia muster, who not a little question the influence upon those taking part in it or even witnessing it, and look with regret upon the expenditure of money and time.

If such be the condition of the public mind, the Government must recognize it. The soul of all effective laws is an animating public sentiment. This gives vitality to what else would be a dead letter. In vain enact what is not inspired by this spirit. No skill in the device of the system, no penalties, no bounties even, can uphold it. Happily, we are not without remedy. If State Legislatures are disposed to provide a substitute for this questionable or offensive agency, as conservator of domestic quiet, it is entirely within their competency. Let the general voice demand the *substitute*.

Among powers reserved to States, under the National Constitution, is that of *Internal Police*. Within its territorial limits, a State has municipal power to be exercised according to its own will. In the exercise of this will, it may establish a system, congenial with the sentiment of the age, to supply the place of the militia, as guardian of municipal quiet and instrument of the law. This system may consist of unpaid volunteers, or special constables, like fire companies in the country, or of hired men, enrolled for this particular purpose, and always within call, like fire companies in Boston. They need not be clad in showy costume, or subjected to all the peculiarities of military drill. A system so simple, practical, efficient, unostentatious, and cheap, especially as compared with the militia, would be in harmony with existing sentiment, while it could not fail to remedy the evils sometimes feared from present neglect of the militia. Many attempts have been made to reform the militia. *It remains, that a proper effort should be made to provide a substitute for it.*

An eminent English jurist of the last century, — renowned as scholar also, — Sir William Jones, — in a learned and ingenious tract, entitled "An Inquiry into the Legal Mode of Suppressing Riots, with a Constitutional Plan of Future Defence," after developing the obligations of the citizen, under the Common Law, as part of the Power of the County, presents a system of organization independent of the military. It is not probable that this system would be acceptable in all its details to the people of our community, but there is one of his recommendations which seems to harmonize with existing sentiment. "Let companies," he says, "be taught, in the most private and orderly manner, for two or three hours early every morning, until they are competently skilled in the use of their arms; *let them not unnecessarily march through streets or high-roads, nor make any the least military parade, but consider themselves entirely as part of the civil state.*"[1] Thus is the soldier kept out of sight, while the citizen becomes manifest; and this is the true idea of republican government. In the midst of arms the laws are silent. Not "arms," but "laws," should command our homage and quicken the patriotism of the land.

1 Works, Vol. VIII. p. 494.

While divorcing the Police from the unchristian and barbarous War System, I confess the vital importance of maintaining law and order. Life and property should be guarded. Peace must be preserved in our streets. And it is the duty of Government to provide such means as are most expedient, if those established are in any respect inadequate, or uncongenial with the Spirit of the Age.

I must not close this exposition without an attempt to display the inordinate expenditure by which the War System is maintained. And here figures appear to lose their functions. They seem to pant, as they toil vainly to represent the enormous sums consumed in this unparalleled waste. Our own experience, measured by the concerns of common life, does not allow us adequately to conceive the sums. Like the periods of geological time, or the distances of the fixed stars, they baffle imagination. Look, for an instant, at the cost to us of this system. Without any allowance for the loss sustained by the withdrawal of active men from productive industry, we find, that, from the adoption of the National Constitution down to 1848, there has been paid directly from the National Treasury, —

For the Army and Fortifications,	$475,936,475
For the Navy and its operations,	209,994,428
	$685,930,903[1]

This immense amount is not all. Regarding the militia as part of the War System, we must add a moderate estimate for its cost during this period, being, according

1 American Almanac, 1849, p. 162. United States Executive Documents: 28th Cong. 1st Sess., No. 15, pp. 1018-19; 35th Cong. 1st Sess., No. 60, pp. 6, 7.

to the calculations of an able and accurate economist, as much as $ 1,500,000,000.[1] The whole presents an inconceivable sum-total of *more than two thousand millions* of dollars already dedicated by our Government to the support of the War System, — nearly twelve times as much as was set apart, during the same period, to all other purposes whatsoever!

Look now at the Commonwealth of Europe. I do not intend to speak of War Debts, under whose accumulated weight these nations are now pressed to earth, being the terrible legacy of the Past. I refer directly to the existing War System, the establishment of the Present. According to recent calculations, its annual cost is not less than a *thousand millions* of dollars. Endeavor, for a moment, by comparison with other interests, to grapple with this sum.

It is larger than the entire profit of all the commerce and manufactures of the world.

It is larger than all the expenditure for agricultural labor, producing the food of man, upon the whole face of the globe.

It is larger, by a hundred millions, than the value of all the exports sent forth by all the nations of the earth.

It is larger, by more than five hundred millions, than the value of all the shipping belonging to the civilized world.

It is larger, by nine hundred and ninety-seven millions, than the annual combined charities of Europe and America for preaching the Gospel to the Heathen.

Yes! the Commonwealth of Christian Nations, in-

[1] Jay's War and Peace, p. 13, note; and "True Grandeur of Nations," *ante*, p. 79.

cluding our own country, appropriates, without hesitation, as a matter of course, upwards of a thousand millions of dollars annually to the maintenance of the War System, and vaunts its three millions of dollars, laboriously collected, for diffusing the light of the Gospel in foreign lands! With untold prodigality of cost, it perpetuates the worst Heathenism of War, while, by charities insignificant in comparison, it doles to the Heathen a message of Peace. At home it breeds and fattens a cloud of eagles and vultures, trained to swoop upon the land; to all the Gentiles across the sea it dismisses a solitary dove.

Still further: every ship-of-war that floats costs more than a well-endowed college.

Every sloop-of-war that floats costs more than the largest public library in our country.

It is sometimes said, by persons yet in leading-strings of inherited prejudice, and with little appreciation of the true safety afforded by the principles of Peace, that all these comprehensive preparations are needed for protection against enemies from abroad. Wishing to present the cause without any superfluous question on what are called, apologetically, "defensive wars," let me say, in reply, — *and here all can unite*, — that, if these preparations are needed at any time, according to the aggressive martial interpretation of self-defence in its exigencies, there is much reason to believe it is because the unchristian spirit in which they have their birth, lowering and scowling in the very names of the ships, provokes the danger, — as the presence of a bravo might challenge the attack he was hired to resist.

Frederick of Prussia, sometimes called the Great, in

a singular spirit of mingled openness and effrontery, deliberately left on record, most instructively prominent among the real reasons for his war upon Maria Theresa, *that he had troops always ready to act.* Thus did these *Preparations* unhappily become, as they too often show themselves, *incentives* to War. Lord Brougham justly dwells on this confession as a lesson of history. Human nature, as manifest in the conduct of individuals or communities, has its lesson also. The fatal War Spirit is born of these preparations, out of which it springs full-armed. Here also is its great aliment; here are the seeds of the very evil it is sometimes vainly supposed to avert. Let it never be forgotten, let it be treasured as a solemn warning, that, by the confession of Frederick himself, it was the possession of *troops always ready to act* that helped to inspire that succession of bloody wars, which, first pouncing upon Silesia, mingled at last with the strifes of England and France, even in distant colonies across the Atlantic, ranging the savages of the forest under hostile European banners.[1]

But I deny that these preparations are needed for just self-defence. It is difficult, if not impossible, to suppose any such occasion in the Fraternity of Christian Nations, *if War ceases to be an established Arbitrament,*

[1] "Que l'on joigne à ces considérations *des troupes toujours prêtes d'agir*, mon épargne bien remplie, et la vivacité de mon caractère: c'étaient les raisons que j'avais de faire la guerre à Marie-Thérèse, reine de Bohême et d'Hongrie." These are the very words of Frederick, deliberately written in his own account of the war. Voltaire, on revising the work, dishonestly struck out this important confession, but preserved a copy, which afterwards appeared in his own Memoirs. Lord Brougham, in his sketch of Voltaire, says that "the passage thus erased and thus preserved is extremely curious, and for honesty or impudence has no parallel in the history of warriors." — Brougham, Lives of Men of Letters, *Voltaire*, p. 59.

or if any state is so truly great as to decline its umpirage. There is no such occasion among the towns, counties, or states of our extended country; nor is there any such occasion among the counties of Great Britain, or among the provinces of France; but the same goodwill, the same fellowship, and the same ties of commerce, which unite towns, counties, states, and provinces, are fast drawing the whole Commonwealth of Nations into similar communion. France and England, so long regarded as natural enemies, are now better known to each other than only a short time ago were different provinces of the former kingdom. And there is now a closer intimacy in business and social intercourse between Great Britain and our own country than there was at the beginning of the century between Massachusetts and Virginia.

Admitting that an enemy might approach our shores for piracy or plunder or conquest, who can doubt that the surest protection would be found, not in the waste of long-accumulating preparation, not in idle fortresses along the coast, built at a cost far surpassing all our lighthouses and all our colleges, but in the intelligence, union, and pacific repose of good men, with the unbounded resources derived from uninterrupted devotion to productive industry? I think it may be assumed as beyond question, according to the testimony of political economy, that the people who spend most sparingly in Preparations for War, all other things being equal, must possess the most enduring means of actual self-defence at home, on their own soil, before their own hearths, if any such melancholy alternative should occur. Consider the prodigious sums, exceeding in all two thousand millions of dollars, squandered by the United States, since the adoption of the National Constitution, for the sake of the War System. Had such means been devoted to railroads and canals, schools and colleges, the country would possess, at the present moment, an accumulated material power grander far than any it now boasts. There is another power, of more unfailing temper, which would not be wanting. Overflowing with intelligence, with charity, with civilization, with all that constitutes a generous state, ours would be peaceful triumphs, transcending all yet achieved, and surrounding the land with an invincible self-defensive might, while the unfading brightness of a new era made the glory of War impossible. Well does the poet say with persuasive truth, —

> "What constitutes a State?
> Not high-raised battlement or labored mound,
> Thick wall or moated gate;
> Not cities proud with spires and turrets crowned;
> Not bays and broad-armed ports,
> Where, laughing at the storm, rich navies ride:
> No: MEN, high-minded MEN." [1]

Such men will possess a Christian greatness, rendering them unable to do an injury; while their character, instinct with all the guardian virtues, must render their neighbors unable to do an injury to them.

The injunction, "In time of Peace prepare for War," is of Heathen origin.[2] As a rule of international conduct, it is very questionable in a Christian age, being vindicated on two grounds only: first, by assuming that the Arbitrament of War is the proper tribunal for international controversies, and therefore the War Sys-

[1] Sir William Jones, Ode in Imitation of Alcæus: Works, Vol. X. p. 389.

[2] True Grandeur of Nations, *ante*, pp. 97, seqq.

tem is to be maintained and strengthened, as the essential means of international justice; or, secondly, by assuming the rejected dogma of an Atheist philosopher, Hobbes, that War is the natural state of man. Whatever may be the infirmities of our passions, it is plain that the natural state of man, assuring the highest happiness, and to which he tends by an irresistible heavenly attraction, is Peace. This is true of communities and nations, as of individuals. The proper rule is, In time of Peace cultivate the arts of Peace. So doing, you will render the country truly strong and truly great; not by arousing the passions of War, not by nursing men to the business of blood, not by converting the land into a flaming arsenal, a magazine of gunpowder, or an "infernal machine," just ready to explode, but by dedicating its whole energies to productive and beneficent works.

The incongruity of this system may be illustrated by an example. Look into the life of that illustrious philosopher, John Locke, and you will find, that, in the journal of his tour through France, describing the arches of the amphitheatre at Nismes, he says, "In all those arches, to support the walls over the passage where you go round, there is a stone laid, about twenty inches or two feet square, and about six times the length of *my sword, which was near about a philosophical yard long.*"[1] Who is not struck with the unseemly incongruity of the exhibition, as he sees the author of the "Essay concerning Human Understanding" travelling with a sword by his side? But here the philosopher only followed the barbarous custom of his time. Individuals then

[1] King's Life of Locke, Vol. I. p. 99.

lived in the same relations towards each other which now characterize nations. The War System had not yet entirely retreated from Municipal Law and Custom, to find its last citadel and temple in the Law and Custom of Nations. Do not forget, that, at the present moment, our own country, the great author, among the nations, of a new Essay concerning Human Understanding, not only travels with a sword by the side, like John Locke, but lives encased in complete armor, burdensome to limbs and costly to treasury.

Condemning the War System as barbarous and most wasteful, the token and relic of a society alien to Christian civilization, we except the Navy, so far as necessary in arrest of pirates, of traffickers in human flesh, and generally in preserving the police of the sea. But it is difficult for the unprejudiced mind to regard the array of fortifications and of standing armies otherwise than obnoxious to the condemnation aroused by the War System. Fortifications are instruments, and standing armies are hired champions, in the great Duel of Nations.

Here I quit this part of the subject. Sufficient has been said to expose the War System of the Commonwealth of Nations. It stands before us, a colossal image of International Justice, *with the sword, but without the scales,*— like a hideous Mexican idol, besmeared with human blood, and surrounded by the sickening stench of human sacrifice. But this image, which seems to span the continents, while it rears aloft its flashing form of brass and gold, hiding far in the clouds "the round and top of sovereignty," can be laid low; for its feet are clay.

II.

I COME now to the means by which the War System can be overthrown. Here I shall unfold the tendencies and examples of nations, and the sacred efforts of individuals, constituting the Peace Movement, now ready to triumph, — with practical suggestions on our duties to this cause, and a concluding glance at the barbarism of Military Glory. In this review I cannot avoid details incident to a fruitfulness of topics; but I shall try to introduce nothing not bearing directly on the subject.

Civilization now writhes in travail and torment, and asks for liberation from oppressive sway. Like the slave under a weary weight of chains, it raises its exhausted arms, and pleads for the angel Deliverer. And, lo! the beneficent angel comes, — not like the Grecian God of Day, with vengeful arrows to slay the destructive Python, — not like the Archangel Michael, with potent spear to transfix Satan, — but with words of gentleness and cheer, saying to all nations, and to all children of men, "Ye are all brothers, of *one* flesh, *one* fold, *one* shepherd, children of *one* Father, heirs to *one* happiness. By your own energies, through united fraternal endeavor, will the tyranny of War be overthrown, and its Juggernaut in turn be crushed to earth."

In this spirit, and with this encouragement, we must labor for that grand and final object, watchword of all ages, the Unity of the Human Family. Not in benevolence, but in selfishness, has Unity been sought in times past, — not to promote the happiness of all, but to establish the dominion of one. It was the mad lust of power which carried Alexander from conquest to conquest, till he boasted that the whole world was one empire, with the Macedonian phalanx as citadel. The same passion animated Rome, till, at last, while Christ lay in a manger, this single city swayed a broader empire than that of Alexander. The Gospel, in its simple narrative, says, "And it came to pass in those days that there went out a decree from Cæsar Augustus that *all the world* should be taxed." History recalls the exile of Ovid, who, falling under the displeasure of the same emperor, was condemned to close his life in melancholy longings for Rome, far away in Pontus, on the Euxine Sea. With singular significance, these two contemporaneous incidents reveal the universality of Roman dominion, stretching from Britain to Parthia. The mighty empire crumbled, to be reconstructed for a brief moment, in part by Charlemagne, in part by Tamerlane. In our own age, Napoleon made a last effort for Unity founded on Force. And now, from his utterances at St. Helena, the expressed wisdom of his unparalleled experience, comes the remarkable confession, worthy of constant memory: "The more I study the world, the more am I convinced of the inability of brute force to create anything durable." From the sepulchre of Napoleon, now sleeping on the banks of the Seine, surrounded by the trophies of battle, nay, more, from the sepulchres of all these departed empires, may be heard the words, "They that take the sword shall perish by the sword."

Unity is the longing and tendency of Humanity: not the enforced Unity of military power; not the Unity of might triumphant over right; not the Unity of Inequality; not the Unity which occupied the soul of Dante, when, in his treatise *De Monarchia*, the earliest political work of modern times, he strove to show that all the world belonged to a single ruler, the successor of the Roman Emperor: not these; but the voluntary Unity of nations in fraternal labor; the Unity promised, when it was said, "There is neither Jew nor Greek, there is neither bond nor free, there is neither male nor female, for ye are all one in Christ Jesus"; the Unity which has filled the delighted vision of good men, prophets, sages, and poets, in times past; the Unity which, in our own age, prompted Béranger, the incomparable lyric of France, in an immortal ode, to salute the Holy Alliance of the Peoples,[1] summoning them in all lands, and by whatever names they may be called, French, English, Belgian, German, Russian, to give each other the hand, that the useless thunderbolts of War may all be quenched, and Peace sow the earth with gold, with flowers, and with corn; the Unity which prompted an early American diplomatist and poet to anticipate the time when nations shall meet in Congress, —

> "To give each realm its limit and its laws,
> Bid the last breath of dire contention cease,
> And bind all regions in the leagues of Peace;
> Bid one great empire, with extensive sway,
> Spread with the sun, and bound the walks of day,
> One centred system, one all-ruling soul,
> Live through the parts, and regulate the whole";[2]

the Unity which inspired our contemporary British poet of exquisite genius, Alfred Tennyson, to hail the certain day, —

> "When the war-drum throb no longer, and the battle-flags be furled,
> In the Parliament of Man, the Federation of the World."[3]

1 "Peuples, formez une sainte alliance,
Et donnez-vous la main."
La Sainte Alliance des Peuples.

2 Barlow, Vision of Columbus, Book IX. 432 – 438.

3 Locksley Hall.

Such is Unity in the bond of Peace. The common good and mutual consent are its enduring base, Justice and Love its animating soul. These alone can give permanence to combinations of men, whether in states or confederacies. Here is the vital elixir of nations, the true philosopher's stone of divine efficacy to enrich the civilization of mankind. So far as these are neglected or forgotten, will the people, though under one apparent head, fail to be really united. So far as these are regarded, will the people, within the sphere of their influence, constitute one body, and be inspired by one spirit. And just in proportion as these find recognition from individuals and from nations will War be impossible.

Not in vision, nor in promise only, is this Unity discerned. Voluntary associations, confederacies, leagues, coalitions, and congresses of nations, though fugitive and limited in influence, all attest the unsatisfied desires of men solicitous for union, while they foreshadow the means by which it may be permanently accomplished. Of these I will enumerate a few. 1. The *Amphictyonic Council*, embracing at first twelve, and finally thirty-one communities, was established about the year 1100 before Christ. Each sent two deputies, and had two votes in the Council, which was empowered to restrain the violence of hostility among the associates. 2. Next comes the *Achæan League*, founded at a very early period, and renewed in the year 281 before Christ. Each member was independent, and yet all together constituted one inseparable body. So great was the fame of their justice and probity, that the Greek cities of Italy were glad to invite their peaceful arbitration. 3. Passing over other confederacies of Antiquity, I mention next the *Hanseatic League,* begun in the twelfth century, completed in the middle of the thirteenth, and comprising at one time no less than eighty-five cities. A system of International Law was adopted in their general assemblies, and also *courts of arbitration, to determine controversies among the cities.* The decrees of these courts were enforced by placing the condemned city under the ban, a sentence equivalent to excommunication. 4. At a later period, other cities and nobles of Germany entered into alliance and association for mutual protection, under various names, as *the League of the Rhine,* and *the League of Suabia.* 5. To these I add the combination of *Armed Neutrality* in 1780, uniting, in declared support of certain principles, a large cluster of nations, — Russia, France, Spain, Holland, Sweden, Denmark, Prussia, and the United States. 6. And still further, I refer to Congresses at Westphalia, Utrecht, Aix-la-Chapelle, and Vienna, after the wasteful struggles of War, to arrange terms of Peace and to arbitrate between nations.

These examples, belonging to the Past, reveal tendencies and capacities. Other instances, having the effect of living authority, show practically how the War System may be set aside. There is, *first,* the Swiss Republic, or *Helvetic Union,* which, beginning so long ago as 1308, has preserved Peace among its members during the greater part of five centuries. Speaking of this Union, Vattel said, in the middle of the last century, "The Swiss have had the precaution, in all their alliances among themselves, and even in those they have contracted with the neighboring powers, *to agree beforehand on the manner in which their disputes were to be submitted to arbitrators, in case they could not adjust them in an amicable manner.*" And this publicist proceeds to testify that "this wise precaution has not a little contributed to maintain the Helvetic Republic in that flourishing condition which secures its liberty, and renders it respectable throughout Europe."[1] Since these words were written, there have been many changes in the Swiss Constitution; but its present Federal System, established on the downfall of Napoleon, confirmed in 1830, and now embracing twenty-five different States, provides that differences among the States shall be referred to "special arbitration." This is an instructive example. But, *secondly*, our own happy country furnishes one yet more so. The United States of America are a National Union of thirty different States,—each having peculiar interests,—in pursuance of a Constitution, established in 1788, which not only provides a high tribunal for the adjudication of controversies between the States, but expressly *disarms* the individual States, declaring that "*no State shall, without the consent of Congress, keep troops or ships of war in time of peace, or engage in war, unless actually invaded, or in such imminent danger as will not admit of delay.*" A *third* example, not unlike that of our own country, is the *Confederation of Germany*, composed of thirty-eight sovereignties, who, by reciprocal stipulation in their Act of Union, on the 8th of June, 1815, deprived each sovereignty of the *right of war* with its confederates. The words of this stipulation, which, like those of the Constitution of the United States, might furnish a model to the Commonwealth of Nations, are as follows: "*The Confederate States likewise engage under no pretext to make war upon*

1 Law of Nations, Book II. ch. 18, § 329.

one another, nor to pursue their differences by force of arms, but to submit them to the Diet. The latter shall endeavor to mediate between the parties by means of a commission. Should this not prove successful, and a judicial decision become necessary, provision shall be made therefor through a well-organized Court of Arbitration, to which the litigants shall submit themselves without appeal."[1]

Such are authentic, well-defined examples. This is not all. It is in the order of Providence, that individuals, families, tribes, and nations should tend, by means of association, to a final Unity. A law of mutual attraction, or affinity, first exerting its influence upon smaller bodies, draws them by degrees into well-established fellowship, and then, continuing its power, fuses the larger bodies into nations; and nations themselves, stirred by this same sleepless energy, are now moving towards that grand system of combined order which will complete the general harmony: —

> "Spiritus intus alit, totamque infusa per artus
> Mens agitat molem, et magno se corpore miscet."[2]

History bears ample testimony to the potency of this attraction. Modern Europe, in its early periods, was filled with petty lordships, or communities constituting so many distinct units, acknowledging only a vague nationality, and maintaining, as we have already seen, the "liberty" to fight with each other. The great nations of our day have grown and matured into their present form by the gradual absorption of these political bodies.

[1] Acte pour la Constitution Fédérative de l'Allemagne du 8 Juin, 1815, Art. XI. par. 4: Archives Diplomatiques, Vol. IV. p. 15.

[2] Æneid, Lib. VI. 726, 727.

Territories, once possessing an equivocal and turbulent independence, feel new power and happiness in peaceful association. Spain, composed of races dissimilar in origin, religion, and government, slowly ascended by progressive combinations among principalities and provinces, till at last, in the fifteenth century, by the crowning union of Castile and Aragon, the whole country, with its various sovereignties, was united under one common rule. Germany once consisted of more than three hundred different principalities, each with the *right of war.* These slowly coalesced, forming larger principalities; till at last the whole complex aggregation of states, embracing abbeys, bishoprics, archbishoprics, bailiwicks, counties, duchies, electorates, margraviates, and free imperial cities, was gradually resolved into the present Confederation, where each state expressly renounces the *right of war* with its associates. France has passed through similar changes. By a power of assimilation, in no nation so strongly marked, she has absorbed the various races and sovereignties once filling her territory with violence and conflict, and has converted them all to herself. The Roman or Iberian of Provence, the indomitable Celtic race, the German of Alsace, have all become Frenchmen,— while the various provinces, once inspired by such hostile passions, Brittany and Normandy, Franche-Comté and Burgundy, Gascony and Languedoc, Provence and Dauphiné, are now blended in one powerful, united nation. Great Britain, too, shows the influence of the same law. The many hostile principalities of England were first merged in the Heptarchy; and these seven kingdoms became *one* under the Saxon Egbert. Wales, forcibly attached to England under Edward the First, at last assimilated with her conqueror; Ireland, after a protracted resistance, was absorbed under Edward the Third, and at a later day, after a series of bitter struggles, was united, I do not say how successfully, under the Imperial Parliament; Scotland was connected with England by the accession of James the First to the throne of the Tudors, and these two countries, which had so often encountered in battle, were joined together under Queen Anne, by an act of peaceful legislation.

Thus has the tendency to Unity predominated over independent sovereignties and states, slowly conducting the constant process of crystallization. This cannot be arrested. The next stage must be the peaceful association of the Christian nations. In this anticipation we but follow analogies of the material creation, as seen in the light of chemical or geological science. Everywhere Nature is busy with combinations, exerting an occult incalculable power, drawing elements into new relations of harmony, uniting molecule with molecule, atom with atom, and, by progressive change, in the lapse of time, producing new structural arrangements. Look still closer, and the analogy continues. At first we detect the operation of cohesion, rudely acting upon particles near together,—then subtler influences, slowly imparting regularity of form,—while heat, electricity, and potent chemical affinities conspire in the work. As yet there is only an incomplete body. *Light* now exerts its mysterious powers, and all assumes an organized form. So it is with mankind. First appears the rude cohesion of early ages, acting only upon individuals near together. Slowly the work proceeds. But time and space, the great obstructions, if not annihilated, are now subdued, giving free scope to the powerful affinities of civilization. At last, light, thrice holy light, in whose glad beams are knowledge, justice, and beneficence, with empyrean sway will combine those separate and distracted elements into one organized system.

Thus much for examples and tendencies. In harmony with these are *efforts of individuals*, extending through ages, and strengthening with time, till now at last they swell into a voice that must be heard. A rapid glance will show the growth of the cause we have met to welcome. Far off in the writings of the early Fathers we learn the duty and importance of Universal Peace. Here I might accumulate texts, each an authority, while you listened to Justin Martyr, Irenæus, Tertullian, Origen, Augustine, Aquinas. How beautiful it appears in the teachings of St. Augustine! How comprehensive the rules of Aquinas, who spoke with the authority of Philosophy and the Church, when he said, in phrase worthy of constant repetition, that the perfection of joy is Peace![1] But the rude hoof of War trampled down these sparks of generous truth, destined to flame forth at a later day. In the fifteenth century, *The good Man of Peace* was described in that work of unexampled circulation, translated into all modern tongues, and republished more than a thousand times, "The Imitation of Christ," by Thomas-à-Kempis.[2] A little later the cause found important support from the pen of a great scholar, the gentle and learned Erasmus. At last it obtained a specious advocacy from the throne. Henry the Fourth,

[1] "*Perfectio gaudii est pax.*"—Aquinas, Summa Theologica, Prima Secundæ, Quæst. LXX., Art. III. Concl.

[2] De Imitatione Christi, Lib. II. cap. 3.

of France, with the coöperation of his eminent minister, Sully, conceived the beautiful scheme of blending the Christian nations in one confederacy, with a high tribunal for the decision of controversies between them, and had drawn into his plan Queen Elizabeth, of England. All was arrested by the dagger of Ravaillac. This gay and gallant monarch was little penetrated by the divine sentiment of Peace; for at his death he was gathering materials for fresh War; and it is too evident that the scheme of a European Congress was prompted less by comprehensive humanity than by a selfish ambition to humble the House of Austria. Even with this drawback it did great good, by holding aloft before Christendom the exalted idea of a tribunal for the Commonwealth of Nations.

Universal Peace was not to receive thus early the countenance of Government. Meanwhile private efforts began to multiply. Grotius, in his wonderful work on "The Rights of War and Peace," while lavishing learning and genius on the Arbitrament of War, bears testimony in favor of a more rational tribunal. His virtuous nature, wishing to save mankind from the scourge of War, foreshadowed an Amphictyonic Council. "It would be useful, and in some sort necessary," he says, — in language which, if carried out practically, would sweep away the War System and all the *Laws of War*, — "to have Congresses of the Christian Powers, where differences might be determined by the judgment of those not interested in them, and means found to constrain parties into acceptance of peace on just conditions."[1] To the discredit of his age, these moderate words, so much in harmony with his other effort for the union

[1] De Jure Belli ac Pacis, Lib. II. cap. 23, § 8.

of Christian sects, were derided, and the eminent expounder was denounced as rash, visionary, and impracticable. The sentiment in which they had their origin found other forms of utterance. Before the close of the seventeenth century, Nicole, the friend of Pascal, belonging to the fellowship of Port-Royal, and one of the highest names in the Church of France, gave to the world a brief "Treatise on the Means of preserving Peace among Men,"[1] which Voltaire, with exaggerated praise, terms "a masterpiece, to which nothing equal has been left to us by Antiquity." Next appeared a little book, which is now a bibiographical curiosity, entitled "The New Cineas,"[2] — after the pacific adviser of Pyrrhus, the warrior king of Epirus, — where the humane author counsels sovereigns to govern in Peace, submitting their differences to an established tribunal. In Germany, at the close of the seventeenth century, as we learn from Leibnitz, who mentions the preceding authority also, a retired general, who had commanded armies, the Landgrave Ernest of Hesse Rhinfels, in a work entitled "The Discreet Catholic," suggested a plan for Perpetual Peace by means of a tribunal established by associate sovereigns.[3] England testified also by William Penn, who adopted and enforced what he called the "great design"

[1] Traité des Moyens de conserver la Paix avec les Hommes: Essais de Morale, Tom. I. pp. 192-318. This little treatise has been printed in a recent edition of the *Pensées* of Pascal. Notwithstanding this great company, and the praise of Voltaire in his *Écrivains du Siècle de Louis XIV.*, the reader of our day will be disappointed. See Hallam, Introduction to the Literature of Europe, Part IV. ch. 4, Vol. III. p. 393.

[2] Le Nouveau Cynée, ou Discours des Occasions et Moyens d'establir une Paix générale et la Liberté du Commerce par tout le Monde: Paris, 1623. A copy, found in one of the stalls of Paris, is now before me.

[3] Leibnitz, Observations sur le Projet d'une Paix Perpétuelle de l'Abbé de S. Pierre: Opera (ed. Dutens), Tom. V. pp. 56, 57

of Henry the Fourth. In a work entitled "An Essay towards the Present and Future Peace of Europe," the enlightened Quaker proposed a Diet, or Sovereign Assembly, into which the princes of Europe should enter, as men enter into society, for the love of peace and order, — that its object should be justice, and that all differences not terminated by embassies should be brought before this tribunal, whose judgment should be so far binding, that, in the event of contumacy, it should be enforced by the united powers.[1] Thus, by writings, as also by illustrious example in Pennsylvania, did Penn show himself the friend of Peace.

These were soon followed in France by the untiring labors of the good Abbé Saint-Pierre, — the most devoted among the apostles of Peace, and not to be confounded with the eloquent and eccentric Bernardin de Saint-Pierre, author of "Paul and Virginia," who, at a later day, beautifully painted the true Fraternity of Nations.[2] Of a genius less artistic and literary, the Abbé consecrated a whole life, crowned with venerable years, to the improvement of mankind. There was no humane cause he did not espouse: now it was the poor; now it was education; and now it was to exhibit the grandeur and sacredness of human nature; but he was especially filled with the idea of Universal Peace, and the importance of teaching nations, not less than individuals, the duty of doing as they would be done by. This was his passion, and it was elaborately presented in a work of three volumes, entitled "The Project of Per-

[1] Clarkson, Life of William Penn, Ch. VI. Vol. II. pp. 82 – 85.

[2] Harmonies de la Nature: Œuvres, Tom. X. p. 138. Vœux d'un Solitaire: Ibid., Tom. XI. p. 168.

petual Peace,"[1] where he proposes a Diet or Congress of Sovereigns, for the adjudication of international controversies without resort to War. Throughout his voluminous writings he constantly returns to this project, which was a perpetual vision, and records his regret that Newton and Descartes had not devoted their exalted genius to the study and exposition of the laws determining the welfare of men and nations, believing that they might have succeeded in organizing Peace. He dwells often on the beauty of Christian precepts in government, and the true glory of beneficence, while he exposes the vanity of military renown, and does not hesitate to question that false glory which procured for Louis the Fourteenth the undeserved title of Great, echoed by flattering courtiers and a barbarous world. The French language owes to him the word *Bienfaisance;* and D'Alembert said "it was right he should have invented the word who practised so largely the virtue it expresses."[2]

Though thus of benevolence all compact, Saint-Pierre was not the favorite of his age. A profligate minister, Cardinal Dubois, ecclesiastical companion of a vicious regent in the worst excesses, condemned his efforts in a phrase of satire, as "the dreams of a good man." The pen of La Bruyère wantoned in a petty portrait of per-

[1] Le Projet de Paix Perpétuelle. — A collection of the works of Saint-Pierre, in fourteen volumes, entitled *Œuvres de Politique*, appeared at Amsterdam in the middle of the last century. But this collection is not complete; I have several other volumes. Brunet introduces him into his Bibliographical Pantheon among "Modern Reformers"; but the space allowed is very scanty by the side of his namesake. His works are sympathetically described and analyzed in a volume published since this Address, entitled *L'Abbé de Saint-Pierre, sa Vie et ses Œuvres*, par G. de Molinari.

[2] Éloge de Saint-Pierre: Œuvres, Tom. XI. p. 113. See, also, Bescherelle, Dictionnaire National, under *Bienfaisance.*

sonal peculiarities.[1] Many turned the cold shoulder. The French Academy, of which he was a member, took from him his chair, and on the occasion of his death forbore the eulogy which is its customary tribute to a departed academician. But an incomparable genius in Germany,—an authority not to be questioned on any subject upon which he spoke,—the great and universal Leibnitz, bears his testimony to the "Project of Perpetual Peace," and, so doing, enrolls his own prodigious name in the catalogue of our cause. In observations on this Project, communicated to its author, under date of February 7, 1715, while declaring that it is supported by the practical authority of Henry the Fourth, that it justly interests the whole human race, and is not foreign to his own studies, as from youth he had occupied himself with law, and particularly with the Law of Nations, Leibnitz says: "*I have read it with attention, and am persuaded that such a project, on the whole, is feasible, and that its execution would be one of the most useful things in the world.* Although my suffrage cannot be of any weight, I have nevertheless thought that gratitude obliged me not to withhold it, and to join some remarks for the satisfaction of a meritorious author, who ought to have much reputation and firmness, to have dared and been able to oppose with success the prejudiced crowd, and the unbridled tongue of mockers."[2] Such testimony from Leibnitz must have been grateful to Saint-Pierre.

I cannot close this brief record of a philanthropist, constant in an age when War was more regarded than

[1] Les Caractères, *Du Mérite Personnel*, Tom. I. p. 93.

[2] Observations sur le Projet d'une Paix Perpétuelle; Lettre à l'Abbé de S. Pierre: Opera (ed Dutens), Tom. V. pp. 56-62.

Humanity, without offering him an unaffected homage. To this faithful man may be addressed the sublime salutation which hymned from the soul of Milton: —

> "Servant of God, well done! well hast thou fought
> The better fight, who single hast maintained
> Against revolted multitudes the cause
> Of Truth, in word mightier than they in arms,
> And for the testimony of truth hast borne
> . . . . reproach, far worse to bear
> Than violence: for this was all thy care,
> To stand approved in sight of God, though worlds
> Judged thee perverse." [1]

Waking hereafter from its martial trance, the world will rejoice to salute the greatness of his career.[2] It may well measure advance in civilization by the appreciation of his character.

Contemporary with Saint-Pierre was another Frenchman, to whom I have already referred, who flashed his genius upon the game of War. La Bruyère exhibits men, for the sake of a piece of land more or less, *agreeing among themselves* to despoil, burn, and kill each other, even to cutting throats, and, for the doing of this more ingeniously and safely, inventing a beautiful system, known as the Art of War, to the practice of which is attached what is called *Glory.* The same satirist, who lived in an age of War, likens men to animals, even to dogs barking at each other, and then again to cats; and he furnishes a picture of the latter, counted by the thousand, and marshalled on an extended plain, where, after mewing their best, they throw themselves upon each other, tooth and nail, until nine or ten thousand of

1 Paradise Lost, Book VI. 29 – 37.

2 The *Nouvelle Biographie Générale* concludes its notice of him thus: — "Après avoir mérité le beau surnom de *Solliciteur pour le bien public*, l'Abbé de Saint-Pierre mourut, en 1743, à l'âge de quatre-vingt-cinq ans."

them are left dead on the field, infecting the air for ten leagues with an intolerable stench,—and all this for the love of Glory. But how, says the satirist, can we distinguish between those who use only tooth and nail and those others, who, first substituting lances, darts, and swords, now employ destructive balls, small and large, killing at once, while, penetrating a roof, they crash from garret to cellar, sacrificing even women and children? Wherein is the Glory?[1]

Saint-Pierre was followed by that remarkable genius, Jean Jacques Rousseau, in a small work with the modest title, "Extract from the Project of Perpetual Peace by the Abbé Saint-Pierre."[2] Without referring to those higher motives supplied by humanity, conscience, and religion, for addressing which to sovereigns Saint-Pierre incurred the ridicule of what are called practical statesmen, Rousseau appeals to common sense, and shows how much mere worldly interests would be promoted by submission to the arbitration of an impartial tribunal, rather than to the uncertain issue of arms, with no adequate compensation, even to the victor, for blood and treasure sacrificed. If this project fails, it is not, according to him, because chimerical, but because men have lost their wits, and it is a sort of madness to be wise in the midst of fools. As no scheme more grand, more beautiful, or more useful ever occupied the human mind, so, says Rousseau, no author ever deserved attention more than one proposing the means for its practical adoption; nor can any humane and virtuous man fail to regard it with enthusiasm.

[1] Caractères, *Du Souverain*, Tom. I. p. 332; *Des Jugements*, Tom. II. pp. 57 – 59.

[2] Extrait du Projet de Paix Perpétuelle de M. l'Abbé de Saint-Pierre.

The recommendations of Rousseau, reaching Germany, were encountered by a writer now remembered chiefly by this hardihood. I allude to Embser, who treats of Perpetual Peace in a work first published in 1779, under the title of "The Idolatry of our Philosophical Century,"[1] and at a later day with a new title, under the *alias* of the "Refutation of the Project of Perpetual Peace."[2] Objections common with the superficial or prejudiced are vehemently urged; the imputation upon Grotius is reproduced; and the project is pronounced visionary and impracticable, while War is exalted as an instrument more beneficent than Peace in advancing the civilization of mankind. At a later day Hegel gave the same testimony, thus contributing his considerable name to vindicate War.[3]

The cause of Saint-Pierre and Rousseau was not without champions in Germany. In 1763 we meet at Göttingen the work of Totze, entitled "Permanent and Universal Peace, according to the Plan of Henry the Fourth";[4] and in 1767, at Leipsic, an ample and mature treatise by Lilienfeld, under the name of "New Constitution for States."[5] Truth often appears contemporaneously to different minds having no concert with each other; and the latter work, though in remarkable harmony with Saint-Pierre and Rousseau, is said to have been composed without any knowledge of their labors. Lilienfeld exposes the causes and calamities of War, the waste of armaments in time of Peace, and the miserable chances of the battle-field, where, in defiance of all jus-

1 Die Abgötterei unsers Philosophischen Jahrhunderts.

2 Widerlegung des Projects von Ewigen Frieden.

3 Philosophie des Rechts, §§ 321 – 340: Werke, Band VIII. pp. 408 – 423.

4 Ewiger und Allgemeiner Friede nach der Entwurf Heinrichs IV.

5 Neues Staatsgebäude.

tice, controversies are determined as by the throw of dice; and he urges submission to Arbitrators, unless, in their wisdom, nations establish a Supreme Tribunal with the combined power of the Confederacy to enforce its decrees.

It was the glory of another German, in intellectual preëminence the successor of Leibnitz, to illustrate this cause by special and repeated labors. At Königsberg, in a retired corner of Prussia, away from the great lines of travel, Immanuel Kant consecrated his days to the pursuit of truth. During a long, virtuous, and disinterested life, stretching beyond the period appointed for man, — from 1724 to 1804, — in retirement, undisturbed by shock of revolution or war, never drawn by temptation of travel more than seven German miles from the place of his birth, he assiduously studied books, men, and things. Among the fruits of his ripened powers was that system of philosophy known as the "Critique of Pure Reason," by which he was at once established as a master-mind of his country. His words became the text for writers without number, who vied with each other in expounding, illustrating, or opposing his principles. At this period, after an unprecedented triumph in philosophy, when his name had become familiar wherever his mother-tongue was spoken, and while his rare faculties were yet untouched by decay, in the Indian Summer of life, the great thinker published a work "On Perpetual Peace."[1] Interest in the author, or in the cause, was attested by prompt translations into the French, Danish, and Dutch languages. In an

[1] Zum Ewigen Frieden, 1795; Verkündigung des nahen Abschlusses eines Tractats zum Ewigen Frieden in der Philosophie, 1796: Sämmtliche Werke, Band VI. pp. 405-454, 487-498.

earlier work, entitled "Idea for a General History in a Cosmopolitan View,"[1] he espoused the same cause, and at a later day, in his "Metaphysical Elements of Jurisprudence,"[2] he renewed his testimony. In the lapse of time the speculations of the philosopher have lost much of their original attraction; other systems, with other names, have taken their place. But these early and faithful labors for Perpetual Peace cannot be forgotten. Perhaps through these the fame of the applauded philosopher of Königsberg may yet be preserved.

By Perpetual Peace Kant understood a condition of nations where there could be no fear of War; and this condition, he said, was demanded by reason, which, abhorring all War, as little adapted to establish right, must regard this final development of the Law of Nations as a consummation worthy of every effort. The philosopher was right in proposing nothing less than a reform of International Law. To this, according to him, all persons, and particularly all rulers, should bend their energies. A special league or treaty should be formed, which may be truly called a *Treaty of Peace*, having this peculiarity, that, whereas other treaties terminate a single existing War only, this should terminate forever all War between the parties to it. A Treaty of Peace, tacitly acknowledging *the right to wage War*, as all treaties now do, is nothing more than a *Truce*, not Peace. By these treaties an individual War is ended, but not the *state of War*. There may not be constant hostilities; but there will be constant fear of hostilities, with

[1] Idee zu einer Allgemeinen Geschichte in Weltbürgerlicher Absicht: Sämmtliche Werke, Band IV. pp. 141–157.

[2] Metaphysische Anfangsgründe der Rechtslehre, §§ 53–61, *Das Völkerrecht:* Sämmtliche Werke, Band VII. pp. 141–157.

constant threat of aggression and attack. Soldiers and armaments, now nursed as a Peace establishment, become the fruitful parent of new wars. With real Peace, these would be abandoned. Nor should nations hesitate to bow before the *law*, like individuals. They must form one comprehensive federation, which, by the aggregation of other nations, would at last embrace the whole earth. And this, according to Kant, in the succession of years, by a sure progress, is the irresistible tendency of nations. To this end nations must be truly independent; nor is it possible for one nation to acquire another independent nation, whether by inheritance, exchange, purchase, or gift. A nation is not property. The philosophy of Kant, therefore, contemplated not only Universal Peace, but Universal Liberty. The first article of the great treaty would be, that every nation is free.

These important conclusions found immediate support from another German philosopher, Fichte, of remarkable acuteness and perfect devotion to truth, whose name, in his own day, awakened an echo inferior only to that of Kant. In his "Groundwork of the Law of Nature."[1] published in 1796, he urges a Federation of Nations, with a Supreme Tribunal, as the best way of securing the triumph of justice, and of subduing the power of the unjust. To the suggestion, that by this Federation injustice might be done, he replied, that it would not be easy to find any common advantage tempting the confederate nations to do this wrong.

The subject was again treated in 1804, by a learned German, Karl Schwab, whose work, entitled "Of Una-

[1] Grundlage des Naturrechts: *Ueber das Völkerrecht*: Sämmtliche Werke, Band III. pp. 369-382.

voidable Injustice,"[1] deserves notice for practical clearness and directness. Nothing could be better than his idea of the Universal State, where nations will be united, as citizens in the Municipal State; nor have the promises of the Future been more carefully presented. He sees clearly, that, even when this triumph of civilization is won, justice between nations will not be always inviolate,—for, unhappily, between citizens it is not always so; but, whatever may be the exceptions, it will become the general rule. As in the Municipal State War no longer prevails, but offences, wrongs, and sallies of vengeance often proceed from individual citizens, with insubordination and anarchy sometimes,—so in the Universal State War will no longer prevail; but here also, between the different nations, who will be as citizens in the Federation, there may be wrongs and aggressions, with resistance even to the common power. In short, the Universal State will be subject to the same accidents as the Municipal State.

The cause of Permanent Peace became a thesis for Universities. At Stuttgart, in 1796, there was an oration by J. H. La Motte, entitled *Utrum Pax Perpetua pangi possit, nec ne?* And at Leyden, in 1808, there was a Dissertation by Gabinus de Wal, on taking his degree as Doctor of Laws, entitled *Disputatio Philosophico-Juridica de Conjunctione Populorum ad Pacem Perpetuam.*[2] This learned and elaborate performance, after reviewing previous efforts in the cause, accords a

1 Ueber das Unvermeidliche Unrecht.

2 At the Paris Peace Congress of 1849, since the delivery of this Address, with Victor Hugo as President, and Richard Cobden as an active member, Mr. Suringar, of Amsterdam, referred to this Dissertation, and announced a copy of it which had been given him for presentation to the Congress by the son of the author, John de Wal, Professor of Jurisprudence at Leyden. My own copy is a valued present from Elihu Burritt.

preëminence to Kant. Such a voice from the University is the token of a growing sentiment, and an example for the youth of our own day.

Meanwhile in England the cause was espoused by that indefatigable jurist and reformer, Jeremy Bentham, who embraced it in his comprehensive labors. In an Essay on International Law, bearing date 1786–89, and first published in 1839, by his executor, Dr. Bowring,[1] he develops a plan for Universal and Perpetual Peace in the spirit of Saint-Pierre. Such, according to him, is the extreme folly, the madness, of War, that on no supposition can it be otherwise than mischievous. All Trade, in essence, is advantageous, even to the party who profits by it the least; all War, in essence, is ruinous: and yet the great employments of Government are to treasure up occasions of War, and to put fetters upon Trade. To remedy this evil, Bentham proposes, first, "The reduction and fixation of the forces of the several nations that compose the European system"; and in enforcing this proposition, he says: "Whatsoever nation should get the start of the other in making the proposal to reduce and fix the amount of its armed force would crown itself with everlasting honor. The risk would be nothing, the gain certain. This gain would be the giving an incontrovertible demonstration of its own disposition to peace, and of the opposite disposition in the other nation, in case of its rejecting the proposal." He next proposes an International Court of Judicature, with power to report its opinion, and to circulate it in each nation, and, after a certain delay, to put a contumacious nation under the ban. He denies

[1] Bentham's Works, Part VIII. pp. 537–554.

that this system can be styled visionary in any respect: for it is proved, *first,* that it is the interest of the parties concerned; *secondly,* that the parties are already sensible of this interest; and, *thirdly,* that, enlightened by diplomatic experience in difficult and complicated conventions, they are prepared for the new situation. All this is sober and practical.

Coming to our own country, I find many names for commemoration. No person, in all history, has borne his testimony in phrases of greater pungency or more convincing truth than Benjamin Franklin. "In my opinion," he says, "there never was a good War or a bad Peace"; and he asks, "When will mankind be convinced that all Wars are follies, very expensive, and very mischievous, and agree to settle their differences by arbitration? Were they to do it even by the cast of a die, it would be better than by fighting and destroying each other." Then again he says: "We make daily great improvements in natural, there is one I wish to see in moral philosophy, — the discovery of a plan that would induce and oblige nations to settle their disputes without first cutting one another's throats. When will human reason be sufficiently improved to see the advantage of this?"[1] As diplomatist, Franklin strove to limit the evils of War. To him, while Minister at Paris, belongs the honor of those instructions, more glorious for the American name than any battle, where our naval cruisers, among whom was the redoubtable Paul Jones, were directed, in the interest of univer-

[1] Letter to Josiah Quincy, Sept. 11, 1783; to Mrs. Mary Hewson, Jan. 27, 1783; to Richard Price, Feb. 6, 1780: Works, ed. Sparks, Vol. X. p. 11; IX. p. 476; VIII. p. 417.

sal science, to allow a free and undisturbed passage to the returning expedition of Captain Cook, the great circumnavigator, who "steered Britain's oak into a world unknown."[1] To him also belongs the honor of introducing into a treaty with Prussia a provision for the abolition of that special scandal, Private War on the Ocean.[2] In similar strain with Franklin, Jefferson says: "Will nations never devise a more rational umpire of differences than Force? . . . . War is an instrument entirely inefficient towards redressing wrong; it multiplies, instead of indemnifying losses."[3] And he proceeds to exhibit the waste of War, and the beneficent consequences, if its expenditures could be diverted to purposes of practical utility.

To Franklin especially must thanks be rendered for authoritative words and a precious example. But there are three names, fit successors of Saint-Pierre, — I speak only of those on whose career is the seal of death, — which even more than his deserve affectionate regard. I refer to Noah Worcester, William Ellery Channing, and William Ladd. To dwell on the services of these our virtuous champions would be a grateful task. The occasion allows a passing notice only.

In Worcester we behold the single-minded country clergyman, little gifted as preacher, with narrow means, — and his example teaches what such a character may accomplish, — in humble retirement, pained by the reports of War, and at last, as the protracted drama of

1 Franklin's Works, ed. Sparks, Vol. V. pp. 122 – 124. Collections of Mass. Hist. Soc., Vol. IV. pp. 79 – 85.

2 Franklin's Works, ed. Sparks, Vol. II. pp. 485, 486. Lyman's Diplomacy of the United States, Vol. I. pp. 143 – 148.

3 Letter to Sir John Sinclair, March 23, 1798: Transactions of the American Philosophical Society, Vol. IV. pp. 320, 321.

battles was about to close at Waterloo, publishing that appeal, entitled "A Solemn Review of the *Custom* of War," which has been so extensively circulated at home and abroad, and has done so much to correct the inveterate prejudices which surround the cause. He was the founder, and for some time the indefatigable agent, of the earliest Peace Society in the country.

The eloquence of Channing was often, both with tongue and pen, directed against War. He was heart-struck by the awful degradation it caused, rudely blotting out in men the image of God their Father; and his words of flame have lighted in many souls those exterminating fires that can never die, until this evil is swept from the earth.

William Ladd, after completing his education at Harvard University, engaged in commercial pursuits. Early, through his own exertions, blessed with competency, he could not be idle. He was childless; and his affections embraced all the children of the human family. Like Worcester and Channing, his attention was arrested by the portentous crime of War, and he was moved to dedicate the remainder of his days to earnest, untiring effort for its abolition, — going about from place to place inculcating the lesson of Peace, with simple, cheerful manner winning the hearts of good men, and dropping in many youthful souls precious seeds to ripen in more precious fruit. He was the founder of the American Peace Society, in which was finally merged the earlier association established by Worcester. By a long series of practical labors, and especially by developing, maturing, and publishing the plan of an International Congress, has William Ladd enrolled himself among the benefactors of mankind.

Such are some of the names which hereafter, when the warrior no longer usurps the blessings promised to the peacemaker, will be inscribed on immortal tablets.

Now, at last, in the fulness of time, in our own day, by the labors of men of Peace, by the irresistible co-operating affinities of mankind, nations seem to be visibly approaching — even amidst tumult and discord — that Unity so long hoped for, prayed for. By steamboat, railroad, and telegraph, outstripping the traditional movements of government, men of all countries daily commingle, ancient prejudices fast dissolve, while ancient sympathies strengthen, and new sympathies come into being. The chief commercial cities of England send addresses of friendship to the chief commercial cities of France; and the latter delight to return the salutation. Similar cords of amity are twined between cities in England and cities in our own country. The visit to London of a band of French National Guards is reciprocated by the visit to Paris of a large company of Englishmen. Thus are achieved pacific conquests, where formerly all the force of arms could not prevail. Mr. Vattemare perambulates Europe and the United States to establish a system of literary international exchanges. By the daily agency of the press we are sharers in the trials and triumphs of brethren in all lands, and, renouncing the solitude of insulated nationalities, learn to live in the communion of associated states. By multitudinous reciprocities of commerce are developed relations of mutual dependence, stronger than treaties or alliances engrossed on parchment, — while, from a truer appreciation of the ethics of government, we arrive at the conviction, that the divine injunction, "Do unto others as you would have them do unto you," was spoken to nations as well as to individuals.

From increasing knowledge of each other, and from a higher sense of duty as brethren of the Human Family, arises among mankind an increasing interest in each other; and charity, once, like patriotism, exclusively national, is beginning to clasp the world in its embrace. Every discovery of science, every aspiration of philanthropy, no matter what the country of its origin, is now poured into the common stock. Assemblies, whether of science or philanthropy, are no longer municipal merely, but welcome delegates from all the nations. Science has convened Congresses in Italy, Germany, and England. Great causes, grander even than Science, — like Temperance, Freedom, Peace, — have drawn to London large bodies of men from different countries, under the title of *World Conventions,* in whose very name and spirit of fraternity we discern the prevailing tendency. Such a convention, dedicated to Universal Peace, held at London in 1843, was graced by many well known for labors of humanity. At Frankfort, in 1846, was assembled a large Congress from all parts of Europe, to consider what could be done for those in prison. The succeeding year witnessed, at Brussels, a similar Congress, convened in the same charity. At last, in August, 1848, we hail, at Brussels, another Congress, inspired by the presence of a generous American, Elihu Burritt, — who has left his anvil at home to teach the nations how to change their swords into ploughshares and their spears into pruning-hooks, — presided over by an eminent Belgian magistrate, and composed of numerous individuals, speaking various languages, living under diverse forms of government, various in political opinions, differing in religious convictions, but all moved by a common sentiment to seek the abolition of War, and the Disarming of the Nations.

The Peace Congress at Brussels constitutes an epoch. It is a palpable development of those international attractions and affinities which now await their final organization. The resolutions it adopted are so important that I cannot hesitate to introduce them.

"1. That, in the judgment of this Congress, an appeal to arms for the purpose of deciding disputes among nations is a custom condemned alike by religion, reason, justice, humanity, and the best interests of the people, — and that, therefore, it considers it to be the duty of the civilized world to adopt measures calculated to effect its entire abolition.

"2. That it is of the highest importance to urge on the several governments of Europe and America the necessity of introducing a clause into all International Treaties, providing for the settlement of all disputes by Arbitration, in an amicable manner, and according to the rules of justice and equity, by special Arbitrators, or a Supreme International Court, to be invested with power to decide in cases of necessity, as a last resort.

"3. That the speedy convocation of a Congress of Nations, composed of duly appointed representatives, for the purpose of framing a well-digested and authoritative International Code, is of the greatest importance, inasmuch as the organization of such a body, and the unanimous adoption of such a Code, would be an effectual means of promoting Universal Peace.

"4. That this Congress respectfully calls the attention of civilized governments to the necessity of a general and simultaneous disarmament, as a means whereby they may greatly diminish the financial burdens which press upon them, remove a fertile cause of irritation and inquietude, inspire mutual confidence, and promote the interchange of good offices, which, while they advance the interests of each state in particular, contribute largely to the maintenance of general Peace, and the lasting prosperity of nations."

In France these resolutions received the adhesion of Lamartine, — in England, of Richard Cobden. They have been welcomed throughout Great Britain, by large and enthusiastic popular assemblies, hanging with delight upon the practical lessons of peace on earth and good-will to men. At the suggestion of the Congress at Brussels, and in harmony with the demands of an increasing public sentiment, another Congress is called at Paris, in the approaching month of August. The place of meeting is auspicious. There, as in the very cave of Æolus, whence have so often raged forth conflicting winds and resounding tempests, are to gather delegates from various nations, including a large number from our own country, whose glad work will be to hush and imprison these winds and tempests, and to bind them in the chains of everlasting Peace.

Not in voluntary assemblies only has our cause found welcome. Into *legislative halls* it has made its way. A document now before me, in the handwriting of Samuel Adams, an approved patriot of the Revolution, bears witness to his desire for action on this subject in the Congress of the United States. It is in the form of a Letter of Instructions from the Legislature of Massachusetts to the delegates in Congress of this State, and, though without date, seems to have been prepared sometime between the Treaty of Peace in 1783 and the adoption of the National Constitution in 1789. It is as follows.

"GENTLEMEN, — Although the General Court have lately instructed you concerning various matters of very great importance to this Commonwealth, they cannot finish the business of the year until they have transmitted to you a further instruction, which they have long had in contemplation, and which, if their most ardent wish could be obtained, might in its consequences extensively promote the happiness of man.

"You are, therefore, hereby instructed and urged to move the United States in Congress assembled to take into their deep and most serious consideration, whether any measures can by them be used, through their influence with such of the nations in Europe with whom they are united by Treaties of Amity or Commerce, that National Differences may be settled and determined without the necessity of WAR, in which the world has too long been deluged, to the destruction of human happiness and the disgrace of human reason and government.

"If, after the most mature deliberation, it shall appear that no measures can be taken *at present* on this very interesting subject, it is conceived it would redound much to the honor of the United States that it was attended to by their great Representative in Congress, and be accepted as a testimony of gratitude for most signal favors granted to the said States by Him who is the almighty and most gracious Father and Friend of mankind.

"And you are further instructed to move that the foregoing Letter of Instructions be entered on the Journals of Congress, if it may be thought proper, that so it may remain for the inspection of the delegates from this Commonwealth, if necessary, in any *future* time." [1]

I am not able to ascertain whether this document ever became a legislative act; but unquestionably it attests, in authentic form, that a great leader in Mas-

[1] MSS. of Samuel Adams, belonging to the historian, George Bancroft.

sachusetts, after the establishment of that Independence for which he had so assiduously labored, hoped to enlist not only the Legislature of his State, but the Congress of the United States, in efforts for the emancipation of nations from the tyranny of War. For this early effort, when the cause of Permanent Peace had never been introduced to any legislative body, Samuel Adams deserves grateful mention.

Many years later the subject reached Congress, where, in 1838, it was considered in an elaborate report by the late Mr. Legaré, in behalf of the Committee on Foreign Affairs of the House of Representatives, prompted by memorials from the friends of Peace. While injudiciously discountenancing an Association of Nations, as not yet sanctioned by public opinion, the Committee acknowledge "that the union of all nations in a state of Peace, under the restraints and the protection of law, is the ideal perfection of civil society"; that they "concur fully in the benevolent object of the memorialists, and believe that there is a visible tendency in the spirit and institutions of the age towards the practical accomplishment of it at some future period"; that they "heartily concur with the memorialists in recommending a reference to a Third Power of all such controversies as can safely be confided to any tribunal unknown to the Constitution of our own country"; and that "such a practice will be followed by other powers, and will soon grow up into the customary law of civilized nations."[1]

The Legislature of Massachusetts, by a series of resolutions, in harmony with the early sentiments of Samuel Adams, adopted, in 1844, with exceeding unanimity, declare, that they "regard Arbitration as a practical and

1 Reports of Committees, 25th Cong. 2d Sess., No. 979

desirable substitute for War, in the adjustment of international differences"; and still further declare their "earnest desire that the government of the United States would, at the earliest opportunity, take measures for obtaining the consent of the powers of Christendom to the establishment of a general Convention or Congress of Nations, for the purpose of settling the principles of International Law, and of organizing a High Court of Nations to adjudge all cases of difficulty which may be brought before them by the mutual consent of two or more nations."[1] During the winter of 1849 the subject was again presented to the American Congress by Mr. Tuck, who asked the unanimous consent of the House of Representatives to offer the following preamble and resolution: —

"Whereas the evils of War are acknowledged by all civilized nations, and the calamities, individual and general, which are inseparably connected with it, have attracted the attention of many humane and enlightened citizens of this and other countries; and whereas it is the disposition of the people of the United States to coöperate with others in all appropriate and judicious exertions to prevent a recurrence of national conflicts; therefore,

"*Resolved*, That the Committee on Foreign Affairs be directed to inquire into the expediency of authorizing a correspondence to be opened by the Secretary of State with Foreign Governments, on the subject of procuring Treaty stipulations for the reference of all future disputes to a friendly Arbitration, or for the establishment, instead thereof, of a Congress of Nations, to determine International Law and settle international disputes."[2]

1 Mass. House Documents, Sess. 1844, No. 18.

2 Congressional Globe, 30th Cong. 2d Sess., Jan. 16, 1849, p. 267. See also House Journal, Feb. 5, p. 372.

Though for the present unsuccessful, this excellent effort prepares the way for another trial.

Nor does it stand alone. Almost contemporaneously, M. Bouvet, in the National Assembly of France, submitted a proposition of a similar character, as follows: —

"Seeing that War between nations is contrary to religion, humanity, and the public well-being, the French National Assembly decrees: —

"The French Republic proposes to the Governments and Representative Assemblies of the different States of Europe, America, and other civilized countries, to unite, by their representation, in a Congress which shall have for its object a proportional disarmament among the Powers, the abolition of War, and a substitution for that barbarous usage of an Arbitral jurisdiction, of which the said Congress shall immediately fulfil the functions."

In an elaborate report, the French Committee on Foreign Affairs, while declining at present to recommend this proposition, distinctly sanction its object.

At a still earlier date, some time in the summer of 1848, Arnold Ruge brought the same measure before the German Parliament at Frankfort, by moving the following amendment to the Report of the Committee on Foreign Affairs: —

"That, as Armed Peace, by its standing armies, imposes an intolerable burden upon the people of Europe, and endangers civil freedom, we therefore recognize the necessity of calling into existence a *Congress of Nations*, for the purpose of effecting a general disarmament of Europe."

Though this proposition failed, yet the mover is reported to have sustained it by a speech which was received with applause, both in the assembly and gallery. Among other things, he used these important words: —

"There is no necessity for feeding an army of military idlers and eaters. There is nothing to fear from our neighbor barbarians, as they are called. You must give up the idea that the French *will* eat us up, and that the Prussians *can* eat us up. Soldiers must cease to exist; then shall no more cities be bombarded. These opinions must be kept up and propagated by a Congress of Nations. I vote that the nations of Europe disarm at once."

In the British Parliament the cause has found an able representative in Mr. Cobden, whose name is an omen of success. He has addressed many large popular meetings in its behalf, and already, by speech and motion in the House of Commons, has striven for a reduction in the armaments of Great Britain. Only lately he gave notice of the following motion, which he intends to call up in that assembly at the earliest moment: —

"That an humble address be presented to her Majesty, praying that she will be graciously pleased to direct her Principal Secretary of State for Foreign Affairs to enter into communication with Foreign Powers, inviting them to concur in treaties binding the respective parties, in the event of any future misunderstanding which cannot be arranged by amicable negotiation, to refer the matter in dispute to the decision of Arbitrators."

Such is the Peace Movement.[1] With the ever-flowing current of time it has gained ever-increasing strength, and it has now become like a mighty river. At first but a slender fountain, sparkling on some lofty summit, it has swollen with every tributary rill, with the friendly rains and dews of heaven, and at last with the associate waters of various nations, until it washes the feet of

[1] It will be remarked that this history stops with the date of this Address.

populous cities, rejoicing on its peaceful banks. By the voices of poets, — by the aspirations and labors of statesmen, philosophers, and good men, — by the experience of history, — by the peaceful union into nations of families, tribes, and provinces, divesting themselves of "liberty" to wage War, — by the example of leagues, alliances, confederacies, and congresses, — by the kindred movements of our age, all tending to Unity, — by an awakened public sentiment, and a growing recognition of Human Brotherhood, — by the sympathies of large popular assemblies, — by the formal action of legislative bodies, — by the promises of Christianity, are we encouraged to persevere. So doing, we act not *against* Nature, but *with* Nature, making ourselves, according to the injunction of Lord Bacon, its ministers and interpreters. From no single man, from no body of men, does this cause proceed. Not from Saint-Pierre or Leibnitz, from Rousseau or Kant, in other days, — not from Jay or Burritt, from Cobden or Lamartine, in our own. It is the irrepressible utterance of the longing with which the heart of Humanity labors; it is the universal expression of the Spirit of the Age, thirsting after Harmony; it is the heaven-born whisper of Truth, immortal and omnipotent; it is the word of God, published in commands as from the burning bush; it is the voice of Christ, declaring to all mankind that they are brothers, and saying to the turbulent nationalities of the earth, as to the raging sea, "Peace, be still!"

Gentlemen of the Peace Society, — Such is the War System of the Commonwealth of Nations; and such are the means and auguries of its overthrow. To aid and direct public sentiment so as to hasten the coming of this day is the chosen object of this Society. All who have candidly attended me in this exposition will bear witness that our attempt is in no way inconsistent with the human character, — that we do not seek to suspend or hold in check any general laws of Nature, but simply to overthrow a barbarous Institution, having the sanction of International Law, and to bring nations within that system of social order which has already secured such inestimable good to civil society, and is as applicable to nations in their relations with each other as to individuals.

Tendencies of nations, as revealed in history, teach that our aims are in harmony with prevailing laws, which God, in his benevolence, has ordained for mankind.

Examples teach also that we attempt nothing that is not directly practicable. If the several States of the Helvetic Republic, if the thirty independent States of the North American Union, if the thirty-eight independent sovereignties of the German Confederation, can, by formal stipulation, divest themselves of the *right of war with each other,* and consent to submit all mutual controversies to Arbitration, or to a High Court of Judicature, then can the Commonwealth of Nations do the same. Nor should they hesitate, while, in the language of William Penn, such surpassing instances show that *it may be done,* and Europe, by her incomparable miseries, that *it ought to be done.* Nay, more, — if it would be criminal in these several clusters of States to reëstablish the Institution of War as Arbiter of Justice, then is it criminal in the Commonwealth of Nations to continue it.

Changes already wrought in the Laws of War teach that the whole System may be abolished. The existence of laws implies authority that sanctions or enacts, which, in the present case, is the Commonwealth of Nations. This authority can, of course, modify or abrogate what it originally sanctioned or enacted. In the exercise of this power, the Laws of War have been modified, from time to time, in important particulars. Prisoners taken in battle cannot now be killed ; nor can they be reduced to slavery. Poison and assassination can no longer be employed against an enemy. Private property on land cannot be seized. Persons occupied on land exclusively with the arts of Peace cannot be molested. It remains that the authority by which the Laws of War have been thus modified should entirely abrogate them. Their existence is a disgrace to civilization ; for it implies the *common consent* of nations to the Arbitrament of War, as regulated by these laws. Like the Laws of the Duel, they should yield to some arbitrament of reason. If the former, once so firmly imbedded in Municipal Law, could be abolished by individual nations, so also can the Laws of War, which are a part of International Law, be abolished by the Commonwealth of Nations. In the light of reason and religion there can be but one Law of War, — the great law which pronounces it unwise, unchristian, and unjust, and forbids it forever, as a crime.

Thus distinctly alleging the practicability of our aims, I may properly introduce an incontrovertible authority. Listen to the words of an American statesman, whose long life was spent, at home or abroad, in the service of his country, and whose undoubted familiarity with the Law of Nations was never surpassed, — John Quincy Adams. "War," he says, in one of the legacies of his venerable experience, "by the common consent and mere will of civilized man, has not only been divested of its most atrocious cruelties, but for multitudes, growing multitudes of individuals, has already been and is abolished. *Why should it not be abolished for all?* Let it be impressed upon the heart of every one of you, impress it upon the minds of your children, *that this total abolition of War upon earth* is an improvement in the condition of man entirely dependent on his own will. He cannot repeal or change the laws of physical Nature. He cannot redeem himself from the ills that flesh is heir to. But the ills of War and Slavery are all of his own creation; he has but to will, and he effects the cessation of them altogether."[1]

Well does John Quincy Adams say that mankind have but to *will* it, and War is abolished. Will it, and War disappears like the Duel. Will it, and War skulks like the Torture. Will it, and War fades away like the fires of religious persecution. Will it, and War passes among profane follies, like the ordeal of burning ploughshares. Will it, and War hurries to join the earlier institution of Cannibalism. Will it, and War is chastised from the Commonwealth of Nations, as Slavery has been chastised from municipal jurisdictions by England and France, by Tunis and Tripoli.

To arouse this *public will*, which, like a giant, yet sleeps, but whose awakened voice nothing can withstand, should be our endeavor. The true character of the War System must be exposed. To be hated, it needs only to be comprehended; and it will surely be abolished as soon as this is accomplished. See, then, that it is comprehended. Exhibit its manifold atro-

[1] Oration at Newburyport, July 4, 1837, pp. 56, 57.

cities. Strip away all its presumptuous pretences, its specious apologies, its hideous sorceries. Above all, men must no longer deceive themselves by the shallow thought that this System is the necessary incident of imperfect human nature, and thus cast upon God the responsibility for their crimes. They must see clearly that it is a monster of their own creation, born with their consent, whose vital spark is fed by their breath, and without their breath must necessarily die. They must see distinctly, what I have so carefully presented to-night, that War, under the Law of Nations, is nothing but an Institution, and the whole War System nothing but an Establishment for the administration of *international justice,* for which the Commonwealth of Nations is directly responsible, and which that Commonwealth can at any time remove.

Recognizing these things, men must cease to cherish War, and will renounce all appeal to its Arbitrament. They will forego rights, rather than wage an irreligious battle. But, criminal and irrational as is War, unhappily, in the present state of human error, we cannot expect large numbers to appreciate its true character, and to hate it with that perfect hatred making them renounce its agency, unless we offer an approved and practical mode of determining international controversies, as a *substitute* for the imagined necessity of the barbarous ordeal. This we are able to do; and so doing, we reflect new light upon the atrocity of a system which not only tramples upon all the precepts of the Christian faith, but defies justice and discards reason.

1. The most complete and permanent substitute would be a Congress of Nations, with a High Court of Judica-

ture. Such a system, while admitted on all sides to promise excellent results, is opposed on two grounds. *First,* because, as regards the smaller states, it would be a tremendous engine of oppression, subversive of their political independence. Surely, it could not be so oppressive as the War System. But the experience of the smaller States in the German Confederation and in the American Union, nay, the experience of Belgium and Holland by the side of the overtopping power of France, and the experience of Denmark and Sweden in the very night-shade of Russia, all show the futility of this objection. *Secondly,* because the decrees of such a court could not be carried into effect. Even if they were enforced by the combined power of the associate nations, the sword, as the executive arm of the high tribunal, would be only the melancholy instrument of Justice, not the Arbiter of Justice, and therefore not condemned by the conclusive reasons against international appeals to the sword. From the experience of history, and particularly from the experience of the thirty States of our Union, we learn that the occasion for any executive arm will be rare. The State of Rhode Island, in its recent controversy with Massachusetts, submitted with much indifference to the adverse decree of the Supreme Court; and I doubt not that Missouri and Iowa will submit with equal contentment to any determination of their present controversy by the same tribunal. The same submission would attend the decrees of any Court of Judicature established by the Commonwealth of Nations. There is a growing sense of justice, combined with a growing might of public opinion, too little known to the soldier, that would maintain the judgments of the august tribunal assembled in the face of the Nations, better than the swords of all the marshals of France, better than the bloody terrors of Austerlitz or Waterloo.

The idea of a Congress of Nations with a High Court of Judicature is as practicable as its consummation is confessedly dear to the friends of Universal Peace. Whenever this Congress is convened, as surely it will be, I know not all the names that will deserve commemoration in its earliest proceedings; but there are two, whose particular and long-continued advocacy of this Institution will connect them indissolubly with its fame, — the Abbé Saint-Pierre, of France, and William Ladd, of the United States.

2. There is still another substitute for War, which is not exposed even to the shallow objections launched against a Congress of Nations. By formal treaties between two or more nations, Arbitration may be established as the mode of determining controversies between them. In every respect this is a contrast to War. It is rational, humane, and cheap. Above all, it is consistent with the teachings of Christianity. As I mention this substitute, I should do injustice to the cause and to my own feelings, if I did not express our obligations to its efficient proposer and advocate, our fellow-citizen, and the President of this Society, the honored son of an illustrious father, whose absence to-night enables me, without offending his known modesty, to introduce this tribute: I mean William Jay.

The complete overthrow of the War System, involving the disarming of the Nations, would follow the establishment of a Congress of Nations, or any general system of Arbitration. Then at last our aims would be accomplished; then at last Peace would be organized among the Nations. Then might Christians repeat the fitful boast of the generous Mohawk: "We have thrown the hatchet so high into the air, and beyond the skies, that no arm on earth can reach to bring it down." Incalculable sums, now devoted to armaments and the destructive industry of War, would be turned to the productive industry of Art and to offices of Beneficence. As in the dead and rotten carcass of the lion which roared against the strong man of Israel, after a time, were a swarm of bees and honey, so would the enormous carcass of War, dead and rotten, be filled with crowds of useful laborers and all good works, and the riddle of Samson be once more interpreted: "Out of the eater came forth meat, and out of the strong came forth sweetness."

Put together the products of all the mines in the world, — the glistening ore of California, the accumulated treasures of Mexico and Peru, with the diamonds of Golconda, — and the whole shining heap will be less than the means thus diverted from War to Peace. Under the influence of such a change, civilization will be quickened anew. Then will happy Labor find its reward, and the whole land be filled with its increase. There is no aspiration of Knowledge, no vision of Charity, no venture of Enterprise, no fancy of Art, which may not then be fufilled. The great unsolved problem of Pauperism will be solved at last. There will be no paupers, when there are no soldiers. The social struggles, so fearfully disturbing European nations, will die away in the happiness of unarmed Peace, no longer incumbered by the oppressive system of War; nor can there be well-founded hope that these struggles will permanently cease, so long as this system endures. The people ought not to rest, they cannot rest, while this system endures. As King Arthur, prostrate on the earth, with bloody streams pouring from his veins, could not be at ease, until his sword, the terrific Excalibar, was thrown into the flood, so the Nations, now prostrate on the earth, with bloody streams pouring from their veins, cannot be at ease, until they fling far away the wicked sword of War. King Arthur said to his attending knight, "As thou love me, spare not to throw it in"; and this is the voice of the Nations also.

Lop off the unchristian armaments of the Christian Nations, extirpate these martial cancers, that they may feed no longer upon the life-blood of the people, and society itself, now weary and sick, will become fresh and young, — not by opening its veins, as under the incantation of Medea, in the wild hope of infusing new strength, but by the amputation and complete removal of a deadly excrescence, with all its unutterable debility and exhaustion. Energies hitherto withdrawn from proper healthful action will then replenish it with unwonted life and vigor, giving new expansion to every human capacity, and new elevation to every human aim. And society at last shall rejoice, like a strong man, to run its race.

Imagination toils to picture the boundless good that will be achieved. As War with its deeds is infinitely evil and accursed, so will this triumph of Permanent Peace be infinitely beneficent and blessed. Something of its consequences were seen, in prophetic vision, even by that incarnate Spirit of War, Napoleon Bonaparte, when, from his island-prison of St. Helena, looking back upon his mistaken career, he was led to confess the True Grandeur of Peace. Out of his mouth let its praise be spoken. "I had the project," he said, mournfully regretting the opportunity he had lost, "at the general peace of Amiens, of bringing each Power to an immense reduction of its standing armies. I wished a European Institute, with European prizes, to direct, associate, and bring together all the learned societies of Europe. Then, perhaps, through the universal spread of light, it might be permitted to anticipate for the great European Family the establishment of an American Congress, or an Amphictyonic Council; and what a perspective then of strength, of greatness, of happiness, of prosperity! What a sublime and magnificent spectacle!"[1]

Such is our cause. In transcendent influence, it embraces human beneficence in all its forms. It is the comprehensive charity, enfolding all the charities of all. None so vast as to be above its protection, none so lowly as not to feel its care. Religion, Knowledge, Freedom, Virtue, Happiness, in all their manifold forms, depend upon Peace. Sustained by Peace, they lean upon the Everlasting Arm. And this is not all. Law, Order, Government, derive from Peace new sanctions. Nor can they attain to that complete dominion which is our truest safeguard, until, by the overthrow of the War System, they comprehend the Commonwealth of Nations, —

"And Sovereign LAW, *the* WORLD'S *collected will,*
O'er thrones and globes elate,
Sits empress, crowning good, repressing ill."[2]

[1] Las Cases, Memorial de Sainte-Hélène, November, 1816.
[2] Sir William Jones, Ode in Imitation of Alcæus.

In the name of Religion profaned, of Knowledge misapplied and perverted, of Freedom crushed to earth, of Virtue dethroned, of human Happiness violated, in the name of Law, Order, and Government, I call upon you for union to establish the supremacy of Peace. There must be no hesitation. With the lips you confess the infinite evil of War. Are you in earnest? Action must follow confession. All must unite to render the recurrence of this evil impossible. Science and Humanity everywhere put forth all possible energy against cholera and pestilence. Why not equal energy against an evil more fearful than cholera or pestilence? Each man must consider the cause his own. Let him animate his neighbors. Let him seek, in every proper way, to influence the rulers of the Nations, and, above all, the rulers of this happy land.

The old, the middle-aged, and the young must combine in a common cause. The pulpit, the school, the college, and the public street must speak for it. Preach it, minister of the Prince of Peace! let it never be forgotten in conversation, sermon, or prayer; nor any longer seek, by specious theory, to reconcile the monstrous War System with the precepts of Christ! Instil it, teacher of childhood and youth! in the early thoughts of your precious charge; exhibit the wickedness of War and the beauty of Peace; let your warnings sink deep among those purifying and strengthening influences which ripen into true manhood. Scholar! write it in your books, so that all shall read it. Poet! sing it, so that all shall love it. Let the interests of commerce, whose threads of golden tissue interknit the Nations, enlist the traffickers of the earth in its behalf. And you, servant of the law! sharer of my own peculiar toils, mindful that the law is silent in the midst of arms, join to preserve, uphold, and extend its sway. Remember, politician! that our cause is too universal to become the exclusive possession of any political party, or to be confined within any geographical limits. See to it, statesman and ruler! that the principles of Peace are as a cloud by day and a pillar of fire by night. Let the Abolition of War, and the Overthrow of the War System, with the Disarming of the Nations, be your guiding star. Be this your pious diplomacy! Be this your lofty Christian statesmanship!

As a measure simple and practical, obnoxious to no objection, promising incalculable good, and presenting an immediate opportunity for labor, I would invite your coöperation in the effort now making at home and abroad to establish Arbitration Treaties. If in this scheme there is a tendency to avert War, — if, through its agency, we may hope to prevent a single war, — and who can doubt that such may be its result? — we ought to adopt it. Take the initiative. Try it, and nations will never return to the barbarous system. They will begin to learn War no more. Let it be our privilege to volunteer the proposal. Thus shall we inaugurate Permanent Peace in the diplomacy of the world. Nor should we wait for other governments. In a cause so holy, no government should wait for another. Let us take the lead. Let our republic, powerful child of Freedom, go forth, the Evangelist of Peace. Let her offer to the world a Magna Charta of International Law, by which the crime of War shall be forever abolished.

While thus encouraging you in behalf of Universal Peace, the odious din of War, mingled with pathetic appeals for Freedom, reaches us from struggling Italy, from convulsed Germany, from aroused and triumphant Hungary. At bidding of the Russian Autocrat, the populous North threatens to pour its multitudes upon the scene; and a portentous cloud, charged with "red lightning and impetuous rage," hangs over the whole continent of Europe, which echoes again to the tread of mustering squadrons. Alas! must this dismal work be renewed? Can Freedom be born, can nations be regenerated, only through baptism of blood? In our aspirations, I would not be blind to the teachings of History, or to the actual condition of men, so long accustomed to brute force, that, to their imperfect natures, it seems the only means by which injustice can be crushed. With sadness I confess that we cannot expect the *domestic* repose of nations, until tyranny is overthrown, and the principles of *self-government* are established; especially do I not expect imperturbable peace in Italy, so long as foreign Austria, with insolent iron heel, continues to tread any part of that beautiful land. But whatever may be the fate of the present crisis, whether it be doomed to the horrors of prolonged strife, or shall soon brighten into the radiance of enduring concord, I cannot doubt that the Nations are gravitating, with resistless might, even through fire and blood, into peaceful forms of social order, where the War System will cease to be known.

Nay, from the experience of this hour I draw the auguries of Permanent Peace. Not in any international strife, not in duel between nation and nation, not in selfish conflict of ruler with ruler, not in the unwise "game" of War, as played by king with king, do we find the origin of present commotions, "with fear of change perplexing monarchs." It is to overturn the enforced rule of military power, to crush the tyranny of armies, and to supplant unjust government, — whose only stay is physical force, and not the consent of the governed, — that the people have risen in mighty madness. So doing, they wage a battle where all our sympathies must be with Freedom, while, in sorrow at the unwelcome combat, we confess that victory is only less mournful than defeat. Through all these bloody mists the eye of Faith discerns the ascending sun, struggling to shoot its life-giving beams upon the outspread earth, teeming with the grander products of a new civilization. Everywhere salute us the signs of Progress; and the Promised Land smiles at the new epoch. His heart is cold, his eye is dull, who does not perceive the change. Vainly has he read the history of the Past, vainly does he feel the irrepressible movement of the Present. Man has waded through a Red Sea of blood, and for forty centuries wandered through a wilderness of wretchedness and error, but he stands at last on Pisgah: like the adventurous Spaniard, he has wearily climbed the mountain heights, whence he may descry the vast, unbroken Pacific Sea; like the hardy Portuguese, he is sure to double this fearful Cape of Storms, destined ever afterwards to be the Cape of Good Hope. I would not seem too confident. I know not, that, in any brief period, nations, like kindred drops, will commingle into one, — that, like the banyan-trees of the East, they will interlace and interlock, until there are no longer separate trees, but one united wood,

> "a pillared shade
> High overarched, and echoing walks between";

but I rest assured, that, without renouncing any essential qualities of individuality or independence, they may yet, even in our own day, arrange themselves in harmony; as magnetized iron rings, — from which Plato once borrowed an image, — under the influence of potent unseen attraction, while preserving each its own peculiar form, cohere in a united chain of independent circles. From the birth of this new order will spring not only international repose, but domestic quiet also; and Peace will become the permanent rule of civilization. The stone will be rolled away from the sepulchre in which men have laid their Lord, and we shall hear the new-risen voice, saying, in words of blessed truth, "Lo, I am with you alway, even unto the end of the world."

Here I might fitly close. Though admonished that I have already occupied more of your time than I could venture to claim, except for the cause, I cannot forbear to consider, for a brief moment, yet one other topic, which I have left thus far untouched, partly because it is not directly connected with the main argument, and therefore seemed inappropriate to any earlier stage, and partly because I wished to impress it with my last words. I refer to that greatest, most preposterous, and most irreligious of earthly vanities, the monstrous reflection of War, — *Military Glory.*

Let me not disguise the truth. Too true it is that this vanity is still cherished by mankind, — that it is still an object of ambition, — that men follow War, and count its pursuit "honorable," — that feats of brute force are heralded "brilliant," — and that a yet prevailing public opinion animates unreflecting mortals to "seek the bubble *reputation* even in the cannon's mouth." Too true it is that nations persevere in offering praise and thanksgiving — such as no labors of Beneficence can achieve — to the chief whose hands are red with the blood of his fellow-men.

Whatever the usage of the world, whether during the long and dreary Past or in the yet barbarous Present, it must be clear to all who confront this question with candor, and do not turn away from the blaze of truth, that any glory from bloody strife among God's children must be fugitive, evanescent, unreal. It is the offspring of a deluded public sentiment, and will disappear, as we learn to analyze its elements and appreciate its character. Too long has mankind worshipped what St. Augustine called the *splendid vices*, neglecting the simple virtues, — too long cultivated the flaunting and noxious weeds, careless of the golden corn, — too long been insensible to that commanding law and sacred example which rebuke all the pretensions of military glory.

Look face to face at this "glory." Study it in the growing illumination of history. Regarding War as an established Arbitrament, for the adjudication of controversies among nations, — like the Petty Wars of an earlier period between cities, principalities, and provinces, or like the Trial by Battle between individuals, — the conclusion is irresistible, that an enlightened civilization, when the world has reached that Unity to which it tends, must condemn the partakers in its duels, and their vaunted achievements, precisely as we now condemn the partakers in those wretched contests which disfigure the commencement of modern history. The prowess of the individual is forgotten in disgust at an inglorious barbarism.

Observe this "glory" in the broad sunshine of Christian truth. In all ages, even in Heathen lands, there has been a peculiar reverence for the relation of Brotherhood. Feuds among brothers, from that earliest "mutual-murdering" conflict beneath the walls of Thebes, have been accounted ghastly and abhorred, never to be mentioned without a shudder. This sentiment was revived in modern times, and men sought to extend the circle of its influence. Warriors, like Du Guesclin, rejoiced to hail each other as brothers. Chivalry delighted in fraternities of arms sealed by vow and solemnity. According to curious and savage custom, valiant knights were bled together, that their blood, as it spurted forth, might intermingle, and thus constitute them of *one blood,* which was drunk by each. So did the powerful emperor of Constantinople confirm an alliance of friendship with a neighbor king. The two monarchs drank of each other's blood; and then their attendants, following the princely example, caught their own flowing life in a wine-cup, and quaffed a mutual pledge, saying, "We are brothers, of *one blood.*" [1]

By such profane devices men sought to establish that relation, whose beauty they perceived, though they failed to discern, that, by the ordinance of God, without any human stratagem, it justly comprehended all their fellow-men. In the midst of Judaism, which hated Gen-

[1] Du Cange, Dissertations sur l'Histoire de Saint Louys par Jean Sire de Joinville, Diss. XXI. Ibid.: Petitot, Mémoires relatifs à l'Histoire de France, 1re Série, Tom. III. p. 349. Sainte-Palaye, Mémoires sur l'Ancienne Chevalerie, Part. III. Tom. I. p. 225. The same attempt at Brotherhood appears in the "Loka-Lenna, or Strife of Loc," quoted by Sir Walter Scott in his Notes to the Metrical Romance of "Sir Tristrem," p. 350:—

"Father of Slaughter, Odin, say,
Remember'st not the former day,
When in the ruddy goblet stood,
For mutual drink, our blended blood?"

tiles, Christianity proclaimed love to all mankind, and distinctly declared that God had made of *one blood* all the nations of men. As if to keep this sublime truth ever present, the disciples were taught, in the simple prayer of the Saviour, to address God as Father in heaven, — not in phrase of exclusive worship, "*my* Father," but in those other words of peculiar Christian import, "*our* Father," — with the petition, not merely to "forgive *me my* trespasses," but with the diviner prayer, to "forgive *us our* trespasses": thus, in the solitude of the closet, recognizing all alike as children of God, and embracing all alike in the petition for mercy.

Confessing the Fatherhood of God, and the consequent Brotherhood of Man, we find a divine standard of unquestionable accuracy. No brother can win "glory" from the death of a brother. Cain won no "glory," when he slew Abel; nor would Abel have won "glory," had he, in strictest self-defence, succeeded in slaying the wicked Cain. The soul recoils from praise or honor, as the meed of any such melancholy triumph. And what is true of a conflict between *two* brothers is equally true of a conflict between *many*. How can an army win "glory" by dealing death or defeat to an army of its brothers?

The ancient Romans, not knowing this comprehensive relation, and recognizing only the exclusive fellowship of a common country, accounted *civil war fratricidal*, whose opposing forces, even under well-loved names of the Republic, were *impious;* and then, by unerring logic, these masters in War constantly refused "honor," "thanksgiving," or "triumph," to the conquering chief whose sword had been employed against *fellow-citi-*

zens, though traitors and rebels. As the Brotherhood of Man is practically recognized, it becomes impossible to restrict the feeling within any exclusive circle of country, and to set up an unchristian distinction of honor between *civil war* and *international war. As all men are brothers, so, by irresistible consequence,* ALL WAR MUST BE FRATRICIDAL. And can "glory" come from fratricide? None can hesitate in answer, unless fatally imbued with the Heathen rage of nationality, that made the Venetians declare themselves Venetians first and Christians afterwards.

Tell me not of homage yet offered to the military chieftain. Tell me not of "glory" from War. Tell me not of "honor" or "fame" on its murderous fields. All is vanity. It is a blood-red phantom. They who strive after it, Ixion-like, embrace a cloud. Though seeming to fill the heavens, cloaking the stars, it must, like the vapors of earth, pass away. Milton likens the contests of the Heptarchy to "the wars of kites or crows flocking and fighting in the air."[1] But God, and the exalted judgment of the Future, must regard all our bloody feuds in the same likeness,—finding Napoleon and Alexander, so far as engaged in War, only monster crows and kites. Thus must it be, as mankind ascend from the thrall of brutish passion. Nobler aims, by nobler means, will fill the soul. There will be a new standard of excellence; and honor, divorced from blood, will become the inseparable attendant of good works alone. Far better, then, even in the judgment of this world, to have been a doorkeeper in the house of Peace than the proudest dweller in the tents of War.

[1] History of England, Book IV.: Prose Works (ed. Symmons), Vol. IV. p. 158.

There is a pious legend of the early Church, that the Saviour left his image miraculously impressed upon a napkin which had touched his countenance. The napkin was lost, and men attempted to supply the divine lineaments from the Heathen models of Jupiter and Apollo. But the true image of Christ is not lost. Clearer than in the venerated napkin, better than in color or marble of choicest art, it appears in each virtuous deed, in every act of self-sacrifice, in all magnanimous toil, in any recognition of Human Brotherhood. It will be supremely manifest, in unimagined loveliness and serenity, when the Commonwealth of Nations, confessing the True Grandeur of Peace, renounces the War System, and dedicates to Beneficence the comprehensive energies so fatally absorbed in its support. Then, at last, will it be seen, *there can be no Peace that is not honorable, and no War that is not dishonorable.*

There is a pious legend of Mediæval Church, that the Saviour left his image miraculously impressed upon a napkin which had touched his countenance. The napkin was lost, and then attempted to supply the divine lineaments from the Heathen models of Jupiter and Apollo. But the true image of Christ is not lost. Clearer than in the venerated napkin, better than in color or marble or choicest art, it appears in each virtuous deed, in every act of self-sacrifice, in all magnanimous toil, in any recognition of Human Brotherhood. It will be supremely manifest, in unimagined loveliness and grandeur, when the Commonwealth of Nations, confessing the True Grandeur of Peace, renounces the War System, and dedicates to Beneficence the comprehensive energies so fatally absorbed in its support. Then, at last, will it be seen that *there can be no Peace that is not honorable, and no War that is not dishonorable.*

THE

DUEL BETWEEN FRANCE AND GERMANY,

WITH ITS LESSON TO CIVILIZATION.

LECTURE IN THE MUSIC HALL, BOSTON, OCTOBER 26, 1870.

"When kings make war,
No law betwixt two sovereigns can decide,
But that of arms, where Fortune is the judge,
Soldiers the lawyers, and the Bar the field."

DRYDEN, *Love Triumphant*, Act I. Sc. 1.

LECTURE.

MR. PRESIDENT, — I am to speak of the Duel between France and Germany, with its Lesson to Civilization. In calling the terrible war now waging a Duel, I might content myself with classical authority, *Duellum* being a well-known Latin word for War. The historian Livy makes a Roman declare that affairs are to be settled "by a pure and pious duel";[1] the dramatist Plautus has a character in one of his plays who obtains great riches "by the duelling art,"[2] meaning the art of war; and Horace, the exquisite master of language, hails the age of Augustus with the Temple of Janus closed and "free from duels,"[3] meaning at peace, — for then only was that famous temple shut.

WAR UNDER THE LAW OF NATIONS A DUEL.

BUT no classical authority is needed for this designation. War, as conducted under International Law, between two organized nations, is in all respects a duel, according to the just signification of this word, — differing from that between two individuals only in the number of combatants. The variance is of proportion merely, each nation being an individual who appeals to the sword as Arbiter; and in each case the combat is

1 "Puro pioque duello." — *Historiæ*, Lib. I. cap. 32.
2 "Arte duellica." — *Epidicus*, Act. III. Sc. iv. 14.
3 "Vacuum duellis." — *Carmina*, Lib. IV. xv. 8.

subject to rules constituting a code by which the two parties are bound. For long years before civilization prevailed, the code governing the duel between individuals was as fixed and minute as that which governs the larger duel between nations, and the duel itself was simply a mode of deciding questions between individuals. In presenting this comparison I expose myself to criticism only from those who have not considered this interesting subject in the light of history and of reason. The parallel is complete. Modern war is the duel of the Dark Ages, magnified, amplified, extended so as to embrace nations; nor is it any less a duel because the combat is quickened and sustained by the energies of self-defence, or because, when a champion falls and lies on the ground, he is brutally treated. An authentic instance illustrates such a duel; and I bring before you the very pink of chivalry, the Chevalier Bayard, "the knight without fear and without reproach," who, after combat in a chosen field, succeeded by a feint in driving his weapon four fingers deep into the throat of his adversary, and then, rolling with him, gasping and struggling, on the ground, thrust his dagger into the nostrils of the fallen victim, exclaiming, "Surrender, or you are a dead man!"—a speech which seemed superfluous; for the second cried out, "He is dead already; you have conquered." Then did Bayard, brightest among the Sons of War, drag his dead enemy from the field, crying, "Have I done enough?"[1] Now, because the brave knight saw fit to do these things, the combat was not changed in original character. It was a duel at the

[1] La tresjoyeuse, plaisante et recreative Hystoire, composée par le Loyal Serviteur, des Faiz, Gestes, Triumphes et Prouesses du Bon Chevalier sans Paour et sans Reprouche, le Gentil Seigneur de Bayart: Petitot, Collection des Mémoires relatifs à l'Histoire de France, Tom. XV. pp. 241, 242.

beginning and at the end. Indeed, the brutality with which it closed was the natural incident of a duel. A combat once begun opens the way to violence, and the conqueror too often surrenders to the Evil Spirit, as Bayard in his unworthy barbarism.

In likening war between nations to the duel, I follow not only reason, but authority also. No better lawyer can be named in the long history of the English bar than John Selden, whose learning was equalled only by his large intelligence. In those conversations which under the name of "Table-Talk" continue still to instruct, the wise counsellor, after saying that the Church allowed the duel anciently, and that in the public liturgies there were prayers appointed for duellists to say, keenly inquires, "But whether is this lawful?" And then he answers, "If you grant any war lawful, I make no doubt but to convince it."[1] Selden regarded the simple duel and the larger war as governed by the same rule. Of course the exercise of force in the suppression of rebellion, or in the maintenance of laws, stands on a different principle, being in its nature a constabulary proceeding, which cannot be confounded with the duel. But my object is not to question the lawfulness of war; I would simply present an image, enabling you to see the existing war in its true character.

The duel in its simplest form is between two individuals. In early ages it was known sometimes as the Judicial Combat, and sometimes as Trial by Battle. Not only points of honor, but titles to land, grave questions of law, and even the subtilties of theology, were referred to this arbitrament,[2] — just as now kindred

[1] Table-Talk, ed. Singer, (London, 1856,) p. 47, — *Duel.*

[2] Robertson, History of the Reign of Charles V.: View of the Progress of Society in Europe, Section I. Note XXII.

issues between nations are referred to Trial by Battle; and the early rules governing the duel are reproduced in the Laws of War established by nations to govern the great Trial by Battle. Ascending from the individual to corporations, guilds, villages, towns, counties, provinces, we find that for a long period each of these bodies exercised what was called "the Right of War." The history of France and Germany shows how reluctantly this mode of trial yielded to the forms of reason and order. France, earlier than Germany, ordained "Trial by Proofs," and eliminated the duel from judicial proceedings, this important step being followed by the gradual amalgamation of discordant provinces in the powerful unity of the Nation, — so that Brittany and Normandy, Franche-Comté and Burgundy, Provence and Dauphiny, Gascony and Languedoc, with the rest, became the United States of France, or, if you please, France. In Germany the change was slower; and here the duel exhibits its most curious instances. Not only feudal chiefs, but associations of tradesmen and of domestics sent defiance to each other, and sometimes to whole cities, on pretences trivial as those which have been the occasion of defiance from nation to nation. There still remain to us Declarations of War by a Lord of Frauenstein against the free city of Frankfort, because a young lady of the city refused to dance with his uncle, — by the baker and domestics of the Margrave of Baden against Esslingen, Reutlingen, and other imperial cities, — by the baker of the Count Palatine Louis against the cities of Augsburg, Ulm, and Rottweil, — by the shoe-blacks of the University of Leipsic against the provost and other members, — and by the cook of Eppstein, with his scullions, dairy-maids, and dish-washers, against Otho, Count of Solms.[1] This prevalence of the duel aroused the Emperor Maximilian, who at the Diet of Worms put forth an ordinance abolishing the right or liberty of Private War, and instituting a Supreme Tribunal for the determination of controversies without appeal to the duel, and the whole long list of duellists, whether corporate or individual, including nobles, bakers, shoe-blacks, and cooks, was brought under its pacific rule. Unhappily the beneficent reform stopped half-way, and here Germany was less fortunate than France. The great provinces were left in the enjoyment of a barbarous independence, with the "right" to fight each other. The duel continued their established arbiter, until at last, in 1815, by the Act of Union constituting the Confederation or United States of Germany, each sovereignty gave up the right of war with its confederates, setting an example to the larger nations. The terms of this important stipulation, marking a stage in German unity, were as follows: —

> "The members of the Confederation further bind themselves under no pretext to make war upon one another, or to pursue their differences by force of arms, but to submit them to the Diet."[2]

Better words could not be found for the United States of Europe, in the establishment of that Great Era when the Duel shall cease to be the recognized Arbiter of Nations.

With this exposition, which I hope is not too long, it is easy to see how completely a war between two

[1] Coxe, History of the House of Austria, (London, 1820,) Ch. XIX., Vol. I. p. 378.

[2] Acte pour la Constitution fédérative de l'Allemagne du 8 Juin 1815, Art. 11: Archives Diplomatiques, (Stuttgart et Tubingue, 1821-36,) Vol. IV. p. 15.

nations is a duel, — and, yet further, how essential it is to that assured peace which civilization requires, that the duel, which is no longer tolerated as arbiter between individuals, between towns, between counties, between provinces, should cease to be tolerated as such between nations. Take our own country, for instance. In a controversy between towns, the local law provides a judicial tribunal; so also in a controversy between counties. Ascending still higher, suppose a controversy between two States of our Union; the National Constitution establishes a judicial tribunal, being the Supreme Court of the United States. But at the next stage there is a change. Let the controversy arise between two nations, and the Supreme Law, which is the Law of Nations, establishes, not a judicial tribunal, but the duel, as arbiter. What is true of our country is true of other countries where civilization has a foothold, and especially of France and Germany. The duel, though abolished as arbiter at home, is continued as arbiter abroad. And since it is recognized by International Law and subjected to a code, it is in all respects an Institution. War is an institution sanctioned by International Law, as Slavery, wherever it exists, is an institution sanctioned by Municipal Law. But this institution is nothing but the duel of the Dark Ages, prolonged into this generation, and showing itself in portentous barbarism.

WHY THIS PARALLEL NOW?

THEREFORE am I right, when I call the existing combat between France and Germany a Duel. I beg you to believe that I do this with no idle purpose of illustration or criticism, but because I would prepare the way for a proper comprehension of the remedy to be applied. How can this terrible controversy be adjusted? I see no practical method, which shall reconcile the sensibilities of France with the guaranties due to Germany, short of a radical change in the War System itself. That Security for the Future which Germany may justly exact can be obtained in no way so well as by the disarmament of France, to be followed naturally by the disarmament of other nations, and the substitution of some peaceful tribunal for the existing Trial by Battle. Any dismemberment, or curtailment of territory, will be poor and inadequate; for it will leave behind a perpetual sting. Something better must be done.

SUDDENNESS OF THIS WAR.

Never in history has so great a calamity descended so suddenly upon the Human Family, unless we except the earthquake toppling down cities and submerging a whole coast in a single night. But how small all that has ensued from any such convulsion, compared with the desolation and destruction already produced by this war! From the first murmur to the outbreak was a brief moment of time, as between the flash of lightning and the bursting of the thunder.

At the beginning of July there was peace without suspicion of interruption. The Legislative Body had just discussed a proposition for the reduction of the annual Army Contingent. At Berlin the Parliament was not in session. Count Bismarck was at his country home in Pomerania, the King enjoying himself at Ems. How sudden and unexpected the change will appear from an illustrative circumstance. M. Prévost-Paradol, of rare talent and unhappy destiny, newly appointed Minister to the United States, embarked at Havre on the 1st of July, and reached Washington on the morning of the 14th of July. He assured me that when he left France there was no talk or thought of war. During his brief summer voyage the whole startling event had begun and culminated. Prince Leopold of Hohenzollern-Sigmaringen being invited to become candidate for the throne of Spain, France promptly sent her defiance to Prussia, followed a few days later by formal Declaration of War. The Minister was oppressed by the grave tidings coming upon him so unprepared, and sought relief in self-slaughter, being the first victim of the war. Everything moved with a rapidity borrowed from the new forces supplied by human invention, and the Gates of War swung wide open.

CHALLENGE TO PRUSSIA.

A FEW incidents exhibit this movement. It was on the 30th of June, while discussing the proposed reduction of the Army, that Émile Ollivier, the Prime-Minister, said openly: "The Government has no kind of disquietude; at no epoch has the maintenance of peace been more assured; on whatever side you look, you see no irritating question under discussion."[1] In the same debate, Garnier-Pagès, the consistent Republican, and now a member of the Provisional Government, after asking, "Why these armaments?" cried out: "Disarm, without waiting for others: this is practical. Let the people be relieved from the taxes which crush them,

[1] Journal Officiel du Soir, 3 Juillet 1870.

and from the heaviest of all, the tax of blood."[1] The candidature of Prince Leopold seems to have become known at Paris on the 5th of July. On the next day the Duc de Gramont, of a family famous in scandalous history, Minister of Foreign Affairs, hurries to the tribune with defiance on his lips. After declaring for the Cabinet that no foreign power could be suffered, by placing one of its princes on the throne of Charles the Fifth, to derange the balance of power in Europe, and put in peril the interests and the honor of France, he concludes by saying, in ominous words: "Strong in your support, Gentlemen, and in that of the nation, we shall know how to do our duty without hesitation and without weakness."[2] This defiance was followed by what is called in the report, "general and prolonged movement, — repeated applause"; and here was the first stage in the duel. Its character was recognized at once in the Chamber. Garnier-Pagès exclaimed, in words worthy of memory: "It is dynastic questions which trouble the peace of Europe. The people have only reason to love and aid each other."[3] Though short, better than many long speeches. Crémieux, an associate in the Provisional Government of 1848, insisted that the utterance of the Minister was "a menace of war"; and Emmanuel Arago, son of the great Republican astronomer and mathematician, said that the Minister "had declared war."[4] These patriotic representatives were not mistaken. The speech made peace difficult, if not impossible. It was a challenge to Prussia.

[1] Journal Officiel du Soir, 2 Juillet 1870.
[2] Ibid., 8 Juillet. [3] Ibid. [4] Ibid.

COMEDY.

Europe watched with dismay as the gauntlet was thus rudely flung down, while on this side of the Atlantic, where France and Germany commingle in the enjoyment of our equal citizenship, the interest was intense. Morning and evening the telegraph made us all partakers of the hopes and fears agitating the world. Too soon it was apparent that the exigence of France would not be satisfied, while already her preparations for war were undisguised. At all the naval stations, from Toulon to Cherbourg, the greatest activity prevailed. Marshal MacMahon was recalled from Algeria, and transports were made ready to bring back the troops from that colony.

Meanwhile the candidature of Prince Leopold was renounced by him. But this was not enough. The King of Prussia was asked to promise that it should in no event ever be renewed, — which he declined to do, reserving to himself the liberty of consulting circumstances. This requirement was the more offensive, inasmuch as it was addressed exclusively to Prussia, while nothing was said to Spain, the principal in the business. Then ensued an incident proper for comedy, if it had not become the declared cause of tragedy. The French Ambassador, Count Benedetti, who, on intelligence of the candidature, had followed the King to Ems, his favorite watering-place, and there in successive interviews pressed him to order its withdrawal, now, on its voluntary renunciation, proceeding to urge the new demand, and after an extended conversation, and notwithstanding its decided refusal, seeking, nevertheless, another audience the same day on this subject, his Majesty, with perfect politeness, sent him word by an adjutant in attendance, that he had no other answer to make than the one already given: and this refusal to receive the Ambassador was promptly communicated by telegraph, for the information especially of the different German governments.[1]

PRETEXT OF THE TELEGRAM.

THESE simple facts, insufficient for the slightest quarrel, intolerable in the pettiness of the issue disclosed, and monstrous as reason for war between two civilized nations, became the welcome pretext. Swiftly, and with ill-disguised alacrity, the French Cabinet took the next step in the duel. On the 15th of July the Prime-Minister read from the tribune a manifesto setting forth the griefs of France, — being, first, the refusal of the Prussian King to promise for the future, and, secondly, his refusal to receive the French Ambassador, with the communication of this refusal, as was alleged, "officially to the Cabinets of Europe," which was a mistaken allegation:[2] and the paper concludes by announcing that since the preceding day the Government had called in the reserves, and that they would immediately take the measures necessary to secure the interests, the safety, and the honor of France.[3] This was war.

[1] Bismarck to Bernstorff, July 19, 1870, with Inclosures: Parliamentary Papers, 1870, Vol. LXX., — Franco-Prussian War, No. 3, pp. 5-8. Gerolt to Fish, August 11, 1870, with Inclosures: Executive Documents, 41st Cong. 3d Sess., H. of R., Vol. I. No. 1, Part 1, — Foreign Relations, pp. 219-221. The reader will notice that the copy of the Telegram in this latter volume is the paper on p. 221, with the erroneous heading, "*Count Bismarck to Baron Gerolt.*"

[2] Bismarck to Bernstorff, July 18, and to Gerolt, July 19, 1870: Parliamentary Papers and Executive Documents, Inclosures, *ubi supra.*

[3] Journal Officiel du Soir, 17 Juillet 1870.

Some there were who saw the fearful calamity, the ghastly crime, then and there initiated. The scene that ensued belongs to this painful record. The paper announcing war was followed by prolonged applause. The Prime-Minister added soon after in debate, that he accepted the responsibility with "a light heart."[1] Not all were in this mood. Esquiros, the Republican, cried from his seat, in momentous words, "You have a light heart, and the blood of nations is about to flow!" To the apology of the Prime-Minister, "that in the discharge of a duty the heart is not troubled," Jules Favre, the Republican leader, of acknowledged moderation and ability, flashed forth, "When the discharge of this duty involves the slaughter of two nations, one may well have the heart troubled!" Beyond these declarations, giving utterance to the natural sentiments of humanity, was the positive objection, most forcibly presented by Thiers, so famous in the Chamber and in literature, "that the satisfaction due to France had been accorded her, — that Prussia had expiated by a check the grave fault she had committed," — that France had prevailed in substance, and all that remained was "a question of form," "a question of susceptibility," "questions of etiquette." The experienced statesman asked for the dispatches. Then came a confession. The Prime-Minister replied, that he had "nothing to communicate, — that, in the true sense of the term, there had been no dispatches, — that there were only verbal communications gathered up in reports, which, according to diplomatic usage, are not communicated." Here Emmanuel Arago interrupted: "It is on these reports that you make war!" The

1 "De ce jour commence pour les ministres mes collègues, et pour moi, une grande responsibilité. ["Oui!" *à gauche.*] Nous l'acceptons, le cœur léger."

Prime-Minister proceeded to read two brief telegrams from Count Benedetti at Ems, when De Choiseul very justly exclaimed: "We cannot make war on that ground; it is impossible!" Others cried out from their seats,— Garnier-Pagès saying, "These are phrases"; Emmanuel Arago protesting, "On this the civilized world will pronounce you wrong"; to which Jules Favre added, "Unhappily, true!" Thiers and Jules Favre, with vigorous eloquence, charged the war upon the Cabinet: Thiers declaring, "I regret to be obliged to say that we have war by the fault of the Cabinet"; Jules Favre alleging, "If we have war, it is thanks to the politics of the Cabinet; . . . . from the exposition that has been made, so far as the general interests of the two countries are concerned, there is no avowable motive for war." Girault exclaimed, in similar spirit: "We would be among the first to come forward in a war for the country, but we do not wish to come forward in a dynastic and aggressive war." The Duc de Gramont, who on the 6th of July flung down the gauntlet, spoke once more for the Cabinet, stating solemnly, what was not the fact, that the Prussian Government had communicated to all the Cabinets of Europe the refusal to receive the French Ambassador, and then on this misstatement ejaculating: "It is an outrage on the Emperor and on France; and if, by impossibility, there were found in my country a Chamber to bear and tolerate it, I would not remain five minutes Minister of Foreign Affairs." In our country we have seen how the Southern heart was fired; so also was fired the heart of France. The Duke descended from the tribune amidst prolonged applause, with cries of "Bravo!"—and at his seat (so says the report) "received numerous felicitations." Such was the atmosphere of the Chamber at this eventful moment. The orators of the Opposition, pleading for delay in the interest of peace, were stifled; and when Gambetta, the young and fearless Republican, made himself heard in calling for the text of the dispatch communicating the refusal to receive the Ambassador, to the end that the Chamber, France, and all Europe might judge of its character, he was answered by the Prime-Minister with the taunt that "for the first time in a French Assembly there were such difficulties on a certain side in explaining *a question of honor*." Such was the case as presented by the Prime-Minister, and on this question of honor he accepted war "with a light heart." Better say, with no heart at all;—for whoso could find in this condition of things sufficient reason for war was without heart.[1]

During these brief days of solicitude, from the 6th to the 15th of July, England made an unavailing effort for peace. Lord Lyons was indefatigable; and he was sustained at home by Lord Granville, who as a last resort reminded the two parties of the stipulation at the Congress of Paris, which they had accepted, in favor of Arbitration as a substitute for War, and asked them to accept the good offices of some friendly power.[2] This most reasonable proposition was rejected by the French Minister, who gave new point to the French case by charging that Prussia "had chosen to declare that France had been affronted in the person of her Ambassador," and then positively insisting that "it was this boast which was the *gravamen* of the offence." Capping

[1] For the full debate, see the *Journal Officiel du Soir*, 17 Juillet 1870, and *Supplément*.

[2] Earl Granville to Lords Lyons and Loftus, July 15, 1870,—Correspondence respecting the Negotiations preliminary to the War between France and Prussia, p. 35: Parliamentary Papers, 1870, Vol. LXX.

the climax of barbarous absurdity, the French Minister did not hesitate to announce that this "constituted an insult which no nation of any spirit could brook, and rendered it, much to the regret of the French Government, impossible to take into consideration the mode of settling the original matter in dispute which was recommended by her Majesty's Government."[1] Thus was peaceful Arbitration repelled. All honor to the English Government for proposing it!

The famous telegram put forward by France as the *gravamen*, or chief offence, was not communicated to the Chamber. The Prime-Minister, though hard-pressed, held it back. Was it from conviction of its too trivial character? But it is not lost to the history of the duel. This telegram, with something of the brevity peculiar to telegraphic dispatches, merely reports the refusal to see the French Ambassador, without one word of affront or boast. It reports the fact, and nothing else; and it is understood that the refusal was only when this functionary presented himself a second time in one day on the same business. Considering the interests involved, it would have been better, had the King seen him as many times as he chose to call; yet the refusal was not unnatural. The perfect courtesy of his Majesty on this occasion furnished no cause of complaint. All that remained for pretext was the telegram.[2]

[1] Lord Lyons to Earl Granville, July 15, 1870, — Correspondence respecting the Negotiations preliminary to the War between France and Prussia, pp. 39, 40 : Parliamentary Papers, 1870, Vol. LXX.

[2] See references, *ante*, p. 19, Note 1. For this telegram in the original, see Aegidi und Klauhold, *Staatsarchiv*, (Hamburg, 1870,) 19 Band, s. 44, No. 4033.

FORMAL DECLARATION OF WAR.

THE scene in the Legislative Body was followed by the instant introduction of bills making additional appropriations for the Army and Navy, calling out the National Guard, and authorizing volunteers for the war. This last proposition was commended by the observation that in France there were a great many young people liking powder, but not liking barracks, who would in this way be suited; and this was received with applause.[1] On the 18th of July there was a further appropriation to the extent of 500 million francs,—440 millions being for the Army, and 60 for the Navy; and an increase from 150 to 500 millions Treasury notes was authorized.[2] On the 20th of July the Duc de Gramont appeared once more in the tribune, and made the following speech:—

"Conformably to customary rules, and by order of the Emperor, I have invited the *Chargé d'Affaires* of France to notify the Berlin Cabinet of our resolution to seek by arms the guaranties which we have not been able to obtain by discussion. This step has been taken, and I have the honor of making known to the Legislative Body that in consequence a state of war exists between France and Prussia, beginning the 19th of July. This declaration applies equally to the allies of Prussia who lend her the coöperation of their arms against us."[3]

Here the French Minister played the part of trumpeter in the duel, making proclamation before his champion rode forward. According to the statement of Count Bismarck, made to the Parliament at Berlin, this formal

1 Journal Officiel du Soir, 17 Juillet 1870.
2 Ibid., 20 Juillet. 3 Ibid., 23 Juillet.

Declaration of War was the solitary official communication from France in this whole transaction, being the first and only note since the candidature of Prince Leopold.[1] How swift this madness will be seen in a few dates. On the 6th of July was uttered the first defiance from the French tribune; on the 15th of July an exposition of the griefs of France, in the nature of a Declaration of War, with a demand for men and money; on the 19th of July a state of war was declared to exist.

Firmly, but in becoming contrast with the "light heart" of France, this was promptly accepted by Germany, whose heart and strength found expression in the speech of the King at the opening of Parliament, hastily assembled on the 19th of July. With articulation disturbed by emotion and with moistened eyes, his Majesty said: —

"Supported by the unanimous will of the German governments of the South as of the North, we turn the more confidently to the love of Fatherland and the cheerful self-devotion of the German people, with a call to the defence of their honor and their independence."[2]

Parliament responded sympathetically to the King, and made the necessary appropriations. And thus the two champions stood front to front.

[1] Substance of Speech of Bismarck to the Reichstag, [July 20, 1870,] explanatory of Documents relating to the Declaration of War, — Franco-Prussian War, No. 3, p. 29: Parliamentary Papers, 1870, Vol. LXX. Discours du Comte de Bismarck au Reichstag, le 20 Juillet 1870: Angeberg, [Chodzko,] Recueil des Traités, etc., concernant la Guerre Franco-Allemande, Tom. I. p. 215.

[2] Aegidi und Klauhold, Staatsarchiv, 19 Band, s. 107, No. 4056. Parliamentary Papers, 1870, Vol. LXX.: Franco-Prussian War, No. 3, pp. 2–3.

THE TWO HOSTILE PARTIES.

THROUGHOUT France, throughout Germany, the trumpet sounded, and everywhere the people sprang to arms, as if the great horn of Orlando, after a sleep of ages, had sent forth once more its commanding summons. Not a town, not a village, that the voice did not penetrate. Modern invention had supplied an ally beyond anything in fable. From all parts of France, from all parts of Germany, armed men leaped forward, leaving behind the charms of peace and the business of life. On each side the muster was mighty, armies counting by the hundred thousand. And now, before we witness the mutual slaughter, let us pause to consider the two parties, and the issue between them.

France and Germany are most unlike, and yet the peers of each other, while among the nations they are unsurpassed in civilization, each prodigious in resources, splendid in genius, and great in renown. No two nations are so nearly matched. By Germany I now mean not only the States constituting North Germany, but also Würtemberg, Baden, and Bavaria of South Germany, allies in the present war, all of which together make about fifty-three millions of French hectares, being very nearly the area of France. The population of each is not far from thirty-eight millions, and it would be difficult to say which is the larger. Looking at finances, Germany has the smaller revenue, but also the smaller debt, while her rulers, following the sentiment of the people, cultivate a wise economy, so that here again substantial equality is maintained with France. The armies of the two, embracing regular troops and those subject to call, did not differ much in numbers, unless we set aside the authority of the "Almanach de Gotha," which puts the military force of France somewhat vaguely at 1,350,000, while that of North Germany is only 977,262, to which must be added 49,949 for Bavaria, 34,953 for Würtemberg, and 43,703 for Baden, making a sum-total of 1,105,867. This, however, is chiefly on paper, where it is evident France is stronger than in reality. Her available force at the outbreak of the war probably did not amount to more than 350,000 bayonets, while that of Germany, owing to her superior system, was as much as double this number. In Prussia every man is obliged to serve, and, still further, every man is educated. Discipline and education are two potent adjuncts. This is favorable to Germany. In the Chassepot and needle-gun the two are equal. But France excels in a well-appointed Navy, having no less than 55 iron-clads, and 384 other vessels of war, while Germany has but 2 iron-clads, and 87 other vessels of war.[1] Then again for long generations has existed another disparity, to the great detriment of Germany. France has been a nation, while Germany has been divided, and therefore weak. Strong in union, the latter now claims something more than that *dominion of the air* once declared to be hers, while France had the land and England the sea.[2] The dominion of the land is at last contested, and we are saddened inexpressibly, that, from the elevation they

[1] For the foregoing statistics, see *Almanach de Gotha*, 1870, under the names of the several States referred to, — also, for Areas and Population, *Tableaux Comparatifs*, I., II., III., in same volume, pp. 1037 - 38.

[2] "So wie die Franzosen die Herren des Landes sind, die Engländer die des grössern Meeres, wir die der Beide und Alles umfassenden Luft sind." — RICHTER, (Jean Paul,) *Frieden-Predigt an Deutschland*, V.: Sämmtliche Werke, (Berlin, 1826 - 38,) Theil XXXIV. s. 13.

have reached, these two peers of civilization can descend to practise the barbarism of war, and especially that the land of Descartes, Pascal, Voltaire, and Laplace must challenge to bloody duel the land of Luther, Leibnitz, Kant, and Humboldt.

FOLLY.

PLAINLY between these two neighboring powers there has been unhappy antagonism, constant, if not increasing, partly from the memory of other days, and partly because France could not bear to witness that German unity which was a national right and duty. Often it has been said that war was inevitable. But it has come at last by surprise, and on "a question of form." So it was called by Thiers; so it was recognized by Ollivier, when he complained of insensibility to a question of honor; and so also by the Duc de Gramont, when he referred it all to a telegram. This is not the first time in history that wars have been waged on trifles; but since the Lord of Frauenstein challenged the free city of Frankfort because a young lady of the city refused to dance with his uncle, nothing has passed more absurd than this challenge sent by France to Germany because the King of Prussia refused to see the French Ambassador a second time on the same matter, and then let the refusal be reported by telegraph. Here is the folly exposed by Shakespeare, when Hamlet touches a madness greater than his own in that spirit which would "find quarrel in a straw when honor 's at the stake," and at the same time depicts an army

"Led by a delicate and tender prince,
. . . . .
Exposing what is mortal and unsure
To all that Fortune, Death, and Danger dare,
Even for an egg-shell."

There can be no quarrel in a straw or for an egg-shell, unless men have gone mad. Nor can honor in a civilized age require any sacrifice of reason or humanity.

UNJUST PRETENSION OF FRANCE TO INTERFERE WITH THE CANDIDATURE OF HOHENZOLLERN.

If the utter triviality of the pretext were left doubtful in the debate, if its towering absurdity were not plainly apparent, if its simple wickedness did not already stand before us, we should find all these characteristics glaringly manifest in that unjust pretension which preceded the objection of form, on which France finally acted. A few words will make this plain.

In a happy moment Spain rose against Queen Isabella, and, amidst cries of "Down with the Bourbons!" drove her from the throne which she dishonored. This was in September, 1868. Instead of constituting a Republic at once, in harmony with those popular rights which had been proclaimed, the half-hearted leaders proceeded to look about for a King; and from that time till now they have been in this quest, as if it were the Holy Grail, or happiness on earth. The royal family of Spain was declared incompetent. Therefore a king must be found outside, — and so the quest was continued in other lands. One day the throne is offered to a prince of Portugal, then to a prince of Italy, but declined by each, — how wisely the future will show. At last, after a protracted pursuit of nearly two years, the venturesome soldier who is Captain-General and Prime-Minister, Marshal Prim, conceives the idea of offering it to a prince of Germany. His luckless victim is Prince Leopold of Hohenzollern-Sigmaringen, a

Catholic, thirty-five years of age, and colonel of the first regiment of the Prussian foot-guards, whose father, a mediatized German prince, resides at Düsseldorf. The Prince had not the good sense to decline. How his acceptance excited the French Cabinet, and became the beginning of the French pretext, I have already exposed; and now I come to the pretension itself.

By what title did France undertake to interfere with the choice of Spain? If the latter was so foolish as to seek a foreigner for king, making a German first among Spaniards, by what title did any other power attempt to control its will? To state the question is to answer it. Beginning with an outrage on Spanish independence, which the Spain of an earlier day would have resented, the next outrage was on Germany, in assuming that an insignificant prince of that country could not be permitted to accept the invitation, — all of which, besides being of insufferable insolence, was in that worst dynastic spirit which looks to princes rather than the people. Plainly France was unjustifiable. When I say it was none of her business, I give it the mildest condemnation. This was the first step in her monstrous *blunder-crime.*

Its character as a pretext becomes painfully manifest, when we learn more of the famous Prince Leopold, thus invited by Spain and opposed by France. It is true that his family name is in part the same as that of the Prussian king. Each is Hohenzollern; but he adds Sigmaringen to the name. The two are different branches of the same family; but you must ascend to the twelfth century, counting more than twenty degrees, before you come to a common ancestor.[1] And yet on this most

[1] Conversations-Lexikon, (Leipzig, 1866,) 8 Band, art. HOHENZOLLERN. Carlyle's History of Friedrich II., (London, 1858,) Book III. Ch. 1, Vol. I. p. 200.

distant and infinitesimal relationship the French pretension is founded. But audacity changes to the ridiculous, when it is known that the Prince is nearer in relationship to the French Emperor than to the Prussian King, and this by three different intermarriages, which do not go back to the twelfth century. Here is the case. His grandfather had for wife a niece of Joachim Murat,[1] King of Naples, and brother-in-law of the first Napoleon; and his father had for wife a daughter of Stéphanie de Beauharnais, an adopted daughter of the first Napoleon; so that Prince Leopold is by his father great-grand-nephew of Murat, and by his mother he is grandson of Stéphanie de Beauharnais, who was cousin and by adoption sister of Hortense de Beauharnais, mother of the present Emperor; and to this may be added still another connection, by the marriage of his father's sister with Joachim Napoleon, Marquis of Pepoli, grandson of Joachim Murat.[2] It was natural that a person thus connected with the Imperial Family should be a welcome visitor at the Tuileries; and it is easy to believe that Marshal Prim, who offered him the throne, was encouraged to believe that the Emperor's kinsman and guest would be favorably regarded by France. And yet, in the face of these things, and the three several family ties, fresh and modern, binding him to France and the French Emperor, the pretension was set up that his occupation of the Spanish throne would put in peril the interests and the honor of France.

1 Antoinette, daughter of Étienne Murat, third brother of Joachim. — *Biographie Générale*, (Didot,) Tom. XXXVI. col. 984, art. MURAT, note.

2 Almanach de Gotha, 1870, pp. 85–87, art. HOHENZOLLERN-SIGMARINGEN.

BECAUSE FRANCE WAS READY.

In sending defiance to Prussia on this question, the French Cabinet selected their own ground. Evidently a war had been meditated, and the candidature of Prince Leopold from beginning to end supplied a pretext. In this conclusion, which is too obvious, we are hardly left to inference. The secret was disclosed by Rouher, President of the Senate, lately the eloquent and unscrupulous Minister, when, in an official address to the Emperor, immediately after the War Manifesto read by the Prime-Minister, he declared that France quivered with indignation at the flights of an ambition over-excited by the one day's good-fortune at Sadowa, and then proceeded:—

"Animated by that calm perseverance which is true force, your Majesty has known how to wait; but in the last four years you have carried to its highest perfection the arming of our soldiers, and raised to its full power the organization of our military forces. *Thanks to your care, Sire, France is ready.*"[1]

Thus, according to the President of the Senate, France, after waiting, commenced war because she was ready,— while, according to the Cabinet, it was on the point of honor. Both were right. The war was declared because the Emperor thought himself ready, and a pretext was found in the affair of the telegram.

Considering the age, and the present demands of civilization, such a war stands forth terrific in wrong, making the soul rise indignant against it. One reason avowed is brutal; the other is frivolous; both are criminal. If we look into the text of the Manifesto

1 Address at the Palais de Saint-Cloud, July 16, 1870: Journal Officiel du Soir, 18 Juillet 1870.

and the speeches of the Cabinet, it is a war founded on a trifle, on a straw, on an egg-shell. Obviously these were pretexts only. Therefore it is a war of pretexts, the real object being the humiliation and dismemberment of Germany, in the vain hope of exalting the French Empire and perpetuating a bawble crown on the head of a boy. By military success and a peace dictated at Berlin, the Emperor trusted to find himself in such condition, that, on return to Paris, he could overthrow parliamentary government so far as it existed there, and reëstablish personal government, where all depended upon himself,—thus making triumph over Germany the means of another triumph over the French people.

In other times there have been wars as criminal in origin, where trifle, straw, or egg-shell played its part; but they contrasted less with the surrounding civilization. To this list belong the frequent Dynastic Wars, prompted by the interest, the passion, or the whim of some one in the Family of Kings. Others have begun in recklessness kindred to that we now witness,—as when England entered into war with Holland, and for reason did not hesitate to allege "abusive pictures."[1] The England of Charles the Second was

[1] Hume, History of England, Ch. LXV., March 17, 1672.—The terms of the Declaration on this point were,—"Scarce a town within their territories that is not filled with abusive pictures." (Hansard's *Parliamentary History*, Vol. IV. col. 514.) Upon which Hume remarks: "The Dutch were long at a loss what to make of this article, till it was discovered that a portrait of Cornelius de Witt, brother to the Pensionary, painted by order of certain magistrates of Dort, and hung up in a chamber of the Town-House, had given occasion to the complaint. In the perspective of this portrait the painter had drawn some ships on fire in a harbor. This was construed to be Chatham, where De Witt had really distinguished himself," during the previous war, in the way here indicated,—"the disgrace" of which, says Lingard, "sunk deep into the heart of the King and the hearts of his subjects."—*History of England*, Vol. IX. Ch. III., June 13, 1667.

hardly less sensitive than the France of Louis Napoleon, while in each was similar indifference to consequences. But France has precedents of her own. From the remarkable correspondence of the Princess Palatine, Duchess of Orléans, we learn that the first war with Holland under Louis the Fourteenth was brought on by the Minister, De Lionne, to injure a petty German prince who had made him jealous of his wife.[1] The communicative and exuberant Saint-Simon tells us twice over how Louvois, another Minister of Louis the Fourteenth, being overruled by his master with regard to the dimensions of a window at Versailles, was filled with the idea that "on account of a few inches in a window," as he expressed it, all his services would be forgotten, and therefore, to save his place, excited a foreign war that would make him necessary to the King. The flames in the Palatinate, devouring the works of man, attested his continuing power. The war became general, but, according to the chronicler, it ruined France at home, and did not extend her domain abroad.[2] The French Emperor confidently expected to occupy the same historic region so often burnt and ravaged by French armies, with that castle of Heidelberg which repeats the tale of blood, — and, let me say, expected it for no better reason than that of his royal predecessor, stimulated by an unprincipled Minister anxious for personal position. The parallel is continued in the curse which the Imperial arms have brought on France.

[1] Briefe der Prinzessin Elisabeth Charlotte von Orleans an die Raugräfin Louise, 1676-1722, herausg. von W. Menzel, (Stuttgart, 1843,) — Paris, 31 Mertz, 1718, s. 288.

[2] Mémoires, (Paris, 1829,) Tom. VII. pp. 49-51; XIII. pp. 9-10.

PROGRESS OF THE WAR.

How this war proceeded I need not recount. You have all read the record day by day, sorrowing for Humanity, — how, after briefest interval of preparation or hesitation, the two combatants first crossed swords at Saarbrücken, within the German frontier, and the young Prince Imperial performed his part in picking up a bullet from the field, which the Emperor promptly reported by telegraph to the Empress, — how this little military success is all that was vouchsafed to the man who began the war, — how soon thereafter victory followed, first on the hill-sides of Wissembourg and then of Woerth, shattering the army of MacMahon, to which the Empire was looking so confidently, — how another large army under Bazaine was driven within the strong fortress of Metz, — how all the fortresses, bristling with guns and frowning upon Germany, were invested, — how battle followed battle on various fields, where Death was the great conqueror, — how, with help of modern art, war showed itself to be murder by machinery, — how MacMahon, gathering together his scattered men and strengthening them with reinforcements, attempted to relieve Bazaine, — how at last, after long marches, his large army found itself shut up at Sedan with a tempest of fire beating upon its huddled ranks, so that its only safety was capitulation, — how with the capitulation of the army was the submission of the Emperor himself, who gave his sword to the King of Prussia and became prisoner of war, — and how, on the reception of this news at Paris, Louis Napoleon and his dynasty were divested of their powers and the Empire was lost in the Republic. These things you know. I need not dwell on them. Not to battles and their fearful vicissitudes, where all is incarnadined with blood, must we look, but to the ideas which prevail, — as for the measure of time we look, not to the pendulum in its oscillations, but to the clock in the tower, whose striking tells the hours. A great hour for Humanity sounded when the Republic was proclaimed. And this I say, even should it fail again; for every attempt contributes to the final triumph.

A WAR OF SURPRISES.

THE war, from the pretext at its beginning to the capitulation at Sedan, has been a succession of surprises, where the author of the pretext was a constant sufferer. Nor is this strange. Falstaff says, with humorous point, "See now how wit may be made a Jack-a-lent, when 't is upon ill employment!"[1] — and another character, in a play of Beaumont and Fletcher, reveals the same evil destiny in stronger terms, when he says, —

> "Hell gives us art to reach the depth of sin,
> But leaves us wretched fools, when we are in."[2]

And this was precisely the condition of the French Empire. Germany perhaps had one surprise, at the sudden adoption of the pretext for war. But the Empire has known nothing but surprise. A fatal surprise was the promptitude with which all the German States, outside of Austrian rule, accepted the leadership of Prussia, and joined their forces to hers. Differences were forgotten, — whether the hate of Hanover, the

[1] Merry Wives of Windsor, Act V. Sc. 5.
[2] Queen of Corinth, Act IV. Sc. 3.

dread of Würtemberg, the coolness of Bavaria, the opposition of Saxony, or the impatience of the Hanse Towns at lost importance. Hanover would not rise; the other States and cities would not be detached. On the day after the reading of the War Manifesto at the French tribune, even before the King's speech to the Northern Parliament, the Southern States began to move. German unity stood firm, and this was the supreme surprise for France with which the war began. On one day the Emperor in his Official Journal declares his object to be the deliverance of Bavaria from Prussian oppression, and on the very next day the Crown Prince of Prussia, at the head of Bavarian troops, crushes an Imperial army.

Then came the manifest inferiority of the Imperial army, everywhere outnumbered, which was another surprise, — the manifest inferiority of the Imperial artillery, also a surprise, — the manifest inferiority of the Imperial generals, still a surprise. Above these was a prevailing inefficiency and improvidence, which very soon became conspicuous, and this was a surprise. The strength of Germany, as now exhibited, was a surprise. And when the German armies entered France, every step was a surprise. Wissembourg was a surprise; so was Woerth; so was Beaumont; so was Sedan. Every encounter was a surprise. Abel Douay, the French general, who fell bravely fighting at Wissembourg, the first sacrifice on the battle-field, was surprised; so was MacMahon, not only at the beginning, but at the end. He thought that the King and Crown Prince were marching on Paris. So they were, — but they turned aside for a few days to surprise a whole army of more than a hundred thousand men, terrible with cannon and newly invented implements of war, under a Marshal of France, and with an Emperor besides. As this succession of surprises was crowned with what seemed the greatest surprise of all, there remained a greater still in the surprise of the French Empire. No Greek Nemesis with unrelenting hand ever dealt more incessantly the unavoidable blow, until the Empire fell as a dead body falls, while the Emperor became a captive and the Empress a fugitive, with their only child a fugitive also. The poet says:—

> "Sometime let gorgeous Tragedy
> In sceptred pall come sweeping by."[1]

It has swept before the eyes of all. Beneath that sceptred pall is the dust of a great Empire, founded and ruled by Louis Napoleon; if not the dust of the Emperor also, it is because he was willing to sacrifice others rather than himself.

OTHER FRENCH SOVEREIGNS CAPTURED ON THE BATTLE-FIELD.

TWICE before have French sovereigns yielded on the battle-field, and become prisoners of war; but never before was capitulation so vast. Do their fates furnish any lesson? At the Battle of Poitiers, memorable in English history, John, King of France, became the prisoner of Edward the Black Prince. His nobles, one after another, fell by his side, but he contended valiantly to the last, until, spent with fatigue and overcome by numbers, he surrendered. His son, of the same age as the son of the French Emperor, was

[1] Milton, Il Penseroso, 97-98.

wounded while battling for his father. The courtesy of the English Prince conquered more than his arms. I quote the language of Hume: —

> "More touched by Edward's generosity than by his own calamities, he confessed, that, notwithstanding his defeat and captivity, his honor was still unimpaired, and that, if he yielded the victory, it was at least gained by a prince of such consummate valor and humanity."[1]

The King was taken to England, where, after swelling the triumphal pageant of his conqueror, he made a disgraceful treaty for the dismemberment of France, which the indignant nation would not ratify. A captivity of more than four years was terminated by a ransom of three million crowns in gold, — an enormous sum, more than ten million dollars in our day. Evidently the King was unfortunate, for he did not continue in France, but, under the influence of motives differently stated, returned to England, where he died. Surely here is a lesson.

More famous than John was Francis, with salamander crest, also King of France, and rich in gayety, whose countenance, depicted by that art of which he was the patron, stands forth conspicuous in the line of kings. As the French Emperor attacked Germany, so did the King enter Italy, and he was equally confident of victory. On the field of Pavia he encountered an army of Charles the Fifth, but commanded by his generals, when, after fighting desperately and killing seven men with his own hand, he was compelled to surrender. His mother was at the time Regent of France, and to

[1] History of England, (Oxford, 1826,) Ch. XVI., Vol. II. p. 407.

her he is said to have written the sententious letter, "All is lost except honor." No such letter was written by Francis,[1] nor do we know of any such letter by Louis Napoleon; but the situation of the two Regents was identical. Here are the words in which Hume describes the condition of the earlier: —

"The Princess was struck with the greatness of the calamity. She saw the kingdom without a sovereign, without an army, without generals, without money, surrounded on every side by implacable and victorious enemies; and her chief resource, in her present distresses, were the hopes which she entertained of peace, and even of assistance from the King of England."[2]

Francis became the prisoner of Charles the Fifth, and was conveyed to Madrid, where, after a year of captivity, he was at length released, crying out, as he crossed the French frontier, "Behold me King again!"[3] Is not the fate of Louis Napoleon prefigured in the exile and death of his royal predecessor John, rather than in the return of Francis with his delighted cry?

LOUIS NAPOLEON.

THE fall of Louis Napoleon is natural. It is hard to see how it could be otherwise, so long as we continue to

"assert eternal Providence,
And justify the ways of God to men."[4]

Had he remained successful to the end, and died peace-

[1] Sismondi, Histoire des Français, Tom. XVI. pp. 241–42. Martin, Histoire de France, (4ème édit.,) Tom. VIII. pp. 67, 68.

[2] History of England, (Oxford, 1826,) Ch. XXIX., Vol. IV. p. 51.

[3] Sismondi, Tom. XVI. p. 277. Martin, Tom. VIII. p. 90.

[4] Paradise Lost, Book I. 25–26.

fully on the throne, his name would have been a perpetual encouragement to dishonesty and crime. By treachery without parallel, breaking repeated promises and his oath of office, he was able to trample on the Republic. Taking his place in the National Assembly after long exile, the adventurer made haste to declare exultation in regaining his country and all his rights as citizen, with the ejaculation, "The Republic has given me this happiness: let the Republic receive my oath of gratitude, my oath of devotion!" — and next he proclaimed that there was nobody to surpass him in determined consecration "to the defence of order and to the establishment of the Republic."[1] Good words these. Then again, when candidate for the Presidency, in a manifesto to the electors he gave another pledge, announcing that he "would devote himself altogether, without mental reservation, to the establishment of a Republic, wise in its laws, honest in its intentions, great and strong in its acts"; and he volunteered further words, binding him in special loyalty, saying that he "should make it *a point of honor* to leave to his successor, at the end of four years, power strengthened, liberty intact, real progress accomplished."[2] How these plain and unequivocal engagements were openly broken you shall see.

Chosen by the popular voice, his inauguration took place as President of the Republic, when he solemnly renewed the engagements already assumed. Ascending from his seat in the Assembly to the tribune, and holding up his hand, he took the following oath of office: "In presence of God, and before the French people,

[1] Séance du 26 Septembre 1848: Moniteur, 27 Septembre.

[2] A ses Concitoyens: Œuvres, Tom. III. p. 25.

represented by the National Assembly, I swear to remain faithful to the Democratic Republic One and Indivisible, and to fulfil all the duties which the Constitution imposes upon me." This was an oath. Then, addressing the Assembly, he said: "The suffrages of the nation and the oath which I have just taken prescribe my future conduct. My duty is marked out. I will fulfil it as *a man of honor*." Again he attests his honor. Then, after deserved tribute to his immediate predecessor and rival, General Cavaignac, on his loyalty of character, and that sentiment of duty which he declares to be "the first quality in the chief of a State," he renews his vows to the Republic, saying, "We have, Citizen Representatives, a great mission to fulfil; it is to found a Republic in the interest of all"; and he closed amidst cheers for the Republic.[1] And yet, in the face of this oath of office and this succession of most solemn pledges, where he twice attests his honor, he has hardly become President before he commences plotting to make himself Emperor, until, at last, by violence and blood, with brutal butchery in the streets of Paris, he succeeded in overthrowing the Republic, to which he was bound by obligations of gratitude and duty, as well as by engagements in such various form. The Empire was declared. Then followed his marriage, and a dynastic ambition to assure the crown for his son.

Early in life a "Charcoal" conspirator against kings,[2] he now became a crowned conspirator against republics. The name of Republic was to him a reproof, while its glory was a menace. Against the Roman Republic he conspired early; and when the rebellion waged

[1] Séance du 20 Décembre 1848: Moniteur, 21 Décembre.

[2] A member of the secret society of the *Carbonari* in Italy.

by Slavery seemed to afford opportunity, he conspired against our Republic, promoting as far as he dared the independence of the Slave States, and at the same time on the ruins of the Mexican Republic setting up a mock Empire. In similar spirit has he conspired against German Unity, whose just strength promised to be a wall against his unprincipled self-seeking.

This is but an outline of that incomparable perfidy, which, after a career of seeming success, is brought to a close. Of a fallen man I would say nothing; but, for the sake of Humanity, Louis Napoleon should be exposed. He was of evil example, extending with his influence. To measure the vastness of this detriment is impossible. In sacrificing the Republic to his own aggrandizement, in ruling for a dynasty rather than the people, in subordinating the peace of the world to his own wicked ambition for his boy, he set an example of selfishness, and in proportion to his triumph was mankind corrupted in its judgment of human conduct. Teaching men to seek ascendency at the expense of duty, he demoralized not only France, but the world. Unquestionably part of this evil example was his falsehood to the Republic. Promise, pledge, honor, oath, were all violated in this monstrous treason. Never in history was greater turpitude. Unquestionably he could have saved the Republic, but he preferred his own exaltation. As I am a Republican, and believe republican institutions for the good of mankind, I cannot pardon the traitor. The people of France are ignorant; he did not care to have them educated, for their ignorance was his strength. With education bestowed, the Republic would have been assured. And even after the Empire, had he thought more of education and less of his dynasty, there would have been a civilization throughout France making war impossible. Unquestionably the present war is his work, instituted for his imagined advantage. Bacon, in one of his remarkable Essays, tells us that "Extreme self-lovers will set an house on fire, and it were but to roast their eggs."[1] Louis Napoleon has set Europe on fire to roast his.

Beyond the continuing offence of his public life, I charge upon him three special and unpardonable crimes: first, that violation of public duty and public faith, contrary to all solemnities of promise, by which the whole order of society was weakened and human character was degraded; secondly, disloyalty to republican institutions, so that through him the Republic has been arrested in Europe; and, thirdly, this cruel and causeless war, of which he is the guilty author.

RETRIBUTION.

Of familiar texts in Scripture, there is one which, since the murderous outbreak, has been of constant applicability and force. You know it: "All they that take the sword shall perish with the sword":[2] and these words are addressed to nations as to individuals. France took the sword against Germany, and now lies bleeding at every pore. Louis Napoleon took the sword, and is nought. Already in that *coup d'état* by which he overthrew the Republic he took the sword, and now the Empire, which was the work of his hands, expires. In Mexico again he took the sword, and again paid the fearful penalty, — while the Austrian Archduke, who,

1 Of Wisdom for a Man's Self: Essay XXIII.

2 Matthew, xxvi. 52.

yielding to his pressure, made himself Emperor there, was shot by order of the Mexican President, an Indian of unmixed blood. And here there was retribution, not only for the French Emperor, but far beyond. I know not if there be invisible threads by which the Present is attached to the distant Past, making the descendant suffer even for a distant ancestor, but I cannot forget that Maximilian was derived from that very family of Charles the Fifth, whose conquering general, Cortés, stretched the Indian Guatemozin upon a bed of fire, and afterwards executed him on a tree. The death of Maximilian was tardy retribution for the death of Guatemozin. And thus in this world is wrong avenged, sometimes after many generations. The fall of the French Emperor is an illustration of that same retribution which is so constant. While he yet lives, judgment has begun.

If I accumulate instances, it is because the certainty of retribution for wrong, and especially for the great wrong of War, is a lesson of the present duel to be impressed. Take notice, all who would appeal to war, that the way of the transgressor is hard, and sooner or later he is overtaken. The ban may fall tardily, but it is sure to fall.

Retribution in another form has already visited France; nor is its terrible vengeance yet spent. Not only are populous cities, all throbbing with life and filled with innocent households, subjected to siege, but to bombardment also,—being that most ruthless trial of war, where non-combatants, including women and children, sick and aged, share with the soldier his peculiar perils, and suffer alike with him. All are equal before the hideous shell, crashing, bursting, destroying, killing, and changing the fairest scene into blood-spattered wreck. Against its vengeful, slaughterous descent there is no protection for the people, — nothing but an uncertain shelter in cellars, or, it may be, in the common sewers. Already Strasbourg, Toul, and Metz have been called to endure this indiscriminate massacre, where there is no distinction of persons; and now the same fate is threatened to Paris the Beautiful, with its thronging population counted by the million. Thus is the ancient chalice which France handed to others now commended to her own lips. It was France that first in history adopted this method of war. Long ago, under Louis the Fourteenth, it became a favorite; but it has not escaped the judgment of history. Voltaire, with elegant pen, records that "this art, carried soon among other nations, served only to multiply human calamities, and more than once was dreadful to France, where it was invented."[1] The bombardment of Luxembourg in 1683 drew from Sismondi, always humane and refined, words applicable to recent events. "Louis the Fourteenth," he says, "had been the first to put in practice this atrocious and newly invented method of bombarding towns, ... of attacking, not fortifications, but private houses, not soldiers, but peaceable inhabitants, women and children, and of confounding thousands of private crimes, each one of which would cause horror, in one great public crime, one great disaster, which he regarded as nothing more than one of the catastrophes of war."[2] Again is the saying fulfilled, "All they that take the sword shall perish with the sword." No lapse of time

[1] Siècle de Louis XIV., Ch. XIV. : Œuvres, (édit. 1784–89,) Tom. XX. p. 406.

[2] Histoire des Français, Tom. XXV. pp. 452–53.

can avert the inexorable law. Macbeth saw it in his terrible imaginings, when he said, —

> "But in these cases
> We still have judgment here, — that we but teach
> Bloody instructions, which, being taught, return
> To plague the inventor."

And what instruction more bloody than the bombardment of a city, which now returns to plague the French people?

Thus is history something more even than philosophy teaching by example; it is sermon with argument and exhortation. The simple record of nations preaches; and whether you regard reason or the affections, it is the same. If nations were wise or humane, they would not fight.

PEACE AFTER CAPITULATION AT SEDAN.

VAIN are lessons of the past or texts of prudence against that spirit of War which finds sanction and regulation in International Law. So long as the war system continues, men will fight. While I speak, the two champions still stand front to front, Germany exulting in victory, but France in no respect submissive. The duel still rages, although one of the champions is pressed to earth, as in that early combat where the Chevalier Bayard, so eminent in chivalry, thrust his dagger into the nostrils of his fallen foe, and then dragged his dead body off the field. History now repeats itself, and we witness in Germany the very conduct condemned in the famous French knight.

The French Emperor was the aggressor. He began this fatal duel. Let him fall, — but not the people of France. Cruelly already have they expiated their offence in accepting such a ruler. Not always should they suffer. Enough of waste, enough of sacrifice, enough of slaughter have they undergone. Enough have they felt the accursed hoof of War.

It is easy to see now, that, after the capitulation at Sedan, there was a double mistake: first, on the part of Germany, which, as magnanimous conqueror, should have proposed peace, thus conquering in character as in arms; and, secondly, on the part of the Republic, which should have declined to wage a war of Imperialism, against which the Republican leaders had so earnestly protested. With the capitulation of the Emperor the dynastic question was closed. There was no longer pretension or pretext, nor was there occasion for war. The two parties should have come to an understanding. Why continue this terrible homicidal, fratricidal, suicidal combat, fraught with mutual death and sacrifice? Why march on Paris? Why beleaguer Paris? Why bombard Paris? To what end? If for the humiliation of France, then must it be condemned.

THREE ESSENTIAL CONDITIONS OF PEACE.

In arriving at terms of peace, there are at least three conditions which cannot be overlooked in the interest of civilization, and that the peace may be such in reality as in name, and not an armistice only, — three postulates which stand above all question, and dominate this debate, so that any essential departure from them must end in wretched failure.

The first is the natural requirement of Germany, that there shall be completest guaranty against future aggression, constituting what is so well known among us as

"Security for the Future." Count Bismarck, with an exaggeration hardly pardonable, alleges more than twenty invasions of Germany by France, and declares that these must be stopped forever.[1] Many or few, they must be stopped forever. The second condition to be regarded is the natural requirement of France, that the guaranty, while sufficient, shall be such as not to wound needlessly the sentiments of the French people, or to offend any principle of public law. It is difficult to question these two postulates, at least in the abstract. Only when we come to the application is there opportunity for difference. The third postulate, demanded alike by justice and humanity, is the establishment of some rule or precedent by which the recurrence of such a barbarous duel shall be prevented. It will not be enough to obtain a guaranty for Germany; there must be a guaranty for Civilization itself.

On careful inquiry, it will be seen that all these can be accomplished in one way only, which I will describe, when I have first shown what is now put forward and discussed as the claim of Germany, under two different heads, Indemnity and Guaranty.

INDEMNITY OF GERMANY.

I HAVE already spoken of Guaranty as an essential condition. Indemnity is not essential. At the close of our war with Slavery we said nothing of indemnity. For the life of the citizen there could be no indemnity; nor was it practicable even for the treasure sacrificed. Security for the Future was all that our nation required,

[1] Circular of September 16, 1870: Foreign Relations of the United States, — Executive Documents, 41st Cong. 3d Sess., H. of R., Vol. I. No. 1, Part 1, pp. 212-13.

and this was found in provisions of Law and Constitution establishing Equal Rights. From various intimations it is evident that Germany will not be content without indemnity in money on a large scale; and it is also evident that France, the aggressor, cannot, when conquered, deny liability to a certain extent. The question will be on the amount. Already German calculators begin to array their unrelenting figures. One of these insists that the indemnity shall not only cover outlay for the German Army, — pensions of widows and invalids, — maintenance and support of French wounded and prisoners, — compensation to Germans expelled from France, — also damage suffered by the territory to be annexed, especially Strasbourg; but it is also to cover indirect damages, large in amount, — as, loss to the nation from change of productive laborers into soldiers, — loss from killing and disabling so many laborers, — and, generally, loss from suspension of trade and manufactures, depreciation of national property, and diminution of the public revenues: — all of which, according to a recent estimate, reach the fearful sum-total of 4,935,000,000 francs, or nearly one thousand million dollars. Of this sum, 1,255,000,000 francs are on account of the Army, 1,230,000,000 for direct damage, 2,250,000,000 for indirect damage, and 200,000,000 for damage to the reconquered provinces. Still further, the Berlin Chamber of Commerce insists on indemnity not only for actual loss of ships and cargoes from the blockade, but also for damages on account of detention. Much of this many-headed account, which I introduce in order to open the case in its extent, will be opposed by France, as fabulous, consequential, and remote. The practical question will be, Can one nation do wrong to another without paying for the damage, whatever it may be, direct or indirect, — always provided it be susceptible of estimate? Here I content myself with the remark, that, while in the settlement of international differences there is no place for technicality, there is always room for moderation.

GUARANTY OF DISMEMBERMENT.

VAST as may be the claim of indemnity, it opens no question so calculated to touch the sensibilities of France as the claim of guaranty already announced by Germany. On this head we are not left to conjecture. From her first victory we have been assured that Germany would claim Alsace and German Lorraine, with their famous strongholds; and now we have the statement of Count Bismarck, in a diplomatic circular, that he expects to remove the German frontier further west, — meaning to the Vosges Mountains, if not to the Moselle also, — and to convert the fortresses into what he calls "defensive strongholds of Germany."[1] Then, with larger view, he declares, that, "in rendering it more difficult for France, from whom all European troubles have so long proceeded, to assume the offensive, we likewise promote the common interest of Europe, which demands the preservation of peace." Here is just recognition of peace as the common interest of Europe, to be assured by disabling France. How shall this be done? The German Minister sees nothing but dismemberment, consecrated by a Treaty of Peace. With diplomatic shears he would cut off a portion of French territory, and, taking from it the name of France,

[1] Circular of September 16, 1870, — *ubi supra*, p. 49, Note 1.

stamp upon it the trade-mark of Germany. Two of its richest and most precious provinces, for some two hundred years constituent parts of the great nation, with that ancient cathedral city, the pride of the Rhine, long years ago fortified by Vauban as "the strongest barrier of France,"[1] are to be severed, and with them a large and industrious population, which, while preserving the German language, have so far blended with France as to become Frenchmen. This is the German proposition, which I call the Guaranty of Dismemberment.

One argument for this proposition is brushed aside easily. Had the fortune of war been adverse to Germany, it is said, peace would have been dictated at Berlin, perhaps at Königsberg, and France would have carried her frontier eastward to the Rhine, dismembering Germany. Such, I doubt not, would have been the attempt. The conception is entirely worthy of that Imperial levity with which the war began. But the madcap menace of the French Empire cannot be the measure of German justice. It is for Germany to show, that, notwithstanding this wildness, she knows how to be just. Dismemberment on this account would be only another form of retaliation; but retaliation is barbarous.

To the argument, that these provinces, with their strongholds, are needed for the defence of Germany, there is the obvious reply, that, if cut off from France contrary to the wishes of the local population, and with the French people in chronic irritation on this account, they will be places of weakness rather than strength, strongholds of disaffection rather than defence,

[1] Voltaire, Siècle de Louis XIV., Ch. XIV.; Œuvres, (édit. 1784-89,) Tom. XX. p. 403.

to be held always at the cannon's mouth. Does Germany seek lasting peace? Not in this way can it be had. A painful exaction, enforced by triumphant arms, must create a sentiment of hostility in France, suppressed for a season, but ready at a propitious moment to break forth in violence; so that between the two conterminous nations there will be nothing better than a peace where each sleeps on its arms, — which is but an Armed Peace. Such for weary years has been the condition of nations. Is Germany determined to prolong the awful curse? Will her most enlightened people, with poetry, music, literature, philosophy, science, and religion as constant ministers, to whom has been opened in rarest degree the whole book of knowledge, persevere in a brutal policy belonging to another age, and utterly alien to that superior civilization which is so truly theirs?

There is another consideration, not only of justice, but of public law, which cannot be overcome. The people of these provinces are unwilling to be separated from France. This is enough. France cannot sell or transfer them against their consent. Consult the great masters, and you will find their concurring authority. Grotius, from whom on such a question there can be no appeal, adjudges: "In the alienation of a part of the sovereignty it is required *that the part which is to be alienated consent to the act*." According to him, it must not be supposed "that the body should have the right of cutting off parts from itself and giving them into the authority of another."[1] Of the same opinion is Pufendorf, declaring: "The sovereign who attempts to transfer his kingdom to another by his sole authority does

[1] De Jure Belli et Pacis, tr. Whewell, Lib. II. Cap. 6, § 4.

an act in itself null and void, and not binding on his subjects. To make such a conveyance valid, the consent of the people is required, as well as of the prince."[1] Vattel crowns this testimony, when he adds, that a province or city, "abandoned and dismembered from the State, is not obliged to receive the new master proposed to be given it."[2] Before such texts, stronger than a fortress, the soldiers of Germany must halt.

Nor can it be forgotten how inconsistent is the guaranty of Dismemberment with that heroic passion for national unity which is the glory of Germany. National unity is not less the right of France than of Germany; and these provinces, though in former centuries German, and still preserving the German speech, belong to the existing unity of France, — unless, according to the popular song, the German's Fatherland extends

"Far as the German accent rings";

and then the conqueror must insist on Switzerland; and why not cross the Atlantic, to dictate laws in Pennsylvania and Chicago? But this same song has a better verse, calling that the German's Fatherland

"Where in the heart love warmly lies."

But in these coveted provinces it is the love for France, and not for Germany, which prevails.

GUARANTY OF DISARMAMENT.

THE Guaranty of Dismemberment, when brought to the touchstone of the three essential conditions, is found wanting. Dismissing it as unsatisfactory, I come to

[1] De Jure Naturæ et Gentium, Lib. VIII. Cap. 5, § 9.

[2] Le Droit des Gens, Liv. I. Ch. 21, § 264.

that other guaranty where these conditions are all fulfilled, and we find security for Germany without offence to the just sentiments of France, and also a new safeguard to civilization. Against the Guaranty of Dismemberment I oppose the Guaranty of Disarmament. By Disarmament I mean the razing of the French fortifications and the abolition of the standing army, except that minimum of force required for purposes of police. How completely this satisfies the conditions already named is obvious. For Germany there would be on the side of France absolute repose, so that Count Bismarck need not fear another invasion, — while France, saved from intolerable humiliation, would herself be free to profit by the new civilization.

Nor is this guaranty otherwise than practical in every respect, and the more it is examined the more will its inestimable advantage be apparent.

1. There is, first, its most obvious *economy*, which is so glaring, that, according to a familiar French expression, "it leaps into the eyes." Undertaking even briefly to set it forth, I seem to follow the proverb and "show the sun with a lantern." According to the "Almanach de Gotha," the appropriations for the army of France, during the year of peace before the war, were 588,852,970 francs,[1] — or about one hundred and seventeen millions of dollars. Give up the Standing Army and this considerable sum disappears from the annual budget. But this retrenchment represents only partially the prodigious economy. Beyond the annual outlay is the loss to the nation by the change of producers into non-producers. Admitting that in France the average annual production of a soldier usefully employed would

[1] Almanach de Gotha, 1870, p. 599.

be only fifty dollars, and multiplying this small allowance by the numbers of the Standing Army, you have another amount to be piled upon the military appropriations. Is it too much to expect that this surpassing waste shall be stopped? Must the extravagance born of war, and nursed by long tradition, continue to drain the resources of the land? Where is reason? Where humanity? A decree abolishing the Standing Army would be better for the French people, and more productive, than the richest gold-mine discovered in every department of France. Nor can imagination picture the fruitful result. I speak now only in the light of economy. Relieved from intolerable burden, industry would lift itself to unimagined labors, and society be quickened anew.

2. Beyond this economy, which need not be argued, is the positive *advantage, if not necessity*, of such change for France. I do not speak on general grounds applicable to all nations, but on grounds peculiar to France at the present moment. Emerging from a most destructive war, she will be subjected to enormous and unprecedented contributions of every kind. After satisfying Germany, she will find other obligations at home,—some pressing directly upon the nation, and others upon individuals. Beyond the outstanding pay of soldiers, requisitions for supplies, pensions for the wounded and the families of the dead, and other extraordinary liabilities accumulating as never before in the same time, there will be the duty of renewing that internal prosperity which has received such a shock; and here the work of restoration will be costly, whether to the nation or the individual. Revenue must be regained, roads and bridges repaired, markets supplied; nor can we

omit the large and multitudinous losses from ravage of fields, seizure of stock, suspension of business, stoppage of manufactures, interference with agriculture, and the whole terrible drain of war by which the people are impoverished and disabled. If to the necessary appropriation and expenditure for all these things is superadded the annual tax of a Standing Army, and that other draft from the change of producers into non-producers, plainly here is a supplementary burden of crushing weight. Talk of the last feather breaking the back of the camel, — but never was camel loaded down as France.

3. Beyond even these considerations of economy and advantage I put the transcendent, priceless benefit of Disarmament in the *assurance of peace.* Disarmament substitutes the constable for the soldier, and reduces the Standing Army to a police. The argument assumes, first, the needlessness of a Standing Army, and, secondly, its evil influence. Both of these points were touched at an early day by the wise Chancellor of England, Sir Thomas More, when, in his practical and personal Introduction to "Utopia," he alludes to what he calls the "bad custom" of keeping many servants, and then says: "In France there is yet a more pestiferous sort of people; for the whole country is full of soldiers, that are still kept up in time of peace, — if such a state of a nation can be called a peace." Then, proceeding with his judgment, the Chancellor holds up what he calls those "pretended statesmen" whose maxim is that "it is necessary for the public safety to have a good body of veteran soldiers ever in readiness." And after saying that these pretended statesmen "sometimes seek occasion for making war, that they may train up their

soldiers in the art of cutting throats," he adds, in words soon to be tested, "But France has learned, to its cost, how dangerous it is to feed such beasts."[1] It will be well, if France has learned this important lesson. The time has come to practise it.

All history is a vain word, and all experience is at fault, if large War Preparations, of which the Standing Army is the type, have not been constant provocatives of war. Pretended protectors against war, they have been real instigators to war. They have excited the evil against which they were to guard. The habit of wearing arms in private life exercised a kindred influence. So long as this habit continued, society was darkened by personal combat, street-fight, duel, and assassination. The Standing Army is to the nation what the sword was to the modern gentleman, the stiletto to the Italian, the knife to the Spaniard, the pistol to our slave-master, — furnishing, like these, the means of death; and its possessor is not slow to use it. In stating the operation of this system we are not left to inference. As France, according to Sir Thomas More, shows "how dangerous it is to feed such beasts," so does Prussia, in ever-memorable instance, which speaks now with more than ordinary authority, show precisely how the Standing Army may become the incentive to war. Frederick, the warrior king, is our witness. With honesty or impudence beyond parallel, he did not hesitate to record in his Memoirs, among the reasons for his war upon Maria Theresa, that, on coming to the throne, he found himself with "troops always ready to act." Voltaire, when called to revise the royal memoirs,

[1] Utopia, tr. Burnet, (London, 1845,) Book I. pp. 29, 30.

erased this confession, but preserved a copy;[1] so that by his literary activity we have this kingly authority for the mischief from a Standing Army. How complete a weapon was that army may be learned from Lafayette, who, in a letter to Washington, in 1786, after a visit to the King, described it thus: —

"Nothing can be compared to the beauty of the troops, to the discipline which reigns in all their ranks, to the simplicity of their movements, to the uniformity of their regiments. . . . . All the situations which can be supposed in war, all the movements which these must necessitate, have been by constant habit so inculcated in their heads, that all these operations are done almost mechanically."[2]

Nothing better has been devised since the Macedonian phalanx or the Roman legion. With such a weapon ready to his hands, the King struck Maria Theresa. And think you that the present duel between France and Germany could have been waged, had not both nations found themselves, like Frederick of Prussia, with "troops always ready to act"? It was the possession of these troops which made the two parties rush so swiftly to the combat. Is not the lesson perfect? Already individuals have disarmed. Civilization requires that nations shall do likewise.

Thus is Disarmament enforced on three several grounds: first, economy; secondly, positive advantage, if not necessity, for France; and, thirdly, assurance of peace. No other guaranty promises so much. Does any other guaranty promise anything beyond the acci-

[1] Brougham, Lives of Men of Letters, (London and Glasgow, 1856,) p. 59, —*Voltaire*. See also Voltaire, *Mémoires pour servir à la Vie de, écrits par lui-même*, (édit. 1784-89,) Tom. LXX. p. 279; also Frédéric II., *Histoire de mon Temps*, Œuvres Posthumes, (Berlin, 1789,) Tom. I. Part. I. p. 78.

[2] Mémoires, Tom. II. p. 133.

dent of force? Nor would France be alone. Dismissing to the arts of peace the large army victorious over Slavery, our Republic has shown how disarmament can be accomplished. The example of France, so entirely reasonable, so profitable, so pacific, and so harmonious with ours, would spread. Conquering Germany could not resist its influence. Nations are taught by example more than by precept, and either is better than force. Other nations would follow; nor would Russia, elevated by her great act of Enfranchisement, fail to seize her sublime opportunity. Popular rights, which are strongest always in assured peace, would have new triumphs. Instead of Trial by Battle for the decision of differences between nations, there would be peaceful substitutes, as Arbitration, or, it may be, a Congress of Nations, and the United States of Europe would appear above the subsiding waters. The old juggle of Balance of Power, which has rested like a nightmare on Europe, would disappear, like that other less bloody fiction of Balance of Trade, and nations, like individuals, would all be equal before the law. Here our own country furnishes an illustration. So long as slavery prevailed among us, there was an attempt to preserve what was designated balance of power between the North and South, pivoting on Slavery, — just as in Europe there has been an attempt to preserve balance of power among nations pivoting on War. Too tardily is it seen that this famous balance, which has played such a part at home and abroad, is but an artificial contrivance instituted by power, which must give place to a simple accord derived from the natural condition of things. Why should not the harmony which has begun at home be extended abroad? Practicable and beneficent here, it must be the same there. Then would nations exist without perpetual and reciprocal watchfulness. But the first step is to discard the wasteful, oppressive, and pernicious provocative to war, which is yet maintained at such terrible cost. To-day this glorious advance is presented to France and Germany.

KING WILLIAM AND COUNT BISMARCK.

Two personages at this moment hold in their hands the great question teeming with a new civilization. Honest and determined, both are patriotic rather than cosmopolitan or Christian, believing in Prussia rather than Humanity. And the patriotism so strong in each keeps still the early tinge of iron. I refer to King William and his Prime-Minister, Count Bismarck.

More than any other European sovereign, William of Prussia possesses the infatuation of "divine right." He believes that he was appointed by God to be King — differing here from Louis Napoleon, who in a spirit of compromise entitled himself Emperor "by the grace of God and the national will." This infatuation was illustrated at his coronation in ancient Königsberg, — first home of Prussian royalty, and better famous as birthplace and lifelong home of Immanuel Kant, — when the King enacted a scene of melodrama which might be transferred from the church to the theatre. No other person was allowed to place the crown on his royal head. Lifting it from the altar, where it rested, he placed it on his head himself, in sign that he held it from Heaven and not from man, and next placed another on the head of the Queen, in sign that her dignity was derived from him. Then, turning round, he grasped the sword of state, in testimony of readiness to defend the nation. Since the Battle of Sadowa, when the Austrian Empire was so suddenly shattered, he has believed himself providential sword-bearer of Germany, destined, perhaps, to revive the old glories of Barbarossa. His habits are soldierly, and, notwithstanding his seventy-three winters, he continues to find pleasure in wearing the spiked helmet of the Prussian camp. Republicans smile when he speaks of "my army," "my allies," and "my people"; but this egotism is the natural expression of the monarchical character, especially where the monarch believes that he holds by "divine right." His public conduct is in harmony with these conditions. He is a Protestant, and rules the land of Luther, but he is no friend to modern Reform. The venerable system of war and prerogative is part of his inheritance handed down from fighting despots, and he evidently believes in it.

His Minister, Count Bismarck, is the partisan of "divine right," and, like the King, regards with satisfaction that hierarchical feudalism from which they are both derived. He is noble, and believes in nobility. He believes also in force, as if he had the blood of the god Thor. He believes in war, and does not hesitate to throw its "iron dice," insisting upon the rigors of the game. As the German question began to lower, his policy was most persistent. "Not by speeches and votes of the majority," he said in 1862, "are the great questions of the time decided, — that was the error of 1848 and 1849, — *but by iron and blood.*"[1] Thus expli-

[1] "Nicht durch Reden und Majoritätsbeschlüsse werden die grossen Fragen der Zeit entschieden, — das ist der Fehler von 1848 und 1849 gewesen, — sondern durch Eisen und Blut." — *Aeusserungen in der Budgetkommission,* September, 1862.

cit was he. Having a policy, he became its representative, and very soon thereafter controlled the counsels of his sovereign, coming swiftly before the world; and yet his elevation was tardy. Born in 1815, he did not enter upon diplomacy until 1851, when thirty-six years of age, and only in 1862 became Prussian Minister at Paris, whence he was soon transferred to the Cabinet at Berlin as Prime-Minister. Down to that time he was little known. His name is not found in any edition of the bulky French Dictionary of Contemporaries,[1] not even its "Additions and Rectifications," until the Supplement of 1863. But from this time he drew so large a share of public attention that the contemporary press of the world became the dictionary where his name was always found. Nobody doubts his intellectual resources, his courage, or strength of will; but it is felt that he is naturally hard, and little affected by human sympathy. Therefore is he an excellent war minister. It remains to be seen if he will do as much for peace. His one idea has been the unity of Germany under the primacy of Prussia; and here he encountered Austria, as he now encounters France. But in that larger unity where nations will be conjoined in harmony he can do less, so long at least as he continues a fanatic for kings and a cynic towards popular institutions.

Such is the King, and such his Minister. I have described them that you may see how little help the great ideas already germinating from bloody fields will receive from them. In this respect they are as one.

[1] Vapereau, Dictionnaire Universel des Contemporains.

TWO INFLUENCES *VERSUS* WAR SYSTEM.

BEYOND the most persuasive influence of civilization, pleading, as never before, with voice of reason and affection, that the universal tyrant and master-evil of Christendom, the War System, may cease, and the means now absorbed in its support be employed for the benefit of the Human Family, there are two special influences which cannot be without weight at this time. The first is German authority in the writings of philosophers, by whom Germany rules in thought; and the second is the uprising of the working-men: both against war as acknowledged arbiter between nations, and insisting upon peaceful substitutes.

AUTHORITY OF THE GERMAN MIND.

MORE than any other nation Germany has suffered from war. Without that fatal gift of beauty, "a dowry fraught with never-ending pain," which tempted the foreigner to Italy, her lot has been hardly less wretched; but Germany has differed from Italy in the successful bravery with which she repelled the invader. Tacitus says of her people, that, "surrounded by numerous and very powerful nations, they are safe, not by obsequiousness, but by battles and braving danger";[1] and this same character, thus epigrammatically presented, has continued ever since. Yet this was not without that painful experience which teaches what Art has so often attempted to picture and Eloquence to describe, "The Miseries of War." Again in that same

1 "Plurimis ac valentissimis nationibus cincti, non per obsequium, sed prœliis et periclitando tuti sunt." — *Germania*, Cap. XL.

fearless spirit has Germany driven back the invader, while War is seen anew in its atrocious works. But it was not merely the Miseries of War which Germans regarded. The German mind is philosophical and scientific, and it early saw the irrational character of the War System. It is well known that Henry the Fourth of France conceived the idea of Harmony among Nations without War; and his plan was taken up and elaborated in numerous writings by the good Abbé de Saint-Pierre, so that he made it his own. Rousseau, in his treatise on the subject,[1] popularized Saint-Pierre. But it is to Germany that we must look for the most complete and practical development of this beautiful idea. If French in origin, it is German now in authority.

The greatest minds in Germany have dealt with this problem, and given to its solution the exactness of science. No greater have been applied to any question. Foremost in this list, in time and in fame, is Leibnitz, that marvel of human intelligence, second, perhaps, to none in history, who, on reading the "Project of Perpetual Peace" by the Abbé de Saint-Pierre, pronounced this judgment: "I have read it with attention, and am persuaded that such a project is on the whole feasible, and that its execution would be one of the most useful things in the world."[2] Thus did Leibnitz affirm its feasibility and its immense usefulness. Other minds followed, in no apparent concert, but in unison. I may be pardoned, if, without being too bibliographical, I name some of these witnesses.

1 J. J. Rousseau, Extrait du Projet de Paix Perpétuelle de M. l'Abbé de Saint-Pierre; avec Lettre à M. de Bastide, et Jugement sur la Paix Perpétuelle: Œuvres, (édit. 1788-93,) Tom. VII. pp. 339-418.

2 Observations sur le Projet d'une Paix Perpétuelle de M. l'Abbé de Saint-Pierre: Opera, ed. Dutens, (Genevæ, 1768,) Tom. V. p. 56.

At Göttingen, renowned for its University, the question was opened, at the close of the Seven Years' War in 1763, in a work by Totze, whose character appears in its title, "Permanent and Universal Peace in Europe, according to the Plan of Henry IV."[1] At Leipsic, also the seat of a University, the subject was presented in 1767 by Lilienfeld, in a treatise of much completeness, under the name of "New Constitution for States,"[2] where, after exposing the wretched chances of the battle-field and the expense of armaments in time of peace, the author urges submission to Arbitrators, unless a Supreme Tribunal is established to administer International Law and to judge between nations. In 1804 appeared another work, of singular clearness and force, by Karl Schwab, entitled "Of Unavoidable Injustice,"[3] where the author describes what he calls the Universal State, in which nations will be to each other as citizens in the Municipal State. He is not so visionary as to imagine that justice will always be inviolate between nations in the Universal State, for it is not always so between citizens in the Municipal State; but he confidently looks to the establishment between nations of the rules which now subsist between citizens, whose differences are settled peaceably by judicial tribunals.

These works, justly important for the light they shed, and as expressions of a growing sentiment, are eclipsed in the contributions of the great teacher, Immanuel Kant, who, after his fame in philosophy was established, so that his works were discussed and expounded not only throughout Germany, but in other lands, in 1795

[1] Der ewige und allgemeine Friede in Europa, nach dem Entwurf Heinrichs IV.

[2] Neues Staatsgebäude.

[3] Ueber das unvermeidliche Unrecht.

gave to the world a treatise entitled "On Perpetual Peace,"[1] which was promptly translated into French, Danish, and Dutch. Two other works by him attest his interest in the subject, the first entitled "Idea for a General History in a Cosmopolitan View,"[2] and the other, "Metaphysical Elements of Jurisprudence."[3] His grasp was complete. A treaty of peace which tacitly acknowledges the right to wage war, as all treaties now do, according to Kant is nothing more than a truce. An individual war may be ended, but not the *state of war*; so that, even after cessation of hostilities, there will be constant fear of their renewal, while the armaments known as Peace Establishments will tend to provoke them. All this should be changed, and nations should form one comprehensive Federation, which, receiving other nations within its fold, will at last embrace the civilized world; and such, in the judgment of Kant, was the irresistible tendency of nations. To a French poet we are indebted for the most suggestive term, "United States of Europe";[4] but this is nothing but the Federation of the illustrious German philosopher. Nor was Kant alone among his great contemporaries. That other philosopher, Fichte, whose name at the time was second only to that of Kant, in his "Groundwork of the Law of Nature,"[5] published in 1796, also urges a Federation of Nations, with an established tribunal to which all should submit. Much better for civilization, had the King at Königsberg, in-

[1] Zum ewigen Frieden.

[2] Idee zu einer allgemeinen Geschichte in weltbürgerlicher Absicht.

[3] Metaphysische Anfangsgründe der Rechtslehre.

[4] Victor Hugo, Discours d'Ouverture du Congrès de la Paix à Paris, 21 Août 1849 : Treize Discours, (Paris, 1851,) p. 19.

[5] Grundlage des Naturrechts.

stead of grasping the sword, hearkened to the voice of Kant, renewed by Fichte.

With these German oracles in its support, the cause cannot be put aside. Even in the midst of war, Philosophy will be heard, especially when she speaks words of concurring authority that touch a chord in every heart. Leibnitz, Kant, and Fichte, a mighty triumvirate of intelligence, unite in testimony. As Germany, beyond any other nation, has given to the idea of Organized Peace the warrant of philosophy, it only remains now that she should insist upon its practical application. There should be no delay. Long enough has mankind waited while the river of blood flowed on.

UPRISING OF WORKING-MEN.

THE working-men of Europe, not excepting Germany, respond to the mandate of Philosophy, and insist that the War System shall be abolished. At public meetings, in formal resolutions and addresses, they have declared war against War, and they will not be silenced. This is not the first time that working-men have made themselves heard for international justice. I cannot forget, that, while Slavery was waging war against our nation, the working-men of Belgium in public meeting protested against that precocious Proclamation of Belligerent Rights by which the British Government gave such impulse to the Rebellion; and now, in the same spirit, and for the sake of true peace, they declare themselves against that War System by which the peace of nations is placed in such constant jeopardy. They are right; for nobody suffers in war as the working-man, whether in property or in person. For him war is a ravening monster, devouring his substance, and changing him from citizen to military serf. As victim of the War System he is entitled to be heard.

The working-men of different countries have been organizing in societies, of which it is difficult at present to tell the number and extent. It is known that these societies exist in Germany, France, Spain, Italy, and England, as well as in our own country, and that they have in some measure an international character. In France, before the war, there were 433,785 men in the organization, and in Germany 150,000.[1] Yet this is but the beginning.

At the menace of the present war, all these societies were roused. The society known as the International Working-Men's Association, by their General Council, issued an address, dated at London, protesting against it as a war of dynasties, denouncing Louis Napoleon as an enemy of the laboring classes, and declaring "the war-plot of July, 1870, but an amended edition of the *coup d'état* of December, 1851." The address then testifies generally against war, saying, —

"They feel deeply convinced, that, whatever turn the impending horrid war may take, *the alliance of the working classes of all countries will ultimately kill war*."[2]

At the same time the Paris branch of the International Association put forth a manifesto addressed "To the Working-Men of all Countries," from which I take these passages: —

[1] La Solidarité, 25 Juin 1870, — as cited by Testu, *L'Internationale*, (7ème édit.,) p. 275.

[2] The General Council of the International Working-Men's Association on the War, (London, July 23, 1870,) p. iv.

"Once more, under the pretext of European equilibrium, of national honor, political ambitions menace the peace of the world.

"French, German, Spanish working-men! *let our voices unite in a cry of reprobation against war!*

. . . .

"War for a question of preponderance, or of dynasty, can, in the eyes of working-men, be nothing but a criminal absurdity.

"In response to the warlike acclamations of those who exonerate themselves from the impost of blood, or who find in public misfortunes a source of new speculations, we protest, — we who wish for peace, work, and liberty.

. . . .

"Brothers of Germany! . . . . our divisions would only bring about *the complete triumph of despotism on both sides of the Rhine.*

. . . .

"Working-men of all countries! whatever may be the result of our common efforts, we, members of the International Association of Working-Men, who know no frontiers, we send you, as a pledge of indissoluble solidarity, the good wishes and the salutations of the working-men of France."[1]

To this appeal, so full of truth, touching to the quick the pretence of balance of power and questions of dynasty as excuses for war, and then rising to "a cry of reprobation against war," the Berlin branch of the International Association replied: —

"We join with heart and hand in your protestation. . . . . Solemnly we promise you that neither the noise of drums nor the thunder of cannon, neither victory nor defeat, shall turn us aside from our work for the union of the proletaries of all countries."[2]

[1] Testu, L'Internationale, pp. 279–80. The General Council of the International Working-Men's Association on the War, p. ii.

[2] Testu, pp. 284–85. The General Council, etc., p. iii.

Then came a meeting of delegates at Chemnitz, in Saxony, representing fifty thousand Saxon working-men, which put forth the following hardy words: —

"We are happy to grasp the fraternal hand stretched out to us by the working-men of France. . . . . Mindful of the watchword of the International Working-Men's Association, *Proletarians of all countries, unite!* we shall never forget that the working-men of all countries are our friends, and the despots of all countries our enemies."[1]

Next followed, at Brunswick, in Germany, on the 16th of July, — the very day after the reading of the war document at the French tribune, and the "light heart" of the Prime-Minister, — a mass meeting of the working-men there, which declared its full concurrence with the manifesto of the Paris branch, spurned the idea of national antagonism to France, and wound up with these solid words: —

"We are enemies of all wars, but above all of dynastic wars."[2]

The whole subject is presented with admirable power in an address from the Workmen's Peace Committee to the Working-Men of Great Britain and Ireland, duly signed by their officers. Here are some of its sentences: —

"Without us war must cease; for without us standing armies could not exist. It is out of our class chiefly that they are formed."

"We would call upon and implore the peoples of France and Germany, in order to enable their own rulers to realize

1 The General Council of the International Working-Men's Association on the War, p. iii.

2 Ibid.

these their peace-loving professions, *to insist upon the abolition of standing armies,* as both the source and means of war, nurseries of vice, and locust-consumers of the fruits of useful industry."

"What we claim and demand — what we would implore the peoples of Europe to do, without regard to Courts, Cabinets, or Dynasties — is *to insist upon Arbitration as a substitute for war,* with peace and its blessings for them, for us, for the whole civilized world." [1]

The working-men of England responded to this appeal, in a crowded meeting at St. James's Hall, London, where all the speakers were working-men and representatives of the various handicrafts, except the Chairman, whose strong words found echo in the intense convictions of the large assemblage: —

"One object of this meeting is to make the horror universally inspired by the enormous and cruel carnage of this terrible war the groundwork for appealing to the working classes and the people of all other European countries to join in protesting against war altogether, [*prolonged cheers,*] as the shame of Christendom, and direst curse and scourge of the human race. Let the will of the people sweep away war, which cannot be waged without them. ['*Hear!*'] Away with enormous standing armies, ['*Hear!*'] the nurseries and instruments of war, — nurseries, too, of vice, and crushing burdens upon national wealth and prosperity! Let there go forth from the people of this and other lands one universal and all-overpowering cry and demand for the blessings of peace!" [2]

At this meeting the Honorary Secretary of the Workmen's Peace Committee, after announcing that the work-

[1] Herald of Peace for 1870, September 1st, pp. 101 - 2.

[2] Ibid., October 1st, p. 125.

ing-men of upwards of three hundred towns had given their adhesion to the platform of the Committee, thus showing a determination to abolish war altogether, moved the following resolution, which was adopted: —

"That war, especially with the present many fearful contrivances for wholesale carnage and destruction, is repugnant to every principle of reason, humanity, and religion; and this meeting earnestly invites all civilized and Christian peoples to insist upon the abolition of standing armies, and the settlement by arbitration of all international disputes."[1]

Thus clearly is the case stated by the Working-Men, now beginning to be heard; and the testimony is reverberated from nation to nation. They cannot be silent hereafter. I confidently look to them for important coöperation in this great work of redemption. Could my voice reach them now, wherever they may be, in that honest toil which is the appointed lot of man, it would be with words of cheer and encouragement. Let them proceed until civilization is no longer darkened by war. In this way will they become not only saviours to their own households, but benefactors of the whole Human Family.

ABOLITION OF THE WAR SYSTEM.

Such is the statement, with its many proofs, by which war is exhibited as the Duel of Nations, being the Trial by Battle of the Dark Ages. You have seen how nations, under existing International Law, to which all are parties, refer their differences to this insensate arbitrament, — and then how, in our day and before our own eyes, two nations eminent in civilization have furnished

[1] Herald of Peace for 1870, October 1st, p. 125.

an instance of this incredible folly, waging together a world-convulsing, soul-harrowing, and most barbarous contest. All ask how long the direful duel will be continued. Better ask, How long will be continued that War System by which such a duel is authorized and regulated among nations? When will this legalized, organized crime be abolished? When at last will it be confessed that the Law of Right is the same for nations as for individuals, so that, if Trial by Battle be impious for individuals, it is so for nations likewise? Against it are Reason and Humanity, pleading as never before,— Economy, asking for mighty help,— Peace, with softest voice praying for safeguard,— and then the authority of Philosophy, speaking by some of its greatest masters,— all reinforced by the irrepressible, irresistible protest of working-men in different nations.

Precedents exist for the abolition of this duel, so completely in point, that, according to the lawyer's phrase, they "go on all fours" with the new case. Two of these have been already mentioned: first, when, at the Diet of Worms, in 1495, the Emperor Maximilian proclaimed a permanent peace throughout Germany, and abolished the "liberty" of Private War; and, secondly, when, in 1815, the German Principalities stipulated "under no pretext to make war upon one another, or to pursue their differences by force of arms."[1] But first in time, and perhaps in importance, was the great Ordinance of St. Louis, King of France, promulgated at a Parliament in 1260, where he says: "*We forbid battles* [*i.e.* TRIALS BY BATTLE] *to all persons throughout our dominions, ... and in place of battles we put proofs by witnesses. . . . .* AND THESE BATTLES WE ABOLISH IN

[1] See, *ante*, p. 247.

our Dominions forever."[1] These at the time were great words, and they continue great as an example. Their acceptance by any two nations would begin the work of abolition, which would be completed on their adoption by a Congress of Nations, taking from war its existing sanction.

THE WORLD A GLADIATORIAL AMPHITHEATRE.

The growing tendencies of mankind have been quickened by the character of the present war, and the unexampled publicity with which it has been waged. Never before were all nations, even those separated by great spaces, whether of land or ocean, the daily and excited spectators of the combat. The vast amphitheatre within which the battle is fought, with the whole heavens for its roof, is coextensive with civilization itself. The scene in that great Flavian Amphitheatre, the famous Colosseum, is a faint type of what we are witnessing; but that is not without its lesson. Bloody games, where human beings contended with lions and tigers, imported for the purpose, or with each other, constituted an institution of ancient Rome, only mildly rebuked by Cicero,[2] and adopted even by Titus, in that short reign so much praised as unspotted by the blood of the citizen.[3] One

[1] "Nous deffendons à tous les batailles par tout nostre demengne, ... et en lieu des batailles nous meton prüeves de tesmoins. . . . . Et ces batailles nous ostons en nostre demaigne à toûjours." — *Recueil Général des Anciennes Lois Françaises*, par Jourdan, etc., (Paris, 1822-33,) Tom. I. pp. 283-90.

[2] "Crudele gladiatorum spectaculum et inhumanum nonnullis videri solet: et haud scio an ita sit, ut nunc fit." — *Tusculanæ Quæstiones*, Lib. II. Cap. XVII. 41.

[3] Suetonius: *Titus*, Cap. IX. Merivale, History of the Romans under the Empire, (London, 1862,) Ch. LX., Vol. VII. p. 56.

hundred thousand spectators looked on, while gladiators from Germany and Gaul joined in ferocious combat; and then, as blood began to flow, and victim after victim sank upon the sand, the people caught the fierce contagion. A common ferocity ruled the scene. As Christianity prevailed, the incongruity of such an institution was widely felt; but still it continued. At last an Eastern monk, moved only by report, journeyed a long way to protest against the impiety. With noble enthusiasm he leaped into the arena, where the battle raged, in order to separate the combatants. He was unsuccessful, and paid with life the penalty of his humanity.[1] But the martyr triumphed where the monk had failed. Shortly afterwards, the Emperor Honorius, by solemn decree, put an end to this horrid custom. "The first Christian Emperor," says Gibbon, "may claim the honor of the first edict which condemned the art and amusement of shedding human blood."[2] Our amphitheatre is larger than that of Rome; but it witnesses scenes not less revolting; nor need any monk journey a long way to protest against the impiety. That protest can be uttered by every one here at home. We are all spectators; and since by human craft the civilized world has become one mighty Colosseum, with place for everybody, may we not insist that the bloody games by which it is yet polluted shall cease, and that, instead of mutual-murdering gladiators filling the near-brought scene with death, there shall be a harmonious people, of different nations, but one fellowship, vying together only in works of industry and art, inspired and exalted by a divine beneficence?

1 St. Telemachus, A. D. 404. Gibbon, Decline and Fall of the Roman Empire, ed. Milman, (London, 1846,) Ch. XXX., Vol. III. p. 70. Smith, Dict. Gr. and Rom. Biog. and Myth., art. TELEMACHUS.

2 Decline and Fall of the Roman Empire, *ubi supra.*

In presenting this picture I exaggerate nothing. How feeble is language to depict the stupendous barbarism! How small by its side the bloody games which degraded ancient Rome! How pygmy the one, how colossal the other! Would you know how the combat is conducted? Here is the briefest picture of the arena by a looker-on:—

"Let your readers fancy masses of colored rags glued together with blood and brains, and pinned into strange shapes by fragments of bones, — let them conceive men's bodies without heads, legs without bodies, heaps of human entrails attached to red and blue cloth, and disembowelled corpses in uniform, bodies lying about in all attitudes, with skulls shattered, faces blown off, hips smashed, bones, flesh, and gay clothing all pounded together as if brayed in a mortar extending for miles, not very thick in any one place, but recurring perpetually for weary hours, — and then they cannot, with the most vivid imagination, come up to the sickening reality of that butchery."[1]

Such a sight would have shocked the Heathen of Rome. They could not have looked on while the brave gladiator was thus changed into a bloody hash; least of all could they have seen the work of slaughter done by machinery. Nor could any German gladiator have written the letter I proceed to quote from a German soldier:—

"I do not know how it is, but one wholly forgets the danger one is in, and thinks only of the effect of one's own bullets, rejoicing like a child at the sight of the enemy falling like skittles, and having scarcely a compassionate glance to spare for the comrade falling at one's side. One ceases to be a human being, and turns into a brute, a complete brute."

[1] Scene after the Battle of Sedan: Herald of Peace for 1870, October 1st, p. 121.

Plain confession! And yet the duel continues. Nor is there death for the armed man only. Fire mingles with slaughter, as at Bazeilles. Women and children are roasted alive, filling the air with suffocating odor, while the maddened combatants rage against each other. All this is but part of the prolonged and various spectacle, where the scene shifts only for some other horror. Meanwhile the sovereigns of the world sit in their boxes, and the people everywhere occupy the benches.

PERIL FROM THE WAR SYSTEM.

THE duel now pending teaches the peril from continuance of the present system. If France and Germany can be brought so suddenly into collision on a mere pretext, what two nations are entirely safe? Where is the talisman for their protection? None, surely, except Disarmament, which, therefore, for the interest of all nations, should be commenced. Prussia is now an acknowledged military power, armed "in complete steel," — but at what cost to her people, if not to mankind! Military citizenship, according to Prussian rule, is military serfdom, and on this is elevated a military despotism of singular grasp and power, operating throughout the whole nation, like martial law or a state of siege. In Prussia the law tyrannically seizes every youth of twenty, and, no matter what his calling or profession, compels him to military service for seven years. Three years he spends in active service in the regular army, where his life is surrendered to the trade of blood; then for four years he passes to the reserve, where he is subject to periodic military drills; then for five years longer to the *Landwehr*, or militia, with liability to service in the *Landsturm*, in case of war, until sixty. Wherever he may be in foreign lands, his military duty is paramount.

But if this system be good for Prussia, then must it be equally good for other nations. If this economical government, with education for all, subordinates the business of life to the military drill, other nations will find too much reason for doing the same. Unless the War System is abandoned, all must follow the successful example, while the civilized world becomes a busy camp, with every citizen a soldier, and with all sounds swallowed up in the tocsin of war. Where, then, are the people? Where are popular rights? Montesquieu has not hesitated to declare that the peril to free governments proceeds from armies, and that this peril is not corrected even by making them depend directly on the legislative power. This is not enough. The armies must be reduced in number and force.[1] Among his papers, found since his death, is the prediction, "France will be ruined by the military."[2] It is the privilege of genius like that of Montesquieu to lift the curtain of the future; but even he did not see the vastness of suffering in store for his country through those armies against which he warned. For years the engine of despotism at home, they became the sudden instrument of war abroad. Without them Louis Napoleon could not have made himself Emperor, nor could he have hurried France into the present duel. If needed in other days, they are not needed now. The War System, always barbarous, is an anachronism, full of peril both to peace and liberal institutions.

[1] De l'Esprit des Lois, Liv. XI. Ch. 6.

[2] "La France se perdra par les gens de guerre." — *Pensées Diverses, — Variétés;* Œuvres Mêlées et Posthumes, (Paris, 1807, Didot,) Tom. II. p. 138.

PEACE.

An army is a despotism; military service is a bondage; nor can the passion for arms be reconciled with a true civilization. The present failure to acknowledge this incompatibility is only another illustration how the clear light of truth is discolored and refracted by an atmosphere where the cloud of war still lingers. Soon must this cloud be dispersed. From war to peace is a change indeed; but Nature herself testifies to change. Sirius, brightest of all the fixed stars, was noted by Ptolemy as of reddish hue,[1] and by Seneca as redder than Mars;[2] but since then it has changed to white. To the morose remark, whether in the philosophy of Hobbes or the apology of the soldier, that man is a fighting animal and that war is natural, I reply, — Natural for savages rejoicing in the tattoo, natural for barbarians rejoicing in violence, but not natural for man in a true civilization, which I insist is the natural state to which he tends by a sure progression. The true state of Nature is not war, but peace. Not only every war, but every recognition of war as the mode of determining international differences, is evidence that we are yet barbarians, — and so also is every ambition for empire founded on force, and not on the consent of the people. A ghastly, bleeding, human head was discovered by the early Romans, as they dug the foundations of that Capitol which finally swayed the world.[3] That ghastly, bleeding, human head is the fit symbol of military power.

[1] Almagest, ed. et tr. Halma, (Paris, 1816-20,) Tom. II. pp. 72, 73.

[2] Naturales Quæstiones, Lib. I. Cap. 1.

[3] Dionysius Halicarnassensis, Antiquitates Romanæ, Lib. IV. Capp. 59-61.

Let the War System be abolished, and, in the glory of this consummation, how vulgar all that comes from battle! By the side of this serene, beneficent civilization, how petty in its pretensions is military power! how vain its triumphs! At this moment the great general who has organized victory for Germany is veiled, and his name does not appear even in the military bulletins. Thus is the glory of arms passing from sight, and battle losing its ancient renown. Peace does not arrest the mind like war. It does not glare like battle. Its operations, like those of Nature, are gentle, yet sure. It is not the tumbling, sounding cataract, but the tranquil, fruitful river. Even the majestic Niagara, with thunder like war, cannot compare with the peaceful plains of water which it divides. How easy to see that the repose of nations, like the repose of Nature, is the great parent of the most precious bounties vouchsafed by Providence! Add Peace to Liberty, —

"And with that virtue, every virtue lives."

As peace is assured, the traditional sensibilities of nations will disappear. Their frontiers will no longer frown with hostile cannon, nor will their people be nursed to hate each other. By ties of constant fellowship will they be interwoven together, no sudden trumpet waking to arms, no sharp summons disturbing the uniform repose. By steam, by telegraph, by the press, have they already conquered time, subdued space, — thus breaking down old walls of partition by which they have been separated. Ancient example loses its influence. The prejudices of another generation are removed, and the old geography gives place to a new. The heavens are divided into constellations, with names from beasts, or from some form of brute force, — as Leo,

Taurus, Sagittarius, and Orion with his club; but this is human device. By similar scheme is the earth divided. But in the sight of God there is one Human Family without division, where all are equal in rights; and the attempt to set up distinctions, keeping men asunder, or in barbarous groups, is a practical denial of that great truth, religious and political, the Brotherhood of Man. The Christian's Fatherland is not merely the nation in which he was born, but the whole earth appointed by the Heavenly Father for his home. In this Fatherland there can be no place for unfriendly boundaries set up by any, — least of all, place for the War System, making nations as hostile camps.

At Lassa, in Thibet, there is a venerable stone in memory of the treaty between the courts of Thibet and China, as long ago as 821, bearing an inscription worthy of a true civilization. From Eastern story learn now the beauty of peace. After the titles of the two august sovereigns, the monument proceeds: "These two wise, holy, spiritual, and accomplished princes, foreseeing the changes hidden in the most distant futurity, touched with sentiments of compassion towards their people, and not knowing, in their beneficent protection, any difference between their subjects and strangers, have, after mature reflection and by mutual consent, resolved to give peace to their people. . . . . In perfect harmony with each other, they will henceforth be good neighbors, and will do their utmost to draw still closer the bonds of union and friendship. Henceforward the two empires of Han (China) and Pho (Thibet) shall have fixed boundaries. . . . . In preserving these limits, the respective parties shall not endeavor to injure each other; they shall not attack each other in arms, or make any more incursions beyond the frontiers now determined." Then declaring that the two "must reciprocally exalt their virtues and banish forever all mistrust between them, that travellers may be without uneasiness, that the inhabitants of the villages and fields may live at peace, and that nothing may happen to cause a misunderstanding," the inscription announces, in terms doubtless Oriental: "This benefit will be extended to future generations, and the voice of love (towards its authors) will be heard wherever the splendor of the sun and the moon is seen. The Pho will be tranquil in their kingdom, and the Han will be joyful in their empire."[1] Such is the benediction which from early times has spoken from one of the monuments erected by the god Terminus. Call it Oriental; would it were universal! While recognizing a frontier, there is equal recognition of peace as the rule of international life.

THE REPUBLIC.

In the abolition of the War System the will of the people must become all-powerful, exalting the Republic to its just place as the natural expression of citizenship. Napoleon has been credited with the utterance at St. Helena of the prophecy, that "in fifty years Europe would be Republican or Cossack."[2] Evidently Europe

[1] Travels of the Russian Mission through Mongolia to China, and Residence in Peking, in 1820-21, by George Timkowski, Vol. I. pp. 460-64.

[2] See the *New York Times* of August 11, 1870, where the reputed prophecy is cited in these terms, in a letter of the 27th July from the London correspondent of that journal, with remarks indicating an expectation of its fulfilment in the results of the present war. This famous saying has been variously represented; but the following are its original terms, as recorded at the time by Las Cases, to whom it was addressed in conversation,

will not be Cossack, unless the Cossack is already changed to Republican, — as well may be, when it is known, that, since the great act of Enfranchisement, in February, 1861, by which twenty-three millions of serfs were raised to citizenship, with the right to vote, fifteen thousand three hundred and fifty public schools have been opened in Russia. A better than Napoleon, who saw mankind with truer insight, Lafayette, has recorded a clearer prophecy. At the foundation of the monument on Bunker Hill, on the semi-centennial anniversary of the battle, 17th June, 1825, our much-honored national guest gave this toast: "Bunker Hill, and the holy resistance to oppression, which has already enfranchised the American hemisphere. The next half-century Jubilee's toast shall be, — *To Enfranchised Europe.*"[1] The close of that half-century, already so prolific, is at hand. Shall it behold the great Jubilee with all its vastness of promise accomplished? Enfranchised Europe, foretold by Lafayette, means not only the Republic for all, but Peace for all; it means the United States of Europe, with the War System abolished. Against that little faith through which so much fails in life, I declare my unalterable conviction, that "government of the people, by the people, and for the people" — thus simply described by Abraham Lin-

and as authenticated by the Commission appointed by Louis Napoleon for the collection and publication of the matters now composing the magnificent work entitled "Correspondance de Napoléon Ier": —

"*Dans l'état actuel des choses, avant dix ans*, toute l'Europe *peut être* cosaque, ou toute en république." — Las Cases, *Mémorial de Sainte-Hélène*, (Réimpression de 1823 et 1824,) Tom. III. p. 111, — Journal, 18 Avril 1816. *Correspondance de Napoléon Ier*, (Paris, 1858-69,) Tom. XXXII. p. 326.

[1] Columbian Centinel, June 18, 1825.

coln[1] — is a necessity of civilization, not only because of that republican equality without distinction of birth which it establishes, but for its assurance of permanent peace. All privilege is usurpation, and, like Slavery, a state of war, relieved only by truce, to be broken by the people in their might. To the people alone can mankind look for the repose of nations; but the Republic is the embodied people. All hail to the Republic, equal guardian of all, and angel of peace!

Our own part is simple. It is, first, to keep out of war, — and, next, to stand firm in those ideas which are the life of the Republic. Peace is our supreme vocation. To this we are called. By this we succeed. Our example is more than an army. But not on this account can we be indifferent, when Human Rights are assailed or republican institutions are in question. Garibaldi asks for a "word,"[2] that easiest expression of power. Strange will it be, when that is not given. To the Republic, and to all struggling for Human Rights, I give word, with heart on the lips. Word and heart I give. Nor would I have my country forget at any time, in the discharge of its transcendent duties, that, since the rule of conduct and of honor is the same for nations as for individuals, the greatest nation is that which does most for Humanity.

1 Address at the Consecration of the National Cemetery at Gettysburg, November 19, 1863: McPherson's Political History of the United States during the Great Rebellion, p. 606.

2 "The cause of Liberty in Italy needs the *word* of the United States Government, which would be more powerful in its behalf than that of any other." — ***Message to Mr. Sumner from Caprera***, May 24, 1869.

DREW UNIVERSITY LIBRARY
1144 00431217 8